A Guide to INGRES

A user's guide to the INGRES product
(a relational database management
system with built-in application
development facilities) from
Relational Technology Inc.

C. J. Date

The Relational Institute
and
The Codd and Date Consulting Group

ADDISON-WESLEY PUBLISHING COMPANY

Reading, Massachusetts • Menlo Park, California • Don Mills, Ontario
Wokingham, England • Amsterdam • Madrid
San Juan • Bogotá • Sydney • Santiago
Singapore • Tokyo

To my parents,
with thanks for everything

Library of Congress Cataloging-in-Publication Data

Date, C. J.
  A guide to INGRES.

  Includes index.
  1. Data base management.   2. INGRES (Computer system)
  I. Title.
QA76.9.D3D3694 1987   005.74   86-26566
ISBN 0-201-06006-X

Reprinted with corrections May, 1987

Programs presented in this text are printed from
camera-ready material prepared by the author.

BCDEFGHIJ-MA-8987

Preface

The subject of this book, INGRES (pronounced "ingress," with the accent on the first syllable), is, first and foremost, a *relational database management system*. A relational database management system (relational DBMS for short) is a system that allows both end-users and application programmers to store data in, and retrieve data from, databases that are perceived as collections of *relations* or tables. At the time of writing, there are numerous such systems on the market, from many different vendors; however, INGRES can legitimately lay claim to having one of the longest pedigrees in the business. Before going any further, let me justify this statement.

The relational approach to database management was first proposed in 1969–70 by Dr. E. F. Codd, at that time a member of the IBM Research Laboratory in San Jose, California. The basic ideas underlying Codd's proposal were accepted fairly readily in the academic world, and the early and mid 1970s saw the construction of numerous prototype systems in universities and similar research establishments. Among those prototypes were two that were especially worthy of note:

1. The System R prototype, which was built at the IBM San Jose Research Laboratory during the period 1974–77; and

2. The University INGRES prototype, which was built at the University of California at Berkeley during the period 1973–75.*

---

*The dates are only approximate. I do not mean to suggest that all development on these systems ceased in 1977 and 1975, respectively. On the contrary, work continues on both of them (more accurately, on their descendants) right up to the present day.

These two prototypes stood apart from the rest because they were considerably more ambitious than the others. By "more ambitious," I mean that each of the two was always intended to be *a full-function DBMS:* It did not merely provide the simple relational user interface, it also did its best to do so *as efficiently as possible.* In other words, good performance was always recognized as a key objective for both systems. Each also provided all the necessary locking, journaling, recovery, etc., functions that are required in any DBMS (relational or otherwise) if that DBMS is to be anything other than just a toy.

As a result of the foregoing, System R and University INGRES each had a major influence on subsequent developments, both academic and commercial, in the relational field. In particular, of course, each of the two led directly to a significant commercial product—System R to the DB2 product (also the SQL/DS product) from IBM, and University INGRES to the Commercial INGRES product from RTI. (*Note:* "RTI" is an acronym, standing for "Relational Technology Inc.") Indeed, in the case of INGRES, the whole reason for forming the RTI company in the first place was precisely to refine and develop the university prototype into a commercial product, and the RTI founders included some of the original designers and developers of that prototype.

RTI was founded in 1980, and the first INGRES product (for the DEC VAX/VMS environment) was released in 1981. (*Note:* From this point on, I will refer to the commercial product simply as "INGRES." If it is ever necessary to distinguish between the product and the university prototype, I will refer to the latter by the explicitly qualified name "University INGRES.") INGRES now runs in many different environments, including the following among others:

DEC VAX, MicroVAX (etc.)	— VMS, UNIX
AT&T 3B series	— UNIX
IBM 370, 43xx, 30xx	— VM/CMS, MVS/XA [1987]
Motorola MC68000	— UNIX
IBM PC/XT, PC/AT, etc.	— PC/DOS

For most purposes, the differences among the different versions of INGRES are minor and can be ignored. In this book we will be concentrating on the VAX/VMS version, where it makes any difference.

The purpose of this book, then, is to present a detailed (and not wholly uncritical) description of INGRES: what it is and is not, what it is intended for, and how it can be used. The book is aimed at DP management, end-user management, database specialists (including database and system administrators, database designers, and database application programmers),

DP students and teachers, and end-users or DP professionals who wish to broaden their knowledge of the database field by studying a state-of-the-art system. The emphasis throughout is on the *user* (where by ''user'' I mean either an end-user or an application programmer); treatment of user-oriented material, such as the QUEL and SQL languages, is very thorough. By contrast, details that are of interest only to system programmers or machine operators, such as details of system commands, are generally omitted or at best treated only sketchily. Readers are assumed to have an appreciation of the overall structure, concepts, and objectives of database systems in general; however, prior knowledge of relational systems per se is not required.

Note: Some readers may be aware that I have already published a number of other books on database technology, including in particular one called *A Guide to DB2* (Addison-Wesley, 1984). The present book can be regarded as a companion volume to *A Guide to DB2*; its objectives are broadly to do for INGRES what that book did for DB2, and indeed certain portions of the present book are patterned directly after corresponding portions of that earlier book.

While I am on the subject of related publications, let me draw the reader's attention to another Addison-Wesley book, *The INGRES Papers,* edited by Michael Stonebraker (one of the original INGRES architects). That book consists of a comprehensive collection of papers that explain the design and construction of the University INGRES prototype, discuss a variety of INGRES-related research topics, and describe the evolution of the prototype into a successful commercial product. As such, it forms the perfect complement to the present volume.

ACKNOWLEDGMENTS

As usual, I am delighted to acknowledge my debt to the many people involved, directly or indirectly, in the production of this book. First, it is a pleasure to acknowledge the assistance, cooperation, and encouragement I have received from numerous people at RTI, both in the US and in Europe: Nic Birtles, Paul Butterworth, Ed Forman, Derek Frankforth, Neil Goodman, Robin Haines, Peter Kreps, Jeff Lichtman, Randy Livingston, Peter Madams, Corcky McCord, Gary Morgenthaler, Kee Ong, Peter Schmitz, Stu Schuster, Marty Sprinzen, Pete Tierney, Aaron Zornes, and most especially Sandra Duerr and Carol Joyce. Second, I am grateful to Larry Rowe, Mike Stonebraker, and Gene Wong of the University of California at Berkeley for technical discussions on numerous occasions over more than ten years; also to Jeff Lewis, of the University of Denver, for a very helpful review of the manuscript. Third, I am deeply indebted to my long-suffering family and to numerous friends for their support throughout this project. Last, I am (as always) grateful to my editor, Elydia Siegel, and to the staff at Addison-Wesley for their assistance and their high standards of professionalism. It is a pleasure to work with them.

Two final points: First, INGRES (like all software products) is of course evolving all the time, and it is therefore possible that there may be a few detail-level discrepancies between the discussions in the text and the product as it actually exists. However, any such discrepancies are (I hope) minor. The text is intended to be accurate as of year end 1986 (i.e., INGRES Release 6.0). Second, the book was written under a consulting contract with RTI and was checked for technical accuracy by a number of RTI professionals and RTI customers (both INGRES users and INGRES developers). However, the opinions expressed are my own and in no way represent an official statement on the part of RTI. Errors likewise are my own responsibility.

Saratoga, California   C. J. Date

Contents

PART II   THE INGRES DATABASE MANAGEMENT SYSTEM

CHAPTER 11 / **INGRES/SQL**   **181**

CHAPTER 12 / **Storage Structure**   **215**

CHAPTER 13 / **INGRES System Commands**   **231**

PART III THE INGRES APPLICATION DEVELOPMENT SYSTEM

## PART I

AN OVERVIEW
OF INGRES

1

INGRES: A Relational System

1.1 INTRODUCTION

INGRES (pronounced "ingress") is a product of Relational Technology Inc. (RTI). The name INGRES was originally an acronym, standing for *Interactive Graphics and Retrieval System*. As explained in the Preface, INGRES is a database management system (DBMS) that runs under a variety of operating systems, including VMS (for DEC VAX, etc.), VM/CMS and MVS/XA (for IBM System/370, etc.), UNIX (for numerous machines), PC/DOS (for the IBM PC/XT, PC/AT, etc.), and others. More specifically, it is a *relational* DBMS for those environments; in other words, it is a system that allows any number of users (end-users or application programmers or both) in those environments to access any number of relational databases by means of either of the two INGRES relational languages. The two INGRES relational languages are called QUEL ("Query Language") and SQL ("Structured Query Language"; the acronym is usually pronounced "sequel"). Both are described in this book.

What does it mean for a system to be relational? To answer this question in depth, it would unfortunately be necessary to discuss a good deal of preliminary material first. Since any such discussion would be out of place at this early point in the book, we defer it for the time being (see the next section, also Appendix B, for further information); however, we do give a rough-and-ready answer to the question without that discussion here, in the hope that such an answer will help to allay any apprehensions the reader may be feeling at the outset. Briefly, a relational system is a system in which:

(a) The data is perceived by the user as tables (and nothing but tables); and

(b) The operators at the user's disposal (e.g., for retrieval) are operators that generate new tables from old. For example, there will be one operator to extract a subset of the rows of a given table, and another to extract a subset of the columns—and of course a row subset and a column subset of a table can both in turn be regarded as tables themselves.

Figure 1.1 illustrates these two points. The data (see part (a) of the figure) consists of a single table, named CELLAR, with three columns and four rows. Two sample queries—one involving a row-subsetting operation and the other a column-subsetting operation—are shown in part (b) of the figure. *Note*: These two queries are in fact both examples of the RETRIEVE statement of the QUEL language mentioned above.

The purpose of this book, then, is to provide an in-depth tutorial and

(a) Given table:

```
cellar  |wine          |year|bottles|
        |-----------------------------|
        |Zinfandel     |  77|     10|
        |Chardonnay    |  82|      6|
        |Cabernet      |  76|     12|
        |Riesling      |  82|      9|
        |-----------------------------|
```

(b) Operators (examples):

1. Row subset:

```
RETRIEVE ( CELLAR.WINE,
           CELLAR.YEAR,
           CELLAR.BOTTLES )
WHERE      CELLAR.YEAR = 82
```

Result:
```
|wine          |year|bottles|
|-----------------------------|
|Chardonnay    |  82|      6|
|Riesling      |  82|      9|
|-----------------------------|
```

2. Column subset:

```
RETRIEVE ( CELLAR.WINE,
           CELLAR.BOTTLES )
```

Result:
```
|wine          |bottles|
|----------------------|
|Zinfandel     |     10|
|Chardonnay    |      6|
|Cabernet      |     12|
|Riesling      |      9|
|----------------------|
```

Fig. 1.1 Data structure and operators in a relational system (examples)

reference text on the relational system INGRES. It is intended for end-users, application programmers, database administrators, and more generally for anyone who wishes to obtain an understanding of the major concepts of the INGRES system. It is not intended as a substitute for the system manuals provided by RTI; but it *is* intended as a comprehensive, convenient (single-volume) guide to the use of the product. As stated in the Preface, the emphasis is definitely on the user, and therefore on product externals rather than internals, although various internal aspects will be discussed from time to time. The reader is assumed to have an overall appreciation of the structure and objectives of database systems in general, but not necessarily any specific knowledge of relational systems in particular. All applicable relational concepts are introduced in the text as they are needed. In addition, Appendix B provides a more formal summary of those concepts, for purposes of reference.

In this preliminary chapter, we present a brief overview of the INGRES relational DBMS. In particular, we give some idea as to what is involved in creating and accessing data in an INGRES database, and we briefly discuss the status of the two INGRES languages QUEL and SQL. All of these topics, and of course many others, are amplified in later chapters.

1.2 RELATIONAL DATABASES

INGRES databases are relational. *A relational database is a database that is perceived by its users as a collection of tables (and nothing but tables).* An example (the suppliers-and-parts database) is shown in Fig. 1.2.

```
s   |sno |sname |status|city   |        sp   |sno |pno |qty|
    |---------------------------|             |--------------|
    |S1  |Smith |   20|London |               |S1  |P1  |300|
    |S2  |Jones |   10|Paris  |               |S1  |P2  |200|
    |S3  |Blake |   30|Paris  |               |S1  |P3  |400|
    |S4  |Clark |   20|London |               |S1  |P4  |200|
    |S5  |Adams |   30|Athens |               |S1  |P5  |100|
    |---------------------------|             |S1  |P6  |100|
                                              |S2  |P1  |300|
p   |pno |pname |color|weight|city   |        |S2  |P2  |400|
    |----------------------------------|       |S3  |P2  |200|
    |P1  |Nut   |Red  |    12|London |         |S4  |P2  |200|
    |P2  |Bolt  |Green|    17|Paris  |         |S4  |P4  |300|
    |P3  |Screw |Blue |    17|Rome   |         |S4  |P5  |400|
    |P4  |Screw |Red  |    14|London |         |--------------|
    |P5  |Cam   |Blue |    12|Paris  |
    |P6  |Cog   |Red  |    19|London |
    |----------------------------------|
```

Fig. 1.2 The suppliers-and-parts database (sample values)

As you can see, this database consists of three tables, namely S, P, and SP.

- Table S represents suppliers. Each supplier has a supplier number (SNO), unique to that supplier; a supplier name (SNAME), not necessarily unique; a rating or status value (STATUS); and a location (CITY). For the sake of the example, we assume that each supplier is located in exactly one city.

- Table P represents parts (more accurately, kinds of part). Each kind of part has a part number (PNO), which is unique; a part name (PNAME); a color (COLOR); a weight (WEIGHT); and a location where parts of that type are stored (CITY). For the sake of the example, again, we assume that each kind of part comes in exactly one color and is stored in a warehouse in exactly one city.

- Table SP represents shipments. It serves in a sense to connect the other two tables together. For example, the first row of table SP in Fig. 1.2 connects a specific supplier from table S (namely, supplier S1) with a specific part from table P (namely, part P1); in other words, it represents a shipment of parts of kind P1 by the supplier called S1 (and the shipment quantity is 300). Thus, each shipment has a supplier number (SNO), a part number (PNO), and a quantity (QTY). For the sake of the example, once again, we assume that there can be at most one shipment at any given time for a given supplier and a given part; thus, for a given shipment, the combination of SNO value and PNO value is unique with respect to the set of shipments currently appearing in the SP table.

This example is of course extremely simple, much more simple than any real example that you are likely to encounter in practice. Nevertheless, it is adequate to illustrate most of the points that we need to make in this book, and we will use it as the basis for most (not all) of the examples in the following chapters. You should therefore take a little time to familiarize yourself with it now.

Note: There is nothing wrong with using more descriptive names such as SUPPLIERS, PARTS, and SHIPMENTS in place of the rather terse names S, P, and SP; indeed, descriptive names are generally to be recommended in practice. But in the case of the suppliers-and-parts database specifically, the three tables are referenced so frequently in the chapters that follow that very short names seemed desirable. Long names tend to become irksome with much repetition.

There are a few points arising from the example that are worth calling out explicitly:

- First, note that *all data values are atomic*. That is, at every row-and-column position in every table there is always exactly one data value, never a set of values. Thus, for example, in table SP (looking at the first two columns only, for simplicity), we have

```
|sno  |pno  |
|-----------|
|  .  |  .  |
|S2   |P1   |
|S2   |P2   |
|  .  |  .  |
|S4   |P2   |
|S4   |P4   |
|S4   |P5   |
|-----------|
```

instead of

```
|sno  |pno            |
|---------------------|
|  .  |   ...         |
|S2   |{ P1, P2 }     |
|  .  |   ...         |
|S4   |{ P2, P4, P5 } |
|---------------------|
```

A column such as PNO in the second version of this table represents what is sometimes called a "repeating group." A repeating group is a column (or combination of columns) that contains *sets* of data values (different numbers of values in different rows), instead of just one value in each row. *Relational databases do not allow repeating groups.* The second version of the table above would not be permitted in a relational system.

- Second, note that the entire information content of the database is represented as *explicit data values*. This method of representation—viz., as explicit values in column positions within rows of tables—is the *only* method available in a relational database. Specifically, there are no "links" or pointers connecting one table to another. For example, there is a connexion (as already pointed out) between the S1 row of table S and the P1 row of table P, because supplier S1 supplies part P1; but that connexion is represented, not by pointers, but by the existence of a row in table SP in which the SNO value is S1 and the PNO value is P1. In nonrelational systems, by contrast, such information is typically represented by some kind of physical link or pointer that is explicitly visible to the user.

- Third, note that each of the tables in the example has a *unique iden-tifier*—that is, a column (or combination of columns) whose value in any given row is unique with respect to the set of all such values appearing in the table. The unique identifier for table S is SNO; for table P, it is PNO; and for table SP it is the combination (SNO,PNO). For example, values of the SNO column of table S can be used to pinpoint individual supplier records within that table.

The formal relational term for such a unique identifier is *primary key*. INGRES does not enforce the primary key discipline (that is, it does not actually require every table to have a primary key), but users are nevertheless *strongly* recommended to follow such a discipline in practice. We will do so throughout this book. See Appendix B for further discussion.

At this point the reader may be wondering why a database such as that in Fig. 1.2 is called "relational" anyway. The answer is simple: "Relation" is just a mathematical term for a table (to be precise, a table of a certain specific kind—details to follow in Chapter 3). Thus, for example, we can say that the database of Fig. 1.2 consists of three *relations*. For the most part, in fact, we will take "relation" and "table" as synonymous in this book. Relational systems have their origin in the mathematical theory of relations; of course, this does not mean that you need to be a mathematician in order to use a relational system, but it does mean that there is a respectable body of theoretical results that can be applied to practical problems of database usage, such as the problem of database design.

If it is true that a relation is just a table, then why not simply call it a table and have done with it? The answer is that we very often do (and in this book we usually will). However, it is worth taking a moment to understand why the term "relation" was introduced in the first place. Briefly, the explanation is as follows. Relational systems are based on what is called *the relational model of data*. The relational model, in turn, is an abstract theory of data that is based in part on the mathematical theory mentioned earlier. The principles of the relational model were originally laid down in 1969–1970 by one man, Dr. E. F. Codd, at that time an employee of IBM. It was late in 1968 that Codd, a mathematician by training, first realized that the discipline of mathematics could be used to inject some solid principles and rigor into a field—database management—that, prior to that time, was all too deficient in any such qualities. Codd's ideas were first widely disseminated in a now classic paper, "A Relational Model of Data for Large Shared Data Banks" (*Communications of the ACM, Vol. 13*, No. 6, June 1970). Since that time, those ideas (by now almost universally accepted) have had a wide-ranging influence on just about every aspect of database technology, and indeed on certain other fields as well, such as the fields of artificial intelligence and natural language processing.

Now, the relational model as originally formulated by Codd very deliberately made use of certain terms—such as the term "relation" itself—that were not familiar in data processing circles at that time, even though the concepts in some cases were. The trouble was, many of the more familiar terms were very fuzzy; they lacked the precision necessary to a formal theory of the kind that Codd was proposing. For example, consider the term "record." At different times that single term can mean either a record *instance* or a record *type*; a *COBOL-style* record (which allows repeating groups) or a *flat* record (which does not); a *logical* record or a *physical* record; a *stored* record or a *virtual* record; and so on. The formal relational model therefore does not use the term "record" at all; instead, it uses the term "tuple" (short for "*n*-tuple"), which was given a precise definition by Codd when he first introduced it. We do not give that definition here; for our purposes, it is sufficient to say that the term "tuple" corresponds approximately to the notion of a *flat record instance* (just as the term "relation" corresponds approximately to the notion of a table). If you wish to study some of the more formal literature on relational database systems, you will of course have to familiarize yourself with the formal terminology, but in this book we are not trying to be very formal, and we will stick for the most part to terms such as "record" that are reasonably familiar. (One formal term we will use somewhat, however, is the term "primary key" introduced earlier in this section.)

Figure 1.3 shows the terms we will be using most heavily (table, record, row, field, column, also primary key). For interest it also gives the corresponding formal term in each case. Note that we use the terms "record" and "row" interchangeably, and the terms "field" and "column" likewise. Note also, therefore, that we are definitely taking "record" to mean "record instance" and "field" to mean "field type."

Formal relational term	Informal equivalents
relation	table
tuple	record, row
attribute	field, column
primary key	unique identifier

Fig. 1.3 Some terminology

1.3   RELATIONAL OPERATIONS

As already explained, INGRES supports two relational languages, QUEL and SQL. Relational operations—that is, operations that define and manipulate data in the form of relations—can be formulated in either one of the two. For simplicity, the present section concentrates on just one of the two languages, namely QUEL; the role of SQL will be explained in Section 1.4.

First the definitional operations. Figure 1.2, the suppliers-and-parts database, of course represents that database as it appears at some particular instant in time; it is a *snapshot* of the database. Figure 1.4, by contrast, shows the *structure* of that database; it shows how the tables in the database might be defined, or described, using QUEL "data definition" statements.*

As you can see, the definition includes one CREATE statement for each of the three tables. The CREATE statement is, as already indicated, an example of a QUEL data definition statement. Each CREATE statement specifies the name of the table to be created, the names of its columns, and the data types of those columns (possibly some additional information also, not illustrated in Fig. 1.4; see Chapter 3).

It is not our purpose at this juncture to describe the CREATE statement

```
CREATE S
     ( SNO    = CHAR(5),      /* "CHAR" = alphanumeric string */
       SNAME  = CHAR(20),
       STATUS = I2,           /* "I2" = 2-byte binary integer */
       CITY   = CHAR(15) )

CREATE P
     ( PNO    = CHAR(6),
       PNAME  = CHAR(20),
       COLOR  = CHAR(6),
       WEIGHT = I2,
       CITY   = CHAR(15) )

CREATE SP
     ( SNO    = CHAR(5),
       PNO    = CHAR(6),
       QTY    = I4 )          /* "I4" = 4-byte binary integer */
```

Fig. 1.4 The suppliers-and-parts database (data definition)

---

*Throughout this book we show QUEL statements, SQL statements, operating system commands, etc., in upper case, for clarity and emphasis. In practice it is often more convenient to enter all such material in lower case. INGRES will accept both forms.

in detail. That detailed description appears later, in Chapter 3. One point that does need to be stressed right away, however, is that the CREATE statement is *executable*. (In fact, *every* QUEL statement is executable, as we shall see.) If the three CREATE statements in Fig. 1.4 were to be entered at a terminal, exactly as shown, the system would actually build the three tables, then and there. Initially, of course, those tables would be empty— i.e., they would each contain just the row of column headings, no data rows as yet. However, we could immediately go on to insert some data rows (possibly via the QUEL APPEND statement, to be discussed in Chapter 5), and, in just a few minutes' work, we could have a (probably small, but nevertheless useful and usable) database at our disposal, and could start doing some useful things with it. So this simple example illustrates right away one of the advantages of relational systems in general, and INGRES in particular: They are very easy to use (ease of "getting on the air" is of course just one aspect of ease of use in general). As a result, they can make users very productive. We shall see many other advantages later.

To continue with the example: Having created our three tables, and loaded some records into them, we can now start doing useful work with them, using QUEL *data manipulation* statements. One of the things we can do is *data retrieval*, which is specified in QUEL by means of the RE-TRIEVE statement. Figure 1.5 illustrates the use of that statement. *Note*: Certain irrelevant details are deliberately omitted from part (b) of that figure.

A particularly significant feature of many relational systems, and of INGRES in particular, is that the same relational language is available at

(a) Interactive (via the QUEL Terminal Monitor):

```
RETRIEVE ( S.CITY )        Result:   |city    |
WHERE     S.SNO = "S4"                |--------|
                                      |London  |
                                      |--------|
```

(b) Embedded in a host programming language (Ada, BASIC, C, COBOL, FORTRAN, Pascal, or PL/I):

```
##   RETRIEVE ( XCITY = S.CITY )   Result:   |xcity   |
##   WHERE     S.SNO = "S4"                   |--------|
                                              |London  |
                                              |--------|
```

Fig. 1.5 A retrieval example

two different interfaces, namely an interactive interface and an application programming interface. The two interfaces are both illustrated in Fig. 1.5:

(a) Figure 1.5(a) shows an example of the use of the *interactive* interface, which is supported by the QUEL *Terminal Monitor* component. Here, the user has typed the RETRIEVE statement at a terminal, and INGRES has responded—through the Terminal Monitor—by displaying the result ("London") directly at that terminal.

(b) Figure 1.5(b) shows essentially the same RETRIEVE statement *embedded in an application program*. QUEL statements embedded in application programs are referred to as "Embedded QUEL" or *EQUEL* statements. In the example, the EQUEL RETRIEVE statement will be executed when the program is executed, and the result "London" will be returned, not to a terminal, but to the program variable XCITY (by virtue of the *assignment* "XCITY = S.CITY" within the RETRIEVE; XCITY is basically just an input area within the program).

In other words, QUEL can be regarded both as an *interactive query language* and as a *database programming language*. Note that this remark applies to the entire QUEL language; that is, any QUEL statement that can be entered at a terminal can alternatively be embedded in a program. And note in particular that the remark applies even to operations such as creating a new table; you can create tables from within an application program, if it makes sense in your application to do so. INGRES currently supports the following programming languages: Ada, BASIC, C, COBOL, FORTRAN, Pascal, and PL/I.

Note: Interactive QUEL and Embedded QUEL do differ from each other on certain points of detail, of course. For example, each line of an EQUEL statement must be prefixed with the characters "##" in columns 1 and 2 in order to distinguish it from the surrounding host language statements (see Fig. 1.5(b) for an illustration). Also, each field to be retrieved via an EQUEL RETRIEVE statement must have an associated host language variable (designated by means of an assignment within the RETRIEVE) to serve as the necessary input area for that field. So, of course, it is not one hundred percent true to say that the RETRIEVE statement is the same at both interfaces. But it is broadly true, if we overlook the minor differences of detail.

We are now in a position to understand how INGRES looks to the user. By "user" here we mean either an end-user at an online terminal or an application programmer writing in one of the INGRES-supported host programming languages. (We note in passing that the term "user" will be used consistently throughout this book with either or both of these two meanings.) As already explained, each such user will be operating on tables by means of statements of the QUEL language (or the SQL language). See Fig. 1.6.

The first point to be made concerning Fig. 1.6 is that there will normally be many users, of both kinds, all operating on the same data at the same time. INGRES will automatically apply the necessary *locking* controls (see Chapter 9) to ensure that those users are all protected from one another—that is, to guarantee that one user's updates cannot cause another user's operations to produce an incorrect result.

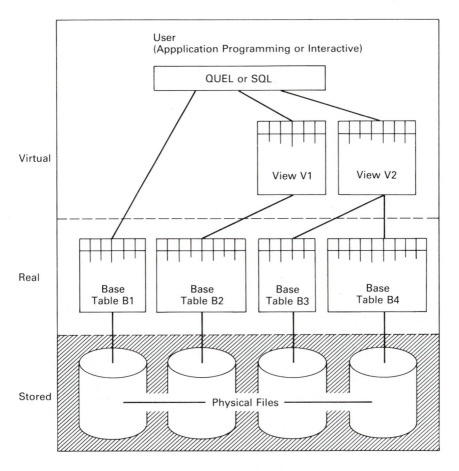

Fig. 1.6 INGRES as perceived by an individual user

Next, note that the tables in the figure are also of two kinds, namely *base tables* and *views*. A base table is a "real" table—i.e., a table that physically exists, in the sense that there exist physically stored records, and possibly physical indexes, in one or more operating system files, that directly represent that table in storage. By contrast, a view is a "virtual" table—i.e., a table that does not directly exist in physical storage, but looks to the user as if it did. Views can be thought of as different ways of looking at the "real" tables. As a trivial example, a given user might have a view of the suppliers base table S in which only those suppliers in London were visible. Views are defined, in a manner to be explained in Chapter 7, in terms of one or more of the underlying base tables.

Note: The foregoing paragraph should not be interpreted as saying that a base table is *physically stored* as a table—i.e., as a set of physically adjacent stored records, with each stored record consisting simply of a direct copy of a row of the base table. There are numerous differences, some to be discussed in Chapter 12, between a base table and its storage representation. The point is, however, that users can always think of base tables as "physically existing," without having to concern themselves with how those tables are actually implemented in storage. In fact, the whole point of a relational database is to allow users to deal with data in the form of tables per se, instead of in terms of the storage representation of such tables. To repeat from Section 1.2: A relational database is a database that is *perceived by its users* as a collection of tables. It is *not* just a database in which data is physically stored as tables.

Like base tables, views can be created at any time. The same is true of indexes. (The CREATE statement discussed earlier is for creating "real" or base tables. There is also a DEFINE VIEW statement for creating views or "virtual" tables, and an INDEX statement for creating indexes. All of these statements will be discussed in detail in later chapters.) Similarly, base tables (and views and indexes) can all be *destroyed* at any time, using the QUEL DESTROY operation. With regard to indexes, however, note carefully that although some user* is responsible for creating and destroying them, users are *not* responsible for saying when those indexes should be used. Indexes are never mentioned in data manipulation statements such as RETRIEVE. The decision as to whether or not to use a particular index in responding to, say, a particular RETRIEVE operation is made by INGRES, not by the user. We shall have more to say on this topic in the next chapter.

The user interface to INGRES is the QUEL language (or the SQL lan-

---

*To be specific, the user who created the table over which the index is to be built. See Chapter 8.

guage—see Section 1.4). We have already indicated (a) that QUEL and SQL can be used in both interactive and embedded environments, and (b) that they provide both data definition and data manipulation functions (in fact, as we shall see later, they provide certain "data control" functions as well). The major QUEL data definition functions—

```
CREATE (base table)
DEFINE VIEW
INDEX
DESTROY (base table, view, index)
```

—have already been touched on. The major data manipulation functions (in effect the only ones, if we temporarily disregard some EQUEL-only functions) are

```
RETRIEVE
APPEND
REPLACE
DELETE
```

Figure 1.7 gives examples of RETRIEVE and REPLACE in order to illustrate an additional point, namely the fact that INGRES data manipulation statements typically operate on *entire sets of records*, instead of just on one record at a time. Given the sample data of Fig. 1.2, the RETRIEVE statement (Fig. 1.7(a)) returns a set of four values, not just a single value; and the REPLACE statement (Fig. 1.7(b)) changes two records, not just one. In other words, QUEL is a *set-level language.*

Set-level languages such as QUEL are sometimes described as "nonprocedural," on the grounds that users specify *what*, not *how* (i.e., they say what data they want, without specifying a procedure for getting it). The process of "navigating" around the physical database to locate the desired

```
(a) RETRIEVE ( SP.SNO )         Result:  | sno |
    WHERE    SP.PNO = "P2"                | ----|
                                          | S1  |
                                          | S2  |
                                          | S3  |
                                          | S4  |
                                          | ----|

(b) REPLACE S ( STATUS =         Result:  Status doubled
               2 * S.STATUS )             for London
    WHERE    S.CITY = "London"            suppliers (i.e.,
                                          S1 and S4)
```

Fig. 1.7 QUEL data manipulation examples

data is performed automatically by the system, not manually by the user. (For this reason, relational systems are sometimes described as "automatic navigation" systems.) However, "nonprocedural" is not really a very satisfactory term, because procedurality and nonprocedurality are not absolutes; the best that can be said is that some language *A* is either more or less procedural than some other language *B*. Perhaps a better way of putting matters is to say that a language such as QUEL is at *a higher level of abstraction* than a language such as COBOL (or a language such as the database languages of nonrelational systems, come to that). With a language like QUEL, in other words, the system handles more of the details than it does with a language like COBOL. Fundamentally, it is this *raising of the level of abstraction* that is responsible for the increased productivity that relational systems like INGRES can provide.

1.4   QUEL vs. SQL

We have mentioned the fact several times that INGRES supports two relational languages, QUEL and SQL. So far, however, all examples have been framed in terms of QUEL. QUEL ("Query Language") was the language originally defined for the University INGRES prototype. It was also the first language implemented in the Commercial INGRES product. By contrast, the "Structured Query Language" SQL was the language originally defined for the IBM System R prototype (see the Preface), and thus became the language implemented in the IBM products SQL/DS and DB2.

During the late 1970s and early 1980s QUEL and SQL were both influential, and both had their followers. Dialects of both were implemented by a number of vendors in a variety of commercial products. In 1986, however, a dialect of SQL (not all that different—perhaps not surprisingly—from the IBM DB2-SQL/DS dialect) was formally adopted by the American National Standards Institute (ANSI) as an official standard language for relational systems. When it became apparent (in late 1984 or thereabouts) that such a development was likely, most relational vendors, even those who were heavily QUEL-oriented, decided that a SQL interface would soon be an essential component in a relational product if that product were to be considered as a serious contender in the marketplace. Thus RTI, like many of its competitors, proceeded to develop a SQL interface for its product—which is why INGRES now supports both languages.

Author's note: Before going any further, I feel compelled to remark that, in the opinion of myself and many other database professionals (and despite the direction being taken by ANSI and the marketplace), QUEL is technically a far superior language. It is considerably easier than SQL to learn and use, and probably to implement also. Given these facts, and given also the fact that QUEL predated SQL in the INGRES world, I feel justified in using QUEL as the basis for the first few chapters of this book. However, there is little doubt that SQL is destined to become the more commercially significant language in the years ahead. Later portions of the book do therefore deal with SQL in some detail. But in order to simplify the presentation as much as possible, SQL will generally be ignored from this point forward until we reach Chapter 11.

1.5 SUMMARY

This brings us to the end of this preliminary chapter, in which we have taken a very quick look at some of the most significant features of the INGRES relational DBMS. We have seen in outline what it means for a system to be relational; we have discussed the relational (tabular) data structure, and we have looked at some of the operators available in QUEL for operating on data in that tabular form. In particular, we have touched on the three categories of QUEL statements (data definition, data manipulation, and data control), and we have seen examples from the first two of those categories. We remind the reader that:

(a) All QUEL statements are executable;

(b) Any statement that can be entered at a terminal can also be embedded in a program, and that program can be written in Ada, BASIC, C, COBOL, FORTRAN, Pascal, or PL/I;

(c) QUEL data manipulation statements (RETRIEVE, REPLACE, etc.) are all set-level;

(d) INGRES also supports the SQL language as an alternative to QUEL.

In the next chapter we will take a brief look at the internal structure of INGRES and some of its principal components.

EXERCISES

1.1 What does it mean to say that INGRES is a relational system?

1.2 Given the sample data of Fig. 1.2, show the effect of each of the following QUEL statements.

```
(a)  RETRIEVE ( S.SNAME )
     WHERE     S.STATUS = 30

(b)  RETRIEVE ( SP.SNO, SP.PNO )
     WHERE     SP.QTY > 200

(c)  REPLACE SP ( QTY = SP.QTY + 300 )
     WHERE     SP.QTY < 300
```

```
(d)  DELETE  P
     WHERE   P.COLOR = "Blue"
     OR      P.COLOR = "Red"

(e)  APPEND TO SP
               ( SNO = "S3", PNO = "P1", QTY = 500 )
```

1.3 What do the following acronyms stand for?

DBMS

INGRES

QUEL

SQL

1.4 What is the INGRES Terminal Monitor?

1.5 What is a repeating group?

1.6 Define the terms *relation* and *relational database*.

1.7 (a) Give a possible CREATE statement for the CELLAR table of Fig. 1.1.
(b) Write an Embedded QUEL (EQUEL) statement to retrieve the number of bottles of 1977 Zinfandel from that table.

1.8 Define the terms *base table* and *view*.

1.9 What do you understand by the term "automatic navigation"?

1.10 Define the term *primary key*.

ANSWERS TO SELECTED EXERCISES

1.1 A relational system such as INGRES is a system in which the data is perceived as tables (and nothing but tables), and the operators available to the user are operators that generate new tables from old.

1.2 (a)
```
|sname |
|------|
|Blake |
|Adams |
|------|
```

(b)
```
|sno |pno |
|---------|
|S1  |P1  |
|S1  |P3  |
|S2  |P1  |
|S2  |P2  |
|S4  |P4  |
|S4  |P5  |
|---------|
```

(c)
```
|sno |pno |qty|
|-------------|
|S1  |P2  |500|
|S1  |P4  |500|
|S1  |P5  |400|
|S1  |P6  |400|
|S3  |P2  |500|
|S4  |P2  |500|
|-------------|
```

(Only altered rows shown.)

(d) Rows for P2, P3, and P5 are deleted from table P.

(e) Row (S3,P1,500) is inserted into table SP.

1.4 Actually there are two Terminal Monitors, one for QUEL and one for SQL. The function of each is to allow INGRES statements (QUEL statements or SQL statements, as applicable) to be entered and executed interactively from an online terminal.

1.5 A repeating group is (conceptually) a column (or combination of columns) of a table that contains multiple data values per row (different numbers of values in different rows). Repeating groups are not permitted in a relational database. *Note*: An explanation of, and justification for, this apparent restriction can be found in C. J. Date, *An Introduction to Database Systems*: *Volume I*, 4th edition (Addison-Wesley, 1986).

1.6 A relation is a table (without repeating groups!). A relational database is a database that is perceived by its users as a collection of relations. *Note*: More precise definitions are given in Appendix B.

1.7 (a)
```
CREATE CELLAR ( WINE    = CHAR(16),
                YEAR    = I2,
                BOTTLES = I2 )
```

    (b)
```
## RETRIEVE ( XBOTT = CELLAR.BOTTLES )
## WHERE    CELLAR.WINE = "Zinfandel"
## AND      CELLAR.YEAR = 77
```

Note: Answer 1.7(b) needs certain additional specifications, beyond the scope of this chapter. See Chapter 10.

1.8 A base table is a "real" table; it has some direct storage representation. A view is a "virtual" table; it does not have any direct storage representation of its own. A view is like a *window* into one or more underlying base tables, through which the data (or some subset of the data) in those underlying tables can be observed, possibly in some rearranged structure.

1.9 "Automatic navigation" means that the system assumes the responsibility of searching through the physical database to locate the data the user has requested. Users specify what they want, not how to get to what they want.

1.10 Informally, a primary key is just a unique identifier for a table. For example, the primary key for the parts table P is the field PNO; given a PNO value *p* say, that value *p* can be used to identify an individual part record and to distinguish that record from all others appearing in the P table.

A more formal definition of the term is given in Appendix B.

2

System Structure

2.1 BACKEND vs. FRONTENDS

The internal structure of INGRES is quite complex, as is only to be expected of a state-of-the-art system that provides all of the functions normally found in a modern DBMS (including, for example, recovery control, concurrency control, authorization control, and so on), and more besides. However, many of those functions, although of course crucial to the overall operation of the system, are of no direct interest to the user in our sense of the term (i.e., an end-user or an application programmer). From a high-level point of view, in fact, the system can be regarded as having a rather simple two-part structure; the two parts are referred to (informally, but very conveniently) as the *backend* and a set of *frontends*. Refer to Fig. 2.1.

- The backend is the INGRES relational DBMS per se. It provides all the basic DBMS functions, including full support for everything in the QUEL language*—data definition, data manipulation, data security and integrity, and so on. It also serves as a transaction manager, providing the necessary concurrency control and recovery support (de-

---

*We remind the reader that we are ignoring SQL for the most part over the next few chapters.

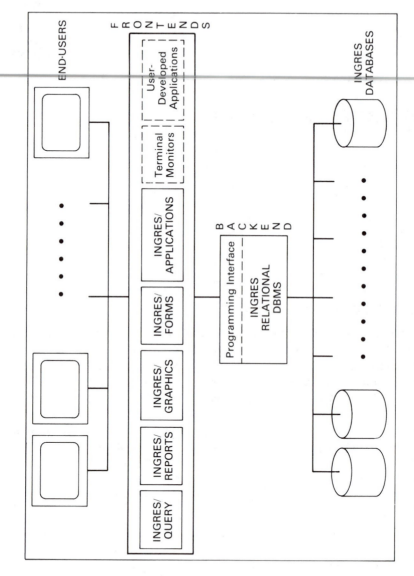

Fig. 2.1 High-level structure of INGRES

scribed in Chapter 9). It also provides support for the INGRES Data Dictionary (described in Chapter 6).

The backend is sometimes called the INGRES *Data Manager.*

- The frontends constitute the INGRES *Application Development System.* In other words, INGRES is not just a relational DBMS—it is a relational DBMS with an extensive array of built-in facilities for assisting in the process of developing database applications. The facilities in question consist of several distinct subsystems, most of them *forms-based* (this term will be explained in Section 2.3). The major subsystems are as follows:

  - INGRES/QUERY   : database retrieval/update, data entry
  - INGRES/REPORTS   : report definition and report writing
  - INGRES/GRAPHICS   : business graphics
  - INGRES/FORMS   : form definition and editing
  - INGRES/APPLICATIONS : application generation

Strictly speaking, the QUEL and SQL Terminal Monitors are also frontend subsystems. However, they are somewhat different in kind from the others; certainly they provide less in the way of genuine application development support than do most of the other frontends.* For the purposes of this book, we shall normally treat the Terminal Monitors as if they were an integral component of the INGRES backend.

Note: From the point of view of the backend, of course, the frontends are nothing more than (RTI-provided) application programs. User-developed applications can also be regarded as INGRES frontends. See Part III of this book.

The division of INGRES into backend and frontends accounts for the structure of this chapter:

- Section 2.2 is concerned with the backend (i.e., the INGRES relational DBMS per se). It explains how the backend executes QUEL statements, and introduces the important notion of *optimization*. It also briefly discusses the concept of *physical data independence*.

- Section 2.3 is concerned with the forms-based frontends (i.e., the INGRES Application Development System). It explains in outline what

---

*In particular, they are not forms-based. Note, however, that they do possess forms-based frontends of their own, called IQUEL and ISQL. See Chapter 15.

a form is and how forms are used in the process of "Visual Programming."

- Section 2.4 shows how the division into backend and frontends facilitates support for distributed processing.

- Finally, Section 2.5 summarizes the major INGRES components.

~~The backend/frontend split also accounts for the structure of the major~~ portion of this book: Part II consists of an in-depth description of the INGRES backend, and Part III consists of a detailed examination of the forms-based frontends. Part IV consists of a single chapter that describes the INGRES distributed database facilities (INGRES/STAR).

2.2 THE INGRES BACKEND: QUERY PROCESSING

In this section we consider in outline what is involved in executing a QUEL statement such as RETRIEVE or REPLACE. This activity is usually referred to as "query processing," though the operation involved need not be a query per se but might be an update, for example. Note that the "query" in question may have been entered interactively via the Terminal Monitor or may have originated from an application program (possibly an RTI-provided application such as INGRES/QUERY) in the form of an EQUEL statement.

The execution of a query involves the following four steps:

1. Parsing
2. Query modification
3. Optimization
4. Execution

We amplify the four steps below.

1. Parsing

INGRES examines the given QUEL statement, reporting on any syntax errors it finds. If there are no errors, the statement is then converted into an internal "parse tree" or "syntax tree" form that is more suitable for subsequent processing.

2. Query modification

The parse tree is modified to incorporate any relevant view definitions and/or security and integrity constraints. See Chapters 7 and 8 for details of this process.

3. Optimization

The INGRES query processing mechanism includes an *optimizer* as an important subcomponent. The function of the optimizer is to choose, for each query it processes, an optimal access strategy for implementing that query. Remember from Chapter 1 that data manipulation statements such as RETRIEVE specify only what data the user wants, not how to get to that data; the *access path* for getting to the data will be chosen by the optimizer. Users and user programs are thus independent of such access paths (for further discussion of this important point, see the conclusion of this section).

By way of illustration of what is involved in the optimization process, consider the following simple RETRIEVE against the suppliers-and-parts database:

```
RETRIEVE ( S.CITY ) WHERE S.SNO = "S4"
```

Even in this very simple case, there are probably at least two ways of performing the required retrieval:

1. By doing a physical sequential scan of (the stored version of) table S until the record for supplier S4 is found;

2. If there is an index or a hash on the SNO column of that table—which there probably will be*—then by using that index or hash and thus going directly to the S4 record.

The optimizer will choose which of these two strategies to adopt. In general, the optimizer will make its choice on the basis of such considerations as which tables are referenced in the query (there may be more than one), how big those tables are, how the tables are physically stored on the disk, what indexes exist, how selective those indexes are, the form of the WHERE clause in the request, and so on.†

---

*Recall that field SNO is the primary key for table S. In practice, an INGRES table will almost always have a UNIQUE index or UNIQUE hash on its primary key. For details, see Chapter 12.

†The question obviously arises: Where does the optimizer get its information? For example, how does it know what indexes exist? The answer is that all such information is recorded in a set of special system tables called the *INGRES Data Dictionary* (dictionary for short). We shall have more to say regarding the dictionary in Chapter 6.

INGRES then generates a *query plan* reflecting the optimizer's choice of strategy. The query plan consists of the internal code needed to implement the original query in accordance with the optimizer's chosen access path(s).

4. Execution

Finally, the query plan generated in the previous step is executed.

We can now see how it is possible for programs to be independent of physical access paths—more specifically, how it is possible to create, change, or destroy such paths without at the same time having to rewrite programs. As stated earlier, INGRES data manipulation statements such as RETRIEVE and REPLACE never include any explicit mention of access paths. Instead, they simply indicate what data the user is interested in; and it is the system's responsibility (actually the optimizer's responsibility) to choose an appropriate access path at the time the statement is processed. We say that systems like INGRES provide a high degree of *physical data independence*: Users and user programs are not dependent on the physical structure of the stored database. The advantage of such a system—a highly significant advantage—is that it is possible to make changes in the physical database (e.g., for performance reasons) *without having to make any corresponding changes in application programs*. In a system without such independence, application programmers may well have to devote some significant portion of their time—a figure of 50 percent is quite typical—to making changes to existing programs that are necessitated merely by changes to the physical database. In a system like INGRES, by contrast, those programmers can concentrate exclusively on "real work"—specifically, on the production of new applications.

2.3   THE INGRES FRONTENDS: FORMS MANAGEMENT

As explained in Section 2.1, the INGRES frontend subsystems are mostly *forms-based*. A *form* in INGRES can be regarded as a display-screen version of a familiar paper form. One advantage of forms is that they can be used both for input and output—i.e., both for entering data into the system and for displaying information to the user. Figure 2.2 shows a simple example* of a form that might be used in conjunction with the parts table P. That form could be used both (a) as a skeleton into which the user could enter values for a new part record that is to be stored in the database, or

---

*We stress the "simple." Real forms are likely to be much more sophisticated in practice.

```
|------------------------------------------------------------------|
| TABLE IS p                                                       |
|                                                                  |
| pno:          pname:                       color:               |
|                                                                  |
| weight:       city:                                             |
|                                                                  |
|                                                                  |
|------------------------------------------------------------------|
```

Fig. 2.2 Example of an INGRES form

(b) as a basis for displaying values from some existing part record in the database to the user. (It could also be used for other purposes, discussed later in this book.) Figure 2.3 shows the same form being used to display the part record for part P1.

Forms represent an attractive style of interface for many applications, because they are so intuitively easy to understand and deal with.* In recognition of this fact, INGRES provides a comprehensive *Forms Management System* to simplify the process of developing and executing forms-based applications. The forms management system consists of:

```
|------------------------------------------------------------------|
| TABLE IS p                                                       |
|                                                                  |
| pno: P1       pname: Nut                    color: Red          |
|                                                                  |
| weight: 12    city: London                                      |
|                                                                  |
|                                                                  |
|------------------------------------------------------------------|
```

Fig. 2.3 Example of an INGRES form, showing sample values

---

*The process of interacting with a forms-based system or application is referred to in INGRES as *Visual Programming*.

(a) A built-in set of forms-based subsystems for performing certain commonly occurring tasks such as data entry and maintenance. Examples of such subsystems are INGRES/QUERY and INGRES/REPORTS, both already mentioned in Section 2.1.

(b) A variety of facilities, most of them forms-based themselves, that allow the installation to construct customized applications that are also forms-based in turn. One such facility is INGRES/APPLICATIONS, already mentioned in Section 2.1. Another (not forms-based in itself, but supporting the construction of forms-based applications) is *EQUEL/ FORMS*. EQUEL/FORMS is to the INGRES Forms Management System what EQUEL is to the INGRES Database Management System; in other words, it provides a set of simple operations (such as GETFORM) that allow application programs to manipulate forms, just as EQUEL provides a set of operations that allow them to manipulate databases. For example, there is an EQUEL/FORMS operation to display the value of some program variable in some field on a form, and another to read a value from some field on a form into some program variable. EQUEL/FORMS is discussed in some detail in Chapter 10.

To conclude this section, we note that *the entire INGRES system* is in fact presented to the online user as a single integrated forms-based application, by virtue of an INGRES component called INGRES/MENU. The user initially invokes INGRES from the terminal by entering the command:

```
INGRES database
```

where "database" is the name of the required database. (*Note*: In some versions of INGRES, the INGRES command is spelled RTINGRES.) INGRES responds with the display shown (slightly modified, for reasons of space) in Fig. 2.4. The user can then perform any of the following operations:

- Execute predefined queries (where "query" includes retrieval, update, and data entry operations)
- Run predefined reports or graphs (i.e., generate reports or graphs in accordance with predefined report or graph specifications)
- Invoke any of the forms-based frontends INGRES/QUERY, INGRES/ REPORTS, INGRES/GRAPHICS, INGRES/FORMS, or INGRES/ APPLICATIONS
- Invoke (the forms-based interface to) the QUEL or SQL Terminal Monitor to enter interactive QUEL or SQL operations

```
|-----------------------------------------------------------------|
|                                                                 |
| INGRES/MENU                                   Database: s_sp_p   |
|                                                                 |
| To run a highlighted command, place the cursor over it and      |
| select the "Go" menu item.                                      |
|                                                                 |
| +---------+---------------------------------------------------+ |
| |Commands |Description                                        | |
| +=========+===================================================+ |
| |QUERY    |RUN QUERY to retrieve, modify, or append data      | |
| |REPORT   |RUN default or saved REPORT                        | |
| |RUNGRAPH |RUN saved GRAPH defined by VIGRAPH                 | |
| |         |                                                   | |
| |QBF      |Use QUERY-BY-FORMS to develop/test query defns     | |
| |RBF      |Use REPORT-BY-FORMS to design/modify reports       | |
| |VIGRAPH  |Use VIGRAPH to design/modify/test graphs           | |
| |ABF      |Use APPLICATIONS-BY-FORMS to design/test applicns  | |
| |         |                                                   | |
| |TABLES   |CREATE, MANIPULATE, or LOOKUP tables in database   | |
| |VIFRED   |EDIT forms by using the VISUAL-FORMS-EDITOR        | |
| |QUEL     |ENTER interactive QUEL statements                  | |
| |SQL      |ENTER interactive SQL statements                   | |
| |SREPORT  |SAVE REPORT-WRITER reports in the database         | |
| +---------+---------------------------------------------------+ |
|                                                                 |
| Go   History   CommandMode  DBswitch   Shell   Help   Quit :    |
|                                                                 |
|-----------------------------------------------------------------|
```

Fig. 2.4 Initial INGRES/MENU form and menu (slightly simplified)

- Define new reports via the Report-Writer
- Perform forms-based data definition operations (e.g., create a new base table by filling in a form)

Note the last of these in particular. Although it is certainly possible, as we have already seen, to create a new table by typing in a CREATE statement via the Terminal Monitor, it is usually much easier to perform that function by filling in an INGRES/MENU form instead. For the next few chapters, however, we shall continue to assume that all such operations are performed directly in QUEL. INGRES/MENU will be discussed in detail in Chapter 15.

2.4 DISTRIBUTED PROCESSING

The term "distributed processing" refers to the ability to connect multiple computers together into some kind of data communications network, such that a single data processing task can span multiple computers in the network. Specifically, a user or user program operating at one computer site should be able to operate on data stored at another such site. The rationale for providing such a facility is fairly obvious: It is quite common for a single enterprise (a bank, for example) to operate many computers, such that the data for one portion of the enterprise is stored on one machine and that for another portion is stored on another machine. It is also quite common for users on one machine to need at least occasional access to data that is stored on another. To pursue the banking example for a moment, it is very likely that users at the bank headquarters will occasionally need access to data stored at one or other of the bank's branch offices.

Ideally, distributed processing should be "transparent to the user"; that is, users should not have to do anything special in order to access remote data, but should be able to behave exactly as if the remote data were in fact stored at their own local site. There are at least two reasons why such *location transparency* is desirable:

- It simplifies application logic.
- It allows data to be moved from site to site as usage patterns change, without necessitating any reprogramming of applications.

In fact, of course, location transparency is nothing more than a special case of physical data independence, as that concept applies to distributed systems.

For reasons that are beyond the scope of this text, relational technology is particularly well suited to distributed processing; indeed, it is the *only* technology that is capable of realizing the potential of such processing to its fullest extent.* As a result, relational systems such as INGRES are well placed to take advantage of the possibilities of distributed processing; and in fact the distributed database version of INGRES ("INGRES/STAR") was the very first product in the marketplace to provide true distributed *database* support (i.e., an environment in which a single database can span multiple sites)—a notable achievement.

There are four levels of distributed processing support in INGRES today:

- INGRES/NET
- INGRES/NET PC
- INGRES/PCLINK
- INGRES/STAR

---

*See C. J. Date, *An Introduction to Database Systems: Volume II* (Addison-Wesley, 1983) for a comprehensive discussion of distributed systems in general, and in particular for evidence in support of the claim that relational technology is essential to the success of such a system.

1. INGRES/NET

The INGRES/NET facility allows any number of INGRES sites (involving various combination of hardware and operating system configurations—for example, any combination of IBM, VAX/VMS, and UNIX sites) to be connected together into a single network. The INGRES frontends at any one site (INGRES/QUERY, INGRES/REPORTS, the QUEL Terminal Monitor, etc.) can then interact with the INGRES backend at a different site (see Fig. 2.5). For example, an interactive QUEL user at site *A* can issue QUEL operations against an INGRES database stored at site *B*. All the user has to do is specify the site name for *B* as a prefix to the database

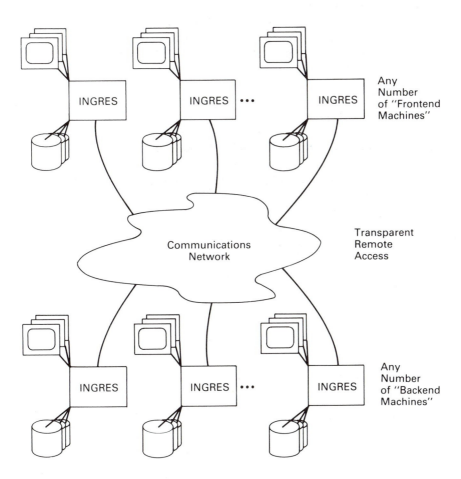

Fig. 2.5 INGRES/NET

name in the command by which INGRES is invoked. It is true that the user at site *A* does need to know the identity of site *B* at the time of invocation; thereafter, however, all QUEL operations on the remote database behave exactly as if the database were local, i.e., as if *A* and *B* were the same site. INGRES/NET thus does provide support for location transparency, except at the time of initial invocation itself.

2. INGRES/NET PC

INGRES/NET PC is similar to INGRES/NET, except that the site running the INGRES frontends (INGRES/QUERY, etc.) can be a personal computer (IBM PC/XT, PC/AT, or compatible). INGRES/NET PC thus allows applications to be developed on a PC and then transported without change to a mainframe (or vice versa). It also allows a PC to serve as a workstation, accessing data in one or more shared databases on one or more connected mainframes and at the same time offloading a considerable amount of processing from those mainframes.

3. INGRES/PCLINK

INGRES/PCLINK is a system that permits a personal computer (IBM PC, PC/XT, PC/AT, or compatible) to download (i.e., retrieve) data from a local or remote host computer running INGRES (see Fig. 2.6). A forms-based query language on the PC called Visual Query Language allows data to be retrieved from the INGRES database on the host and displayed at the PC. The retrieved data can automatically be stored in files at the PC in a form suitable for processing by a variety of commonly used PC products, including Lotus 1-2-3, dBASE II / dBASE III, WordStar, Multiplan, and VisiCalc. (Conversely, data from a PC file can be sent to the host computer for loading into an INGRES table.) The user interface on the PC (query language, menus, function keys, screen manipulation, etc.) is patterned directly after the interface of Lotus 1-2-3.

The PC can also serve as an online terminal to the host by means of the INGRES/PCLINK terminal emulation feature. In this mode, all of the standard INGRES frontend interfaces are available to the PC user to operate on data at the host.

4. INGRES/STAR

INGRES/STAR is a fully distributed version of INGRES. It builds on INGRES/NET. Thus, it assumes an interconnected network of sites, where each site supports one or more local INGRES databases and each local database in turn is available for local or remote processing via the normal facilities of INGRES and INGRES/NET. (In particular, applications existing prior to the introduction of INGRES/STAR will continue to run

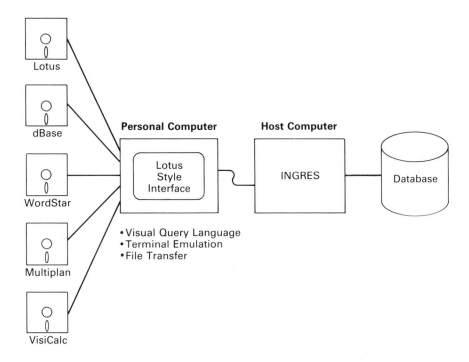

Fig. 2.6 INGRES/PCLINK

without any need for reprogramming.) INGRES/STAR will then allow *any arbitrary collection* of tables from those local databases to be defined as a single distributed database, and will support the standard QUEL data manipulation operations (RETRIEVE, APPEND, REPLACE, DELETE) against that distributed database just as if it were a normal (local) database—with one exception (discussed below).

Example: Suppose we have a network of three sites S1, S2, and S3, with local databases S1L1 and S1L2 at site S1, S2L1 and S2L2 at site S2, and S3L1 and S3L2 at site S3 (see Fig. 2.7). Then we could define a distributed database D1 consisting of local databases S1L1, S2L1, and S3L1, and another distributed database D2 consisting of local databases S1L1, S1L2, S2L2, and S3L2. Note the overlap: Local database S1L1 appears in both D1 and D2. (For simplicity we are assuming that if local database *L* is accessible through distributed database *D*, then *all tables* of *L* are accessible through *D*. In practice, any subset of the tables of *L* can be defined to be accessible through *D*.)

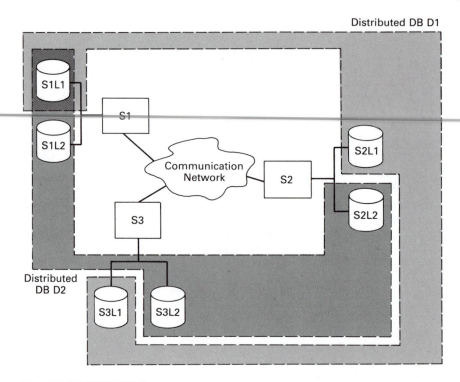

Fig. 2.7 INGRES/STAR

For data manipulation purposes, each of the two distributed databases
D1 and D2 will now (as previously stated) behave basically as if it were an
ordinary local INGRES database. Users of D1, for example, will be able
to issue arbitrary queries against the tables in D1—even if those queries
involve a join* of two tables T1 and T2, and T1 and T2 are in different
local databases at different sites. The one limitation, referred to above, is
that a single transaction† will not be allowed to update tables in more than
one local database. (This is a temporary restriction, due to be lifted in late
1987.)

---

*See Chapter 4 for a discussion of join.

†See Chapter 9 for a discussion of transactions.

2.5 MAJOR SYSTEM COMPONENTS

In this chapter we have examined certain major aspects of the internal structure of INGRES. Fundamentally, INGRES consists of a single backend component, the INGRES relational DBMS per se (sometimes called the INGRES Data Manager), together with a set of frontend components (the INGRES application development subsystems—INGRES/QUERY, INGRES/REPORTS, the QUEL Terminal Monitor, and so on). Section 2.2 showed in outline how queries are processed by the backend, and in particular stressed the importance of the optimizer component. Section 2.3 described the basic concepts of forms-based systems and Visual Programming and introduced the facilities of INGRES/MENU. Finally, Section 2.4 sketched the INGRES facilities for distributed processing. In particular it described:

- INGRES/NET, which allows INGRES frontends on one machine to interact with the INGRES backend on another;

- INGRES/NET PC, a version of INGRES/NET that allows the INGRES frontends to run on a PC and thus permits the PC to serve as a workstation for an INGRES host;

- INGRES/PCLINK, which allows data to be downloaded from an INGRES host and converted into a form suitable for processing by a PC product such as Lotus 1-2-3; and

- INGRES/STAR, which allows an arbitrary collection of tables from databases at multiple sites to function as a single database for data manipulation purposes.

By way of conclusion, we summarize below the principal INGRES subsystems and their components, for purpose of future reference.

- INGRES Data Manager:

  The INGRES relational DBMS, supporting relational operations, the INGRES Data Dictionary, locking, recovery, etc.; includes the INGRES query processing system, and the optimizer as an important subcomponent of that system

- INGRES/EQUEL (including EQUEL/FORMS) and INGRES/ESQL (including ESQL/FORMS):

  Embedded QUEL and SQL preprocessors and run-time support for Ada, BASIC, C, COBOL, FORTRAN, Pascal, PL/I

- INGRES QUEL and SQL Terminal Monitors:

Interactive QUEL and SQL (including forms-based interfaces INGRES/
IQUEL and INGRES/ISQL)

- INGRES/QUERY:

   Query-By-Forms (QBF)

- INGRES/FORMS:

   Visual-Forms-Editor (VIFRED)

- INGRES/REPORTS:

   INGRES Report-Writer and Report-By-Forms (RBF)

- INGRES/GRAPHICS:

   Visual-Graphics-Editor (VIGRAPH)

- INGRES/APPLICATIONS:

   Applications-By-Forms (ABF)

- INGRES/MENU:

   Forms-based interface to INGRES

- INGRES/NET:

   Host-to-host (frontend-to-backend) communication

- INGRES/NET PC:

   PC-to-host (frontend-to-backend) communication

- INGRES/PCLINK:

   PC-to-host (Lotus-to-INGRES, etc.) communication

- INGRES/STAR:

   Data manipulation operations against tables from multiple mutually remote databases as if those tables were all part of a single local database

EXERCISES

2.1 Name the major components of INGRES.

2.2 What is the function of the INGRES optimizer?

2.3 Define *physical data independence*. Explain how such independence is provided
in INGRES. Why is such independence desirable?

2.4 What do you understand by the term "forms-based application"?

2.5 What is the function of INGRES/MENU?

2.6 Define *distributed processing*.

2.7 Define *location transparency*.

2.8 What are the functions of INGRES/NET and INGRES/NET PC?

2.9 What is the function of INGRES/PCLINK?

2.10 What is the function of INGRES/STAR?

ANSWERS TO SELECTED EXERCISES

2.1 See Section 2.5.

2.2 The function of the optimizer is to decide how to implement relational requests. The optimizer's choice of strategy is based on information contained in the dictionary regarding physical storage structures, availability of indexes, data value distributions, etc.

2.3 Physical data independence means that users and user programs do not depend on the physical structure of the database. User requests (e.g., QUEL statements) are formulated purely in terms of the logical structure of the database (i.e., in terms of tables and columns); the choice of physical access paths to implement those requests is made by the system (actually by the optimizer), not by the user. As a result, the physical structure of the database can be changed—e.g., for performance reasons—without requiring any user programs to be rewritten.

2.4 A forms-based application is one that communicates with its user (for both input and output) by means of forms. A form can be thought of as a display-screen version of an ordinary paper form, with boxes or fields to be filled in with actual data values.

2.5 INGRES/MENU is a forms-based frontend to the entire INGRES system.

2.6 Distributed processing means that a single data processing task can span multiple interconnected computer sites (i.e., the task can involve work being performed at each one of those multiple sites).

2.7 Location transparency (in a distributed system) means that users and user programs do not have to know where data is physically stored but can behave as if all the data were in fact stored at their own local site. In other words, it means that a distributed system looks just like a nondistributed system to the user.

2.8 INGRES/NET allows INGRES frontends at one computer site to interact with the INGRES backend at another such site. INGRES/NET PC allows the frontend site in such a system to be a PC.

2.9 INGRES/PCLINK allows a user at a PC to download data from an INGRES database on a host computer and have that data formatted for processing by any of several well-known PC software systems (e.g., Lotus 1–2–3, WordStar, etc.).

2.10 INGRES/STAR allows an arbitrary collection of tables from databases at multiple remote sites to function as a single database for data manipulation purposes.

## PART II

THE INGRES DATABASE MANAGEMENT SYSTEM

3

Data Definition

3.1 INTRODUCTION

In this chapter we examine the data definition portions of QUEL in some detail. It is convenient to divide QUEL data definition statements into two broad classes, which we may very loosely characterize as *logical* and *physical*—"logical" having to do with objects that are genuinely of interest to users, such as base tables and views, and "physical" having to do with objects that are primarily of interest to the system, such as indexes. Needless to say, matters are not quite as clearcut as this simple classification would suggest—some "logical" statements include parameters that are really "physical" in nature, and vice versa, and some statements do not fit neatly into either category. But the classification is convenient as an aid to understanding, and we will stay with it for now. The present chapter is concerned only with "logical" data definition.

The principal logical data definition statements are listed below.*

```
CREATE (base table)
DESTROY (base table)

DEFINE (view)
DESTROY (view)
```

---

*The RETRIEVE INTO statement, discussed in the next chapter, may also be regarded as a data definition statement in some respects.

We defer detailed discussion of views (third and fourth statements above) to Chapter 7; the other two statements are discussed in this chapter.

3.2 BASE TABLES

A base table is an important special case of the more general concept "table." Let us therefore begin by making that more general concept a little more precise.

Definition: A *table* in a relational system consists of a row of *column headings*, together with zero or more rows of *data values* (different numbers of data rows at different times). For a given table:

(a) The column heading row specifies one or more columns (giving, among other things, a data type for each);

(b) Each data row contains exactly one data value for each of the columns specified in the column heading row. Furthermore, all the values in a given column are of the same data type, namely the data type specified for that column in the column heading row.

Two points arise in connexion with the foregoing definition.

1. Note that there is no mention of *row ordering*. Strictly speaking, the rows of a relational table are considered to be unordered, top to bottom. (The rows of a relation constitute a mathematical *set*, and sets in mathematics do not have any ordering.) It is possible, as we shall see in Chapter 4, to *impose* an order on those rows when they are retrieved in response to a query, but such an ordering should be regarded as nothing more than a convenience for the user—it is not intrinsic to the notion of a table.

2. Likewise, the columns of a relational table are also considered to be unordered, left to right. For example, in table S (see Fig. 1.2 in Chapter 1), there is no notion that column SNO is the "first" column or that column SNAME is the "second" column (etc.).

Of course, rows and columns do have a physical ordering in the stored version of the table on the disk; what is more, those physical orderings can and do have a very definite effect on system performance. The point is, however, those physical orderings are always *transparent to the user*.*

To turn now to base tables specifically: A base table is an *autonomous, named* table. By "autonomous" we mean that the table exists in its own

---

*Actually there is one very minor exception to this rule, i.e., one minor situation in which the left-to-right column ordering of a table is visible to the user—namely, when the user issues a RETRIEVE statement of the form "RETRIEVE (R.ALL)" (see Chapter 4).

right—unlike a view, which does not exist in its own right but is derived from one or more base tables (it is merely an alternative way of looking at those base tables). By "named" we mean that the table is explicitly given a name via an appropriate definitional statement—unlike a table that is merely displayed as the result of a query, which does not have any explicit name of its own and has only ephemeral existence (for examples of such unnamed tables, see the two result tables in Fig. 1.1 in Chapter 1).

3.3 CREATING AND DESTROYING BASE TABLES

CREATE

We are now in a position to discuss the CREATE statement in detail. The general format of that statement is

```
CREATE base-table
    ( column-definition [ , column-definition ] ... )
    [ WITH JOURNALING ]
```

where a "column-definition" takes the form

```
column = data-type [ default-spec ]
```

and a "default-spec" (in turn) is one of the following:

```
WITH NULL
NOT NULL
NOT NULL WITH DEFAULT
```

The optional "default-spec" and WITH JOURNALING specifications are explained in the subsection on "Null Values" below and in Chapter 13, respectively. *Note*: Square brackets are used in syntactic definitions throughout this book to indicate that the material enclosed in those brackets is optional (i.e., may be omitted). An ellipsis (...) indicates that the immediately preceding syntactic unit may optionally be repeated one or more times. Material in capitals must be written exactly as shown; material in lower case must be replaced by specific values chosen by the user.

Here is an example, the CREATE statement for the suppliers base table S (now shown complete):

```
CREATE S
    ( SNO    = CHAR(5)  NOT NULL,
      SNAME  = CHAR(20),
      STATUS = I2,
      CITY   = CHAR(15)  )
    WITH JOURNALING
```

The effect of this statement is to create a new, empty base table called S. An entry describing the table is made in the INGRES dictionary. The table has four columns, called SNO, SNAME, STATUS, and CITY,* with the indicated data types (data types are discussed in detail in the next section) and with column SNO defined to be NOT NULL. Journaling is enabled for this table (see Chapter 13).

Once the table has been created, data can be entered into it via the QUEL statements APPEND (discussed in Chapter 5) or COPY (discussed—briefly—in Chapter 13).

Null Values

INGRES supports the concept of a *null data value*. A given column can contain null values if and only if the definition of that column in the CREATE operation for the table explicitly specifies WITH NULL. Null is a special value that is used to represent "value unknown" or "value inapplicable." It is not the same as (e.g.) blank or zero. For example, a shipment record might contain a null QTY value (we know that the shipment exists but we do not know the quantity shipped), or a part record might contain a null COLOR value (perhaps COLOR is irrelevant for some kinds of part).

Referring back to the CREATE for table S shown above, observe that we have specified NOT NULL for field SNO (only). The effect of this specification is to guarantee that every supplier record in base table S will always contain a "genuine" (i.e., nonnull) supplier number value. By contrast, any or all of SNAME, STATUS, and CITY may be null in that same record.

The specification NOT NULL can be extended to include the additional specification WITH DEFAULT—for example:

```
CREATE S
     ( SNO    = CHAR(5)   NOT NULL,
       SNAME  = CHAR(20)  NOT NULL WITH DEFAULT,
       STATUS = I2        NOT NULL WITH DEFAULT,
       CITY   = CHAR(15)  NOT NULL WITH DEFAULT )
     WITH JOURNALING
```

---

*The INGRES rules concerning names are as follows: Database names are unique across the entire INGRES system; table names are unique within the containing database; and column names are unique within the containing table. ("Table" here refers to both base tables and views; i.e., a view cannot have the same name as a base table.) In addition, QUEL keywords (CREATE, INDEX, RETRIEVE, etc.) cannot be used as names. The first character of any name must be alphabetic (A-Z), the remainder, if any, must be alphabetic, numeric (0-9), or the underscore character (not allowed in a table name). All names are limited to a maximum of 24 characters.

The alternative to NOT NULL (WITH DEFAULT or otherwise) is WITH NULL. WITH NULL means that the field in question can accept null values. NOT NULL WITH DEFAULT means that it cannot, and that if an attempt is made to enter a record into the table without a value specified for the field in question, then that field is to be automatically set to one of the following values:

- zero (for numeric and money fields)
- blanks (for fixed length string and date/time fields)
- empty (for varying length string fields)

If no "default-spec" is specified at all for a given field, then NOT NULL WITH DEFAULT is assumed.

Author's note: It is this writer's opinion that null values—at least as currently defined and implemented, not only in INGRES but also in most other systems—are far more trouble than they are worth and should be avoided entirely; they display very strange and inconsistent behavior and can be a rich source of error and confusion. It is frequently preferable in practice to represent unknown or inapplicable information by an ordinary nonnull value such as blank or −1 (minus one). Indeed, in the particular case of a field that participates in a primary key, nulls and nonnull default values should both be disallowed, for reasons that are explained in Appendix B. In this book, therefore, we will always specify NOT NULL for primary key fields and NOT NULL WITH DEFAULT (explicitly or implicitly) for other fields. (Note that the foregoing criticisms apply to any system that supports null values, not just to INGRES specifically. An extensive discussion of the problems that can be caused by null values can be found in the author's book *Relational Database*: *Selected Writings* [Addison-Wesley, 1986].)

We shall have more to say on null values in Chapters 4, 5, 10, and 11.

DESTROY

Just as a new base table can be created at any time via CREATE, so an existing base table can be destroyed at any time via DESTROY:

```
DESTROY base-table
```

The specified base table is removed from the system (more precisely, the description of that table is removed from the dictionary). All views and indexes defined on the table are automatically destroyed also.

3.4 DATA TYPES

QUEL supports the following data types.

CHAR(*n*)	character string of maximum length *n* bytes ($0 < n <\, = 254$), represented as a varying or fixed length item in the database depending on whether or not data compression is specified (see Chapter 12)
VARCHAR(*n*)	character string of maximum length *n* bytes ($0 < n <\, = 2000$), represented as a varying or fixed length item in the database depending on whether or not data compression is specified (again, see Chapter 12)
I1, I2, I4	binary integers of 1, 2, 4 bytes, respectively
F4, F8	floating point numbers of 4, 8 bytes, respectively
MONEY	decimal currency (e.g., dollars and cents), 16 digits (8 bytes), with assumed decimal point two digits from the right
DATE	date and time of 12 bytes (year/month/day/hour/minute/second) representing either an absolute value such as "17-Oct-87 8:30 am" or an interval such as "10 months 17 days 8 hours 30 minutes"

Note: QUEL also supports two additional string data types, C and TEXT. For details of C, the reader is referred to the RTI manuals. TEXT is very similar to VARCHAR. The main difference is in the comparison rules: If two VARCHAR strings of different lengths are compared, the shorter is conceptually padded at the right with blanks to make it the same length as the longer before the comparison is done (see Chapter 4); by contrast, two TEXT strings of different lengths are always considered to be unequal. VARCHAR is usually a better choice than TEXT in practice.

Constants

Although it is something of a digression from the main topic of this section (and chapter), this is a convenient point at which to summarize the various types of *constant* supported in QUEL:

string	written as a sequence of characters enclosed in quotation marks *examples*: "123 Main Street" "PIG"
integer	written as a signed or unsigned decimal integer, with no decimal point *examples*: 4 -95 $+364$ 0

float   written as a signed or unsigned decimal number with a decimal point, or a signed or unsigned decimal number with or without a decimal point followed by the letter E and an integer constant

                    examples: 7.5   12.00   0.001 -4.75

                                 4E3 $-95.7E46$ $+364E-5$ 0.7E1

                    (*note*: the expression xEy represents the value $x * (10 ** y)$)

money   written as an integer or float constant, or as a string constant of the form "[$]integer[.integer]"*

                    examples: 659.00 -45.18 "659"   "-45.18"

date/time   written as a string constant of any of the formats illustrated below,† among others:

Dates:	Times:	Intervals:
"10/17/87"	"8:30:00"	"5 years"
"17-Oct-87"	"8:30 PST"	"3:48:22 hrs"
"15-Oct-1987"	"8:30"	"45 mins"
"10-17-87"	"8:30 pm"	
"87.10.17"		
"101787"	*Dates and times*:	
"10/17"		
"10-17"	"10/17/87 8:30:00"	
"today"	"17-Oct-87 8:30"	
	"now"	

       "today" = today's date

       "now" = today's date and current time

3.5 DISCUSSION

The fact that data definition statements such as CREATE and DESTROY can be executed at any time makes INGRES a very flexible system. For instance, in older (nonrelational) systems, the creation of a new type of

---

*Actually the precise format of money constants depends on the setting of the INGRES "money_format" and "money_prec" options. The explanation given here assumes the default settings for those options, namely US dollars with a leading dollar sign, accurate to the nearest cent. For information regarding other possible settings, the reader is referred to the RTI manuals.

†Actually the precise format of date and time constants depends on the setting of the INGRES "date_format" option. The explanation given here assumes the default setting for that option, namely US format. For information regarding other possible settings, the reader is referred to the RTI manuals.

object, such as a new file or record type—or a new index, come to that, although we have not yet discussed the creation of indexes—is an operation not to be undertaken lightly: Typically it involves bringing the entire system to a halt,* unloading the database, revising and recompiling the database definition, and finally reloading the database in accordance with that revised definition. In such a system it becomes highly desirable to get the database definition (and therefore, much more significantly, the database *design*) *complete* and *correct* once and for all, before starting to load and use the data—which means that (a) the job of getting the system installed and operational can quite literally take months or even years of highly specialized people's time, and (b) once the system is running, it can be difficult and costly, perhaps prohibitively so, to remedy early design errors.

In a system like INGRES, by contrast, it is possible to create and load just a few base tables and then to start using that data right away. Later, new base tables (also new fields) can be added in a piecemeal fashion, without having any effect on existing users of the database. It is also possible to experiment with the physical structure of the database—e.g., to try the effects of having or not having some particular index—again without affecting existing users at all (other than in performance, of course); see Chapter 12. Moreover, as we shall see in Chapter 7, it is even possible under certain circumstances to rearrange the *logical* structure of the database— e.g., to move a field from one table to another—and still not affect the logic of existing programs. In a nutshell, it is not necessary to go through the total database design process before any useful work can be done with the system, nor is it necessary to get everything right the first time. The system is *forgiving*.

Caveat: The foregoing should *not* be taken to mean that database design is unnecessary in a system like INGRES. Of course database design is still necessary. However:

- It doesn't all have to be done at once.

- It doesn't have to be perfect first time.

- Logical and physical design can be tackled separately.

- If requirements change, then the design can change too, in a comparatively painless manner.

---

*We remark in passing that many modern installations simply cannot afford to bring the system to a halt—they require 24-hour operation. For such an installation the comparative inflexibility of nonrelational systems is a major drawback, possibly a complete showstopper.

- Many new applications—typically small-scale applications, involving, for example, personal or departmental databases—become feasible in a system like INGRES that would simply never have been considered under an older (nonrelational) system, because those older systems were just too complicated to make such applications economically worthwhile (in particular, the upfront costs in those systems were prohibitive).

EXERCISES

3.1 Figure 3.1 shows some sample data values for a database containing information concerning suppliers (S), parts (P), and projects (J). Suppliers, parts, and projects are uniquely identified by supplier number (SNO), part number (PNO), and project number (JNO), respectively. The significance of an SPJ (shipment) record is that the specified supplier supplies the specified part to the specified project in the specified quantity (and the combination SNO-PNO-JNO uniquely identifies such a record). Write a suitable set of data definition statements for this database. *Note*: This database will be used in numerous exercises in subsequent chapters.

s

sno	sname	status	city
S1	Smith	20	London
S2	Jones	10	Paris
S3	Blake	30	Paris
S4	Clark	20	London
S5	Adams	30	Athens

p

pno	pname	color	weight	city
P1	Nut	Red	12	London
P2	Bolt	Green	17	Paris
P3	Screw	Blue	17	Rome
P4	Screw	Red	14	London
P5	Cam	Blue	12	Paris
P6	Cog	Red	19	London

j

jno	jname	city
J1	Sorter	Paris
J2	Punch	Rome
J3	Reader	Athens
J4	Console	Athens
J5	Collator	London
J6	Terminal	Oslo
J7	Tape	London

spj

sno	pno	jno	qty
S1	P1	J1	200
S1	P1	J4	700
S2	P3	J1	400
S2	P3	J2	200
S2	P3	J3	200
S2	P3	J4	500
S2	P3	J5	600
S2	P3	J6	400
S2	P3	J7	800
S2	P5	J2	100
S3	P3	J1	200
S3	P4	J2	500
S4	P6	J3	300
S4	P6	J7	300
S5	P2	J2	200
S5	P2	J4	100
S5	P5	J5	500
S5	P5	J7	100
S5	P6	J2	200
S5	P1	J4	100
S5	P3	J4	200
S5	P4	J4	800
S5	P5	J4	400
S5	P6	J4	500

Fig. 3.1 The suppliers-parts-projects database

3.2 Suppose that the suppliers-parts-projects database is to be restructured as follows:

  (a) Field STATUS is to be removed from table S;
  (b) A new field END_DATE is to be added to table J;
  (c) Field QTY of table SPJ is to be renamed SHIP_QTY;
  (d) The data type of field WEIGHT of table P is to be changed to F4.

Write appropriate sets of QUEL statements to accomplish these alterations. *Note:* Although the alterations are logically all alterations to the data definition, you will find you will need certain data manipulation statements—particularly the RETRIEVE INTO statement—in order to answer the exercise. You may prefer to come back to this exercise after reading Chapters 4 and 5.

ANSWERS TO SELECTED EXERCISES

3.1
```
CREATE S
     ( SNO     = CHAR(5) NOT NULL,
       SNAME   = CHAR(20),
       STATUS  = I2,
       CITY    = CHAR(15) )

CREATE P
     ( PNO     = CHAR(6) NOT NULL,
       PNAME   = CHAR(20),
       COLOR   = CHAR(6),
       WEIGHT  = I2,
       CITY    = CHAR(15) )

CREATE J
     ( JNO     = CHAR(4) NOT NULL,
       JNAME   = CHAR(10),
       CITY    = CHAR(15) )

CREATE SPJ
     ( SNO     = CHAR(5) NOT NULL,
       PNO     = CHAR(6) NOT NULL,
       JNO     = CHAR(4) NOT NULL,
       QTY     = I4 )
```

In practice it is quite likely that WITH JOURNALING would be specified for each of these tables also. See Chapter 13.

3.2

  (a)
```
RETRIEVE INTO TEMP1 ( S.SNO, S.SNAME, S.CITY )
DESTROY S
RETRIEVE INTO S ( TEMP1.ALL )
DESTROY TEMP1
```

  (b)
```
RETRIEVE INTO TEMP2 ( J.ALL, END_DATE = "12/31/99" )
DESTROY J
RETRIEVE INTO J ( TEMP2.ALL )
DESTROY TEMP2
```

  (c)
```
RETRIEVE INTO TEMP3 ( SPJ.ALL )
DESTROY SPJ
RETRIEVE INTO SPJ ( TEMP3.SNO, TEMP3.PNO, TEMP3.JNO,
                    SHIP_QTY = TEMP3.QTY )
DESTROY TEMP3
```

(d)
```
RETRIEVE INTO TEMP4 ( P.ALL )
DESTROY P
CREATE P ( PNO    = CHAR(6) NOT NULL,
           PNAME  = CHAR(20),
           COLOR  = CHAR(6),
           WEIGHT = F4,
           CITY   = CHAR(15) )
APPEND TO P ( TEMP4.ALL )
DESTROY TEMP4
```

4

Data Manipulation I:
Retrieval Operations

4.1 INTRODUCTION

QUEL provides four data manipulation statements: RETRIEVE, AP-
PEND, REPLACE, and DELETE. This chapter is concerned with the RE-
TRIEVE statement only; Chapter 5 is concerned with the other three statements. The aim in both chapters is (as always) to be reasonably
comprehensive but *not* to replace the relevant RTI manuals. As usual, all
examples are based on the suppliers-and-parts database. Also, we assume
until further notice that all statements are entered interactively via the Terminal Monitor. The special considerations that apply to embedded QUEL
(EQUEL) are ignored until Chapter 10.

Note: Many of the examples, especially those in the latter parts of this
chapter, are quite complex. The reader should not infer that it is QUEL
itself that is complex. Rather, the point is that common operations are so
simple in QUEL (and indeed in most relational languages) that examples
of such operations tend to be rather uninteresting and do not illustrate the
full power of the language. Of course, we do show some simple examples
first (Section 4.2). The overall plan of the chapter is as follows.

- As just indicated, Section 4.2 is concerned with "simple" queries—in other words, with what are known technically as *single-variable* queries. It introduces several important basic QUEL concepts, among them *predicates*, *scalar expressions*, *scalar functions*, and *target lists*.

- Section 4.3 is concerned with a slightly more complicated (but extremely important) facility known as *join*. Join queries are sometimes referred to as *multi-variable* queries; this section introduces the concept of *range variables* and in so doing explains the "multi-variable" terminology—also the "single-variable" terminology mentioned in the previous paragraph.

- Section 4.4 introduces the QUEL concept of *aggregates*, which are operators such as SUM and AVG whose effect is to reduce an entire set of scalar values (i.e., a column from some table) to a single scalar value.

- Section 4.5 then goes on to discuss aggregate *functions*, which can be regarded (both syntactically and semantically) as extended versions of the simple aggregates of Section 4.4.

- Section 4.6 is concerned with *quantified queries*—that is, queries that involve the special aggregate function ANY.

- Finally, Section 4.7 presents a brief summary of the entire chapter.

As you can see, the chapter is rather long, and you may wish to omit some of the more complicated portions on a first reading. Section 4.6 in particular is probably best skipped on a first pass through.

4.2 SINGLE-VARIABLE QUERIES

We start with a simple example—the query "Get supplier numbers and status for suppliers in Paris," which can be expressed in QUEL as follows:

```
RETRIEVE ( S.SNO, S.STATUS )
WHERE     S.CITY = "Paris"

Result:   |sno |status|
          |-----------|
          |S2  |    10|
          |S3  |    30|
          |-----------|
```

The example illustrates the commonest form of the RETRIEVE statement—"*RETRIEVE* some specified fields from some specified table *WHERE* some specified condition is true." The table in question is specified by means of an appropriate qualifying name on the names of the specified fields. Notice that the result of the query is another table—a table that is derived in some way from the given tables in the database. In other words, the user in a relational system like INGRES is always operating within the simple tabular framework, a very attractive feature of such systems.*

The general form of the RETRIEVE statement is as follows:

```
RETRIEVE [ INTO table ] [ UNIQUE ] ( target-list )
[ WHERE predicate ]
[ SORT BY field(s) ]
```

where "target-list" is a list of *assignments* separated by commas, and each such assignment has the form†

```
[ unqualified-name = ] scalar-expression
```

The "unqualified-name =" portion of such an assignment can be omitted if and only if the result of evaluating "scalar-expression" has an obvious inherited name. In the example at the beginning of this section, there are two scalar-expressions, namely the expressions S.SNO and S.STATUS; evaluating these two expressions produces two values with the obvious inherited names SNO and STATUS, so it is not necessary to introduce new names. Note, however, that it would not be wrong to do so. For example:

---

*Because of this fact, we say that relational tables form a *closed system* under the retrieval operators of a language like QUEL. In general, a closed system is a collection (possibly infinite) of all objects of a certain type, say OBJS, and a corresponding collection of operators, say OPS, such that:

    (a) The operators in OPS apply to the objects in OBJS, and

    (b) The result of applying any operator from OPS to any object(s) in OBJS is another object in OBJS.

The practical significance of this point (in the case of relations specifically) is as follows: Since the result of one RETRIEVE operation is another relation, it is possible, at least in principle, to apply another RETRIEVE operation to that result (provided of course that the result in question has been saved somewhere). It also means, again in principle, that RETRIEVE operations can logically be nested. Examples illustrating these points can be found throughout this book; see, e.g., Example 4.2.6 later in this section, also the examples of Chapter 7.

†A target list can also include an "assignment" of the special form T.ALL (where T identifies some table). See Example 4.2.3, later.

```
RETRIEVE ( X = S.SNO, Y = S.STATUS )
WHERE    S.CITY = "Paris"
```

```
Result:    |x    |y      |
           |------------|
           |S2   |    10 |
           |S3   |    30 |
           |------------|
```

We now proceed to illustrate the major features of the RETRIEVE statement by means of a rather lengthy series of examples.

4.2.1 *Simple Retrieval*. Get part numbers for all parts supplied.

```
RETRIEVE ( SP.PNO )
```

```
Result:    |pno |
           |----|
           |P1  |
           |P2  |
           |P3  |
           |P4  |
           |P5  |
           |P6  |
           |P1  |
           |P2  |
           |P2  |
           |P2  |
           |P4  |
           |P5  |
           |----|
```

Notice the duplication of part numbers in this result. INGRES does not eliminate duplicate rows from the result of a RETRIEVE unless the user explicitly requests it to do so by means of the keyword UNIQUE, as in the next example.*

4.2.2 *Retrieval with Duplicate Elimination*. Get part numbers for all parts supplied, with redundant duplicates eliminated.

```
RETRIEVE UNIQUE ( SP.PNO )
```

```
Result:    |pno |
           |----|
           |P1  |
           |P2  |
           |P3  |
           |P4  |
           |P5  |
           |P6  |
           |----|
```

---

*In earlier INGRES releases, the SORT BY clause (see Example 4.2.5) eliminated duplicates also.

The specification UNIQUE causes retrieved rows to be sorted into ascending order by their value; duplicate rows are then eliminated from the result. *Note*: The result may then be sorted again, if the RETRIEVE includes a SORT BY clause. See Example 4.2.5 below.

4.2.3 Simple Retrieval ("RETRIEVE ALL"). Get full details of all suppliers.

```
RETRIEVE ( S.ALL )
```

Result: A copy of the entire S table.

The special "assignment" T.ALL appearing within a target list is shorthand for a list of all the field names in table T, in the order in which those fields were defined in the statement that originally created that table. The RETRIEVE in the example is thus equivalent to:

```
RETRIEVE ( S.SNO, S.SNAME, S.STATUS, S.CITY )
```

"RETRIEVE ALL" is convenient for interactive queries, since it saves keystrokes. It cannot be used in EQUEL.

Aside. For the benefit of readers who have access to an INGRES system and are trying out some of the examples as they go, we should mention the PRINT statement—syntax:

```
PRINT table
```

(where "table" must identify a base table, not a view). The statement "PRINT T" can be regarded as a convenient shorthand for the statement "RETRIEVE (T.ALL)"; its effect is to display the entire table T on the screen.

4.2.4 Qualified Retrieval. Get supplier numbers for suppliers in Paris with status > 20.

```
     RETRIEVE ( S.SNO )
     WHERE     S.CITY = "Paris"
     AND       S.STATUS > 20
Result:    |sno |
           |----|
           |S3  |
           |----|
```

The condition or *predicate* following WHERE can include fields from the database and/or constants;* the comparison operators =, < > (not

---

*More generally, it may involve *scalar-expressions*. See Example 4.2.7, later.

equals), $>$, $> =$, $<$, and $< =$; the Boolean operators AND, OR, and NOT; and parentheses to indicate a desired order of evaluation. (*Note*: The "not equals" operator can alternatively be written $! =$ or $^\wedge =$.) The values to be compared must be both numeric, both strings, both money values, or both dates/times. The data types of the operands in a comparison are not required to be identical; for performance reasons, however, it is generally a good idea if they are. INGRES evaluates such comparisons as follows:

- Numbers and money values compare algebraically (negative values are considered to be smaller than positive values, regardless of their absolute magnitude).

- Dates and times compare in accordance with the obvious chronologic ordering.

- CHAR and VARCHAR strings compare in accordance with their internal character encoding. If two strings of different lengths are to be compared, the shorter is conceptually padded at the right with blanks to make it the same length as the longer before the comparison is done. Thus, for example, the strings "XYZ" and "XYZbbb" (where "b" stands for a blank character) are considered to be equal to one another.

Note that field names appearing in the predicate must be appropriately qualified, just as they must in the target list.

4.2.5 Retrieval with Ordering.   Get supplier numbers and status for suppliers in Paris, in descending order of status.

```
RETRIEVE ( S.SNO, S.STATUS )
WHERE     S.CITY = "Paris"
SORT BY   STATUS:DESCENDING
```

```
Result:    |sno |status|
           |------------|
           |S3  |    30|
           |S2  |    10|
           |------------|
```

In general, the result of a RETRIEVE is not guaranteed to be in any particular row order. Here, however, the user has specified that the result is to be arranged in a particular sequence before being displayed.* Ordering is specified as follows:

```
field [: direction ] [, field [: direction ] ] ...
```

---

*Note that the ordering applies *only* to the displayed result. *Tables* per se are never considered to have an ordering in INGRES, as explained in Chapter 3.

where "direction" is either ASCENDING or DESCENDING (abbreviations A and D, respectively), and ASCENDING is the default. The left-to-right sequence of naming fields in the SORT BY clause corresponds to major-to-minor ordering in the obvious way.

Note that each "field" specification in a SORT BY clause must identify a field of the *result table*. Thus, for example, the following is *INCORRECT:*

```
RETRIEVE ( S.SNO )
SORT BY  CITY
```

And so is this:

```
RETRIEVE ( Z = S.SNO )
SORT BY  SNO
```

The single field of the result table in this latter example is called Z, not SNO.

4.2.6 Saving the Result of a Query. Get supplier number and status for suppliers in Paris with status > 20 (as in Example 4.2.4), and save the result as a new table TEMP.

```
RETRIEVE INTO TEMP ( S.SNO, S.STATUS )
WHERE    S.CITY = "Paris"
AND      S.STATUS > 20
```

Result: INGRES automatically creates a new table TEMP, with columns SNO and STATUS, and saves the result of the query in that table. That result is *not* displayed at the terminal. Table TEMP must not exist prior to execution of the RETRIEVE.

4.2.7 Retrieval of Expressions. For all parts, get the part number and the weight of that part in grams (part weights are given in table P in pounds). Show the result in descending part number order within ascending weight order.

```
RETRIEVE ( P.PNO, EXPLANATION = "Weight in grams =",
                  GMWT = P.WEIGHT * 454 )
SORT BY  GMWT:A, PNO:D
```

```
Result:  |pno |explanation      |gmwt|
         |--------------------------|
         |P5  |Weight in grams =|5448|
         |P1  |Weight in grams =|5448|
         |P4  |Weight in grams =|6356|
         |P3  |Weight in grams =|7718|
         |P2  |Weight in grams =|7718|
         |P6  |Weight in grams =|8626|
         |--------------------------|
```

Note: It is necessary to introduce names for the second and third columns of the result here, because there are no obvious names they can inherit. Those introduced names can then be referenced in the SORT BY clause, as explained in Example 4.2.5. (Unfortunately they cannot be so referenced in the WHERE clause.)

The expression

```
P.WEIGHT * 454
```

is an example of a *scalar-expression*, i.e., an expression whose operands are simple scalars (i.e., elementary values) and whose value in turn is another such scalar.* Such expressions can appear in the target list and/or in the WHERE clause. (More generally, they can appear wherever a scalar *constant* can appear.) A scalar-expression can involve, not only field names and constants and the usual operators (+, −, *, /, parentheses), but also exponentiation (**), string concatenation (+), and a wide array of *scalar functions*†—e.g., SIN, COS, SQRT (square root), INTERVAL (for date arithmetic), and so on. They can also involve aggregate operators such as SUM and AVG (see Sections 4.4 and 4.5).

One further point arises in connexion with this example: What happens if the weight of some part is null? Remember that null represents an unknown value. Suppose, for example, that the weight of part P1 is given as null in the database, instead of as 12. What then is the value of P.WEIGHT * 454 for part P1? The answer is that it also is null. In general, in fact, *any* scalar expression is considered to evaluate to null if any of the operands in that expression is itself null.

4.2.8 Partial-Match Retrieval.   Get all parts whose names begin with the letter C.

```
        RETRIEVE ( P.ALL )
        WHERE    P.PNAME = "C*"

Result:   ┌─────┬─────┬─────┬──────┬──────┐
          │pno  │pname│color│weight│city  │
          ├─────┴─────┴─────┴──────┴──────┤
          │P5   │Cam  │Blue │    12│Paris │
          │P6   │Cog  │Red  │    19│London│
          └───────────────────────────────┘
```

---

*"Scalar-expression" is not an official INGRES term; we use it because it is more precise than the official term, which is simply "expression."

†Like "scalar-expression," "scalar-function" is not an official INGRES term. We use it to distinguish such functions from other kinds of function, to be introduced in Section 4.5. A full list of INGRES functions can be found in Appendix C. The reader is referred to the RTI manuals for a discussion of which operators and functions apply to which data types.

The following special characters can be used to specify partial match retrieval in a string comparison:*

- The character "?" matches any single character.
- The character "*" matches any sequence of zero or more characters.
- The string "[*xyz*]" (where *xyz* is any set of characters) matches any character in *xyz*.

In the example, therefore, the RETRIEVE statement will retrieve records from table P for which the PNAME value begins with the letter C and has any sequence of zero or more characters following that C.

Here are some more examples of partial-match comparisons:

S.CITY = "*vill*"	—will evaluate to *true* if S.CITY contains the string "vill" anywhere inside it
S.SNO = "S??"	—will evaluate to *true* if S.SNO is exactly 3 characters long and the first is "S"
P.PNAME = "*c???"	—will evaluate to *true* if P.PNAME is 4 characters long or more and the last but three is "c"
S.CITY = "*[qtwz]*"	—will evaluate to *true* if S.CITY includes any of the letters q, t, w, or z
S.CITY = "[A-M]*"	—will evaluate to *true* if S.CITY starts with any letter in the range A, B, C, ..., M

4.2.9 *Retrieval Involving NULL.* Suppose for the sake of the example that part P5 has a weight value of null, rather than 12. Get part numbers for parts with weight greater than 10.

```
RETRIEVE ( P.PNO )
WHERE    P.WEIGHT > 10
```

Part P5 does not qualify. When a null value is compared with some other value in evaluating a predicate, regardless of the comparison operator involved, the result of the comparison is *never* considered to be *true*—even

---

*A special character can be made to behave like an ordinary character—i.e., the special interpretation can be disabled—by preceding it by a backslash character.

if that other value is also null. In other words, if P.WEIGHT happens to be null, then none of the following comparisons evaluates to *true:**

```
P.WEIGHT > 10
P.WEIGHT <= 10
P.WEIGHT = 10
P.WEIGHT <> 10
P.WEIGHT = NULL       /* This is illegal syntax. See below. */
P.WEIGHT <> NULL      /* So is this.                        */
```

Thus, if we issue the query

```
RETRIEVE ( P.PNO )
WHERE     P.WEIGHT <= 10
```

and compare the result with that of the previous query, part P5 will not appear in either of them.

A special comparison of the form

```
x IS [ NOT ] NULL
```

is provided for testing for the presence [or absence] of null values. For example:

```
RETRIEVE ( P.PNO )
WHERE     P.WEIGHT IS NULL
```

The syntax "P.WEIGHT = NULL" is illegal, because *nothing*—not even null itself—is considered to be equal to null.

4.3 MULTI-VARIABLE QUERIES

The ability to "join" two or more tables is one of the most powerful features of relational systems. In fact, it is the availability of the join operation, almost more than anything else, that distinguishes relational from nonrelational systems (see Appendix B). So what is a join? Loosely speaking, it is *a query in which data is retrieved from more than one table.* Here is a simple example.

---

*Actually they all evaluate to the *unknown* truth value. In the presence of null values, it is necessary to adopt a three-valued logic, in which the truth values are *true, false,* and *unknown.* (*Unknown* is really the null truth value, as a matter of fact.) The RETRIEVE statement retrieves records for which the WHERE predicate evaluates to *true,* i.e., not to *false* and not to *unknown.*

4.3.1 Simple Equijoin. Get all combinations of supplier-and-part information such that the supplier and part in question are located in the same city (i.e., are "colocated," to coin an ugly but convenient term).

```
RETRIEVE ( S.ALL, P.ALL )
WHERE     S.CITY = P.CITY
```

Result: *

sno	sname	status	city	pno	pname	color	weight	city
S1	Smith	20	London	P1	Nut	Red	12	London
S1	Smith	20	London	P4	Screw	Red	14	London
S1	Smith	20	London	P6	Cog	Red	19	London
S2	Jones	10	Paris	P2	Bolt	Green	17	Paris
S2	Jones	10	Paris	P5	Cam	Blue	12	Paris
S3	Blake	30	Paris	P2	Bolt	Green	17	Paris
S3	Blake	30	Paris	P5	Cam	Blue	12	Paris
S4	Clark	20	London	P1	Nut	Red	12	London
S4	Clark	20	London	P4	Screw	Red	14	London
S4	Clark	20	London	P6	Cog	Red	19	London

Explanation: It is clear from the English language statement of the problem that the required data comes from two tables, namely S and P. In the QUEL formulation of the query, therefore, we first list the fields of both tables in the target list, and we then express the connexion between the two (i.e., the fact that the CITY values must be equal) in the WHERE predicate. To understand how this works, imagine yourself looking at two rows, one row from each of the two tables—say the two rows shown here:

sno	sname	status	city		pno	pname	color	weight	city
S1	Smith	20	London		P1	Nut	Red	12	London

└─────────────────── identical ───────────────────┘

From these two rows you can see that supplier S1 and part P1 are indeed "colocated." These two rows will generate the result row

sno	sname	status	city	pno	pname	color	weight	city
S1	Smith	20	London	P1	Nut	Red	12	London

---

*Note that the result includes two columns both called CITY. We could avoid this potential ambiguity by explicitly introducing new names, say SCITY and PCITY, for the columns in question. The query would then look like this:

```
RETRIEVE ( S.SNO, S.SNAME, S.STATUS, SCITY = S.CITY,
           P.PNO, P.PNAME, P.COLOR, P.WEIGHT, PCITY = P.CITY )
WHERE     S.CITY = P.CITY
```

For brevity, however, we will stay with our original version of the query.

because they satisfy the predicate in the WHERE clause (namely, S.CITY
= P.CITY). Similarly for all other pairs of rows having matching CITY
values. Notice that supplier S5 (located in Athens) does not appear in the
result, because there are no parts stored in Athens; likewise, part P3 (stored
in Rome) also does not appear in the result, because there are no suppliers
located in Rome.

The result of this query is said to be a *join* of tables S and P over
matching CITY values. The term "join" is also used to refer to the operation of constructing such a result. The condition S.CITY = P.CITY is
said to be a *join condition* or *join predicate*.

A number of further points arise in connexion with this example, some
major, some minor.

- To repeat a point from Section 4.2: The fields to be compared in a join
  predicate must be both numeric, both strings, both money, or both
  dates/times. The data types are not required to be identical; for performance reasons, however, it is generally a good idea if they are.

- There is no requirement that the fields in a join predicate be identically
  named, though they very often will be.

- There is no requirement that the comparison operator in a join predicate be equality, though it very often will be. Examples of where it is
  not are given below (Example 4.3.2 and latter part of Example 4.3.8).
  If it is equality, then the join is sometimes called an *equijoin*.

- The WHERE clause in a join-RETRIEVE can include other conditions
  in addition to the join predicate itself. Example 4.3.3 below illustrates
  this possibility.

- It is of course possible—indeed, it is the normal case—to RETRIEVE
  just specified fields from a join, instead of necessarily having to
  RETRIEVE all of them. Examples 4.3.4–4.3.8 below illustrate this possibility.

- By definition, an *equi*join must produce a result containing two identical columns. If one of those two columns is eliminated, what is left
  is called the *natural* join. To construct the natural join of S and P (over
  cities) in QUEL, we could write:

```
RETRIEVE ( S.SNO, S.SNAME, S.STATUS, P.ALL )
WHERE    S.CITY = P.CITY
```

Natural join is probably the single most useful form of join—so much
so, that we often use the unqualified term "join" to refer to this case
specifically.

- It is also possible to form a join of three, four, ..., or any number of tables. Examples 4.3.6 and 4.3.7 below show joins involving three tables.

- The following is an alternative (and helpful) way to think about how joins may conceptually be constructed. First, form the *Cartesian product* of all tables involved in the request. The Cartesian product of a set of *n* tables is the table consisting of all possible rows *r,* such that *r* is the concatenation of a row from the first table, a row from the second table, ..., and a row from the *n*th table. For example, the Cartesian product of table S and table P (in that order) is the following table (let us call it table CP):

```
|sno |sname |status|city    |pno |pname |color|weight|city    |
|-----------------------------------------------------------------|
|S1  |Smith |    20|London  |P1  |Nut   |Red  |    12|London  |
|S1  |Smith |    20|London  |P2  |Bolt  |Green|    17|Paris   |
|S1  |Smith |    20|London  |P3  |Screw |Blue |    17|Rome    |
|S1  |Smith |    20|London  |P4  |Screw |Red  |    14|London  |
|S1  |Smith |    20|London  |P5  |Cam   |Blue |    12|Paris   |
|S1  |Smith |    20|London  |P6  |Cog   |Red  |    19|London  |
|S2  |Jones |    10|Paris   |P1  |Nut   |Red  |    12|London  |
|S2  |Jones |    10|Paris   |P2  |Bolt  |Green|    17|Paris   |
| .  | .    |    . | .      | .  | .    | .   |    . | .      |
| .  | .    |    . | .      | .  | .    | .   |    . | .      |
| .  | .    |    . | .      | .  | .    | .   |    . | .      |
|S5  |Adams |    30|Athens  |P6  |Cog   |Red  |    19|London  |
|-----------------------------------------------------------------|
```

(The complete table contains $5 * 6 = 30$ rows.)

Now eliminate from this Cartesian product all those rows that do not satisfy the join predicate. What is left is the required join. In the case at hand, we eliminate from CP all those rows in which S.CITY is not equal to P.CITY; and what is left is exactly the join shown earlier.

By the way, it is perfectly possible (though perhaps unusual) to formulate a QUEL query whose result is a Cartesian product. For example:

```
RETRIEVE ( S.ALL, P.ALL )
```

Result: Table CP as shown above.

4.3.2 Greater-Than Join.
Get all combinations of supplier and part information such that the supplier city follows the part city in alphabetical order.

```
RETRIEVE ( S.ALL, P.ALL )
WHERE    S.CITY > P.CITY
```

Result:

sno	sname	status	city	pno	pname	color	weight	city
S2	Jones	10	Paris	P1	Nut	Red	12	London
S2	Jones	10	Paris	P4	Screw	Red	14	London
S2	Jones	10	Paris	P6	Cog	Red	19	London
S3	Blake	30	Paris	P1	Nut	Red	12	London
S3	Blake	30	Paris	P4	Screw	Red	14	London
S3	Blake	30	Paris	P6	Cog	Red	19	London

4.3.3 Join Query with an Additional Condition. Get all combinations of supplier information and part information where the supplier and part concerned are colocated, but omitting suppliers with status 20.

```
RETRIEVE ( S.ALL, P.ALL )
WHERE    S.CITY = P.CITY
AND      S.STATUS <> 20
```

Result:

sno	sname	status	city	pno	pname	color	weight	city
S2	Jones	10	Paris	P2	Bolt	Green	17	Paris
S2	Jones	10	Paris	P5	Cam	Blue	12	Paris
S3	Blake	30	Paris	P2	Bolt	Green	17	Paris
S3	Blake	30	Paris	P5	Cam	Blue	12	Paris

4.3.4 Retrieving Specified Fields from a Join. Get all supplier-number/part-number combinations such that the supplier and part in question are colocated.

```
RETRIEVE ( S.SNO, P.PNO )
WHERE    S.CITY = P.CITY
```

Result:

sno	pno
S1	P1
S1	P4
S1	P6
S2	P2
S2	P5
S3	P2
S3	P5
S4	P1
S4	P4
S4	P6

4.3.5 **_Retrieving Specified Fields from a Join_.**   Get supplier numbers for
suppliers who supply at least one red part.

```
RETRIEVE UNIQUE ( SP.SNO )
WHERE     SP.PNO = P.PNO
AND       P.COLOR = "Red"
```

Result:
```
| sno  |
| ---- |
| S1   |
| S2   |
| S4   |
| ---- |
```

Although there are two tables being joined here, the result values are
all being retrieved from just one of the two. This kind of join query is
probably the one encountered most often in practice. Note that it will often
be desirable to request duplicate elimination (via UNIQUE) in this kind of
query.

We give another example to illustrate the point that the join may involve any number of tables, even if the final result values are extracted from
just one of those tables.

4.3.6 **_Retrieving Specified Fields from a Join_**   (*Join Involving Three Tables*). Get supplier names for suppliers who supply at least one red part.

```
RETRIEVE UNIQUE ( S.SNAME )
WHERE     S.SNO = SP.SNO
AND       SP.PNO = P.PNO
AND       P.COLOR = "Red"
```

Result:
```
| sname  |
| ------ |
| Clark  |
| Jones  |
| Smith  |
| ------ |
```

If the UNIQUE specification had been omitted, the result would have
contained duplicates, as follows:

```
| sname  |
| ------ |
| Smith  |
| Smith  |
| Smith  |
| Jones  |
| Clark  |
| ------ |
```

Exercise for the reader: Do you agree with this latter result?

4.3.7 *Retrieving Specified Fields from a Join (Join Involving Three Tables).* Get all pairs of city names such that a supplier located in the first city supplies a part stored in the second city. For example, supplier S1 supplies part P1; supplier S1 is located in London, and part P1 is stored in London; so (London,London) is a pair of cities in the result.

```
RETRIEVE UNIQUE ( SCITY = S.CITY, PCITY = P.CITY )
WHERE     S.SNO = SP.SNO
AND       SP.PNO = P.PNO
```

Result:

scity	pcity
London	London
London	Paris
London	Rome
Paris	London
Paris	Paris

Here column renaming is definitely a good idea! As an exercise, the reader should decide which particular supplier/part combinations give rise to which particular result rows.

4.3.8 *Joining a Table with Itself.* Get all pairs of supplier numbers such that the two suppliers concerned are colocated.

```
RANGE OF FIRST IS S
RANGE OF SECOND IS S

RETRIEVE ( X = FIRST.SNO, Y = SECOND.SNO )
WHERE     FIRST.CITY = SECOND.CITY
```

This query involves a join of table S with itself (over matching cities), as we now explain. Suppose for a moment that we had two separate copies of table S, the "first" copy and the "second" copy. Then the logic of the query is as follows: We need to be able to examine all possible pairs of supplier rows, one from the first copy of S and one from the second, and to retrieve the two supplier numbers from such a pair of rows when the city values are equal. We therefore need to be able to reference two supplier rows at the same time. In order to distinguish between the two references, we introduce two *range variables* FIRST and SECOND, each of which "ranges over" table S. At any particular time, FIRST represents some row from the "first" copy of table S, and SECOND represents some row from the "second" copy.* The result of the query is found by examining all possible pairs of FIRST/SECOND values and checking the WHERE predicate in every case:

```
| x   | y   |
| --------- |
| S1  | S1  |
| S4  | S1  |
| S2  | S2  |
| S3  | S2  |
| S2  | S3  |
| S3  | S3  |
| S1  | S4  |
| S4  | S4  |
| S5  | S5  |
| --------- |
```

We can tidy up this result by extending the WHERE clause as follows:

```
RETRIEVE ( X = FIRST.SNO, Y = SECOND.SNO )
WHERE     FIRST.CITY = SECOND.CITY
AND       FIRST.SNO < SECOND.SNO
```

The effect of the condition "FIRST.SNO < SECOND.SNO" is twofold: (a) it eliminates pairs of supplier numbers of the form (x,x); (b) it guarantees that the pairs (x,y) and (y,x) will not both appear. Result:

```
| x   | y   |
| --------- |
| S2  | S3  |
| S1  | S4  |
| --------- |
```

This is the first example we have seen in which the explicit use of range variables has been necessary. However, it is never wrong to introduce range variables, even when they are not explicitly required, and sometimes they can help to make the statement clearer. (They can also save writing, if table names are on the lengthy side.) In general, a range variable is a variable that ranges over some specified table—i.e., a variable whose only permitted values are the rows of that table. In other words, if range variable R ranges over table T, then, at any given time, R represents some row or record r of T. For example, the query "Get supplier number and status for suppliers

---

*Of course, INGRES does not really construct two physical copies of the table. Our explanation is purely conceptual in nature.

in Paris'' (the example from the beginning of Section 4.2) could be expressed in QUEL as follows:

```
RANGE OF SX IS S

RETRIEVE ( SX.SNO, SX.STATUS ) WHERE SX.CITY = "Paris"
```

The range variable here is SX, and it ranges over table S. The RETRIEVE statement can be paraphrased: "For each possible value of the variable SX, retrieve the SNO and STATUS components of that value, if and only if the CITY component has the value Paris."

As a matter of fact, QUEL *always* requires queries to be formulated in terms of range variables. If no such variables are specified explicitly, then QUEL assumes the existence of *implicit* variables with the same name(s) as the corresponding table(s). For example, the query

```
RETRIEVE ( S.ALL )
```

is treated by QUEL as if it had been expressed as follows:

```
RANGE OF S IS S

RETRIEVE ( S.ALL )
```

In the second of these two formulations, the symbol "S" in the expression "S.ALL" really means *range variable* S, not *table* S.

To conclude this section: We can now see why what we were calling "simple queries" in the previous section are technically known as "one-variable queries"—they are queries involving a single (implicit or explicit) range variable. By contrast, the queries of the present section have been examples of "two-variable queries" or (in the case of Examples 4.3.6 and 4.3.7) "three-variable queries." More generally, they have all been examples of what are usually called *multi*-variable queries. Note in particular that the query of Example 4.3.8 (joining a table to itself) was a multi-variable query, even though it involved only a single table.

4.4   SIMPLE AGGREGATES

Although quite powerful in many ways, the RETRIEVE statement as described so far is still inadequate for certain problems. For example, even a query as simple as "How many suppliers are there?" cannot be expressed using only the constructs introduced up till now. QUEL therefore provides a number of special operators known as *aggregates* to enhance its basic retrieval power. The operators available are COUNT, SUM, AVG, MAX, and MIN; COUNTU, SUMU, and AVGU, where the trailing "U" stands for "unique" (see Example 4.4.2 below); and ANY. Each of these operators can be used either as a *simple aggregate** or as an *aggregate function*. The present section is concerned with simple aggregates only; aggregate functions are deferred to the next section. Also, the ANY operator, which is something of a special case, is deferred entirely to Section 4.6.

In general, an aggregate is an operator that can be applied to the collection of values in a specified column of some table—most likely a *derived* table, i.e., a table constructed in some way from the given base tables (see Example 4.4.3)—to produce a single scalar value as its result. The general syntax for an aggregate reference is as follows:

```
aggregate ( scalar-expression [ WHERE predicate ] )
```

where "aggregate" is any one of the available aggregate operators. The value of the aggregate reference is defined as follows:

```
COUNT -- number of values in the column

SUM   -- sum of the values in the column

AVG   -- average of the values in the column

MAX   -- largest value in the column

MIN   -- smallest value in the column
```

COUNTU, SUMU, and AVGU are the same as COUNT, SUM, and AVG, respectively, except that redundant duplicate values are eliminated from the argument column before the aggregate is computed. For SUM, AVG, SUMU, and AVGU, the column concerned must contain numeric, money, or date/time interval values. Any null values in the argument column are always eliminated before the aggregate is computed. If the argument column evaluates to the empty set, the aggregate reference returns zero (for numeric, money, or date/time interval arguments), or blank or empty (for other arguments).

Since an aggregate reference returns a single scalar value, it can appear

---

*The official INGRES term is just "aggregate," not "simple aggregate." We will normally follow the official INGRES usage, except where we explicitly wish to distinguish between simple aggregates and aggregate functions. We remark in passing, however, that "aggregate" is not a particularly felicitous term, since it tends to obscure the fact that the aggregate evaluates to a *scalar*.

in a scalar-expression (and hence in a target list or a WHERE predicate or an argument to another aggregate reference) wherever a simple scalar constant is allowed.

4.4.1 Aggregate in the Target List.   Get the total number of suppliers.

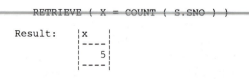

```
          RETRIEVE ( X = COUNT ( S.SNO ) )
Result:      ｜x    ｜
             ｜----｜
             ｜   5｜
             ｜----｜
```

Note that it is necessary to introduce a name (X in the example) for the single column of the result.

Aside: We remark that the field we choose to do the counting on in a COUNT reference is arbitrary; any field of the relevant table would suffice (provided nulls are not allowed for the field in question). For example, the argument S.SNO in the foregoing RETRIEVE could be replaced by any of S.SNAME, S.STATUS, or S.CITY without in any way altering the result of the query. Alternatively (and perhaps more simply), it could be replaced by the expression S.ALL.

4.4.2 Aggregate in the Target List, with Duplicate Elimination.   Get the total number of suppliers currently supplying parts.

```
          RETRIEVE ( Y = COUNTU ( SP.SNO ) )
Result:      ｜Y    ｜
             ｜----｜
             ｜   4｜
             ｜----｜
```

4.4.3 Aggregate in the Target List, with a Predicate.   Get the total quantity of part P2 supplied.

```
          RETRIEVE ( Z = SUM ( SP.QTY WHERE SP.PNO = "P2" ) )
Result:      ｜Z    ｜
             ｜----｜
             ｜1000｜
             ｜----｜
```

This example illustrates the point that the argument to an aggregate can be a column of a *derived* table. The derived table in question is the table that results from evaluating the expression

```
SP.ALL WHERE SP.PNO = "P2"
```

The SUM operator is then applied to the QTY column of this derived table.

4.4.4 Aggregate in the WHERE Clause.   Get supplier numbers for suppliers with status value less than the current maximum status value in the S table.

```
RETRIEVE ( S.SNO )
WHERE     S.STATUS < MAX ( S.STATUS )
```

```
Result:    |sno |
           |----|
           |S1  |
           |S2  |
           |S4  |
           |----|
```

Note carefully that there are two different "S"s in this example—that is, two different range variables, both of which happen to be called "S". The following formulation makes the point explicit:

```
RANGE OF SX IS S
RANGE OF SY IS S

RETRIEVE ( SX.SNO )
WHERE     SX.STATUS < MAX ( SY.STATUS )
```

In general, any range variables (either implicit or explicit) appearing inside the argument to an aggregate are *purely local to that aggregate*; they are distinct from any range variable that may happen to have the same name but appears outside the aggregate—*unless* they are mentioned in a BY clause within the aggregate argument, in which case we are dealing with an aggregate function rather than a simple aggregate. Aggregate functions are discussed in the next section.

4.5 AGGREGATE FUNCTIONS

First, a word of warning: The topic of this section is quite possibly the most confusing part of the entire QUEL language! We will endeavor to avoid as much of that confusion as possible in what follows.

Consider Example 4.4.3 from the previous section once again. That example showed how it is possible to compute the total quantity supplied for some specific part (part P2, in the example). Suppose, by contrast, that it is desired to compute the total quantity supplied for *each* part:

4.5.1   Use of the BY Clause.

For each part supplied, get the part number and the total shipment quantity for that part.

```
RETRIEVE ( SP.PNO, X = SUM ( SP.QTY BY SP.PNO ) )
```

We defer a full explanation of the BY clause to the next example below, Example 4.5.2; for now, we will just assume that its meaning is intuitively obvious. In the case at hand, its effect is to cause QTY values from the SP table to be summed for each distinct value of PNO in that table. Thus the overall result is:

```
¡pno ¡x    ¡
¡----------¡
¡P1   ¡ 600¡
¡P2   ¡1000¡
¡P3   ¡ 400¡
¡P4   ¡ 500¡
¡P5   ¡ 500¡
¡P6   ¡ 100¡
¡----------¡
```

4.5.2   Use of the BY Clause.

For each supplier, get full supplier details, together with a count of the number of parts supplied by that supplier.

```
RETRIEVE ( S.ALL, X = COUNT ( SP.PNO BY S.SNO
                              WHERE SP.SNO = S.SNO ) )
```

Result:

sno	sname	status	city	x
S1	Smith	20	London	6
S2	Jones	10	Paris	2
S3	Blake	30	Paris	1
S4	Clark	20	London	3
S5	Adams	30	Athens	0

We now explain the action of the BY clause in detail. For simplicity we assume that the BY clause in question names only a single field;* the generalization to multiple fields is tedious but straightforward.

First of all, an aggregate operator whose argument includes a BY clause is known in QUEL as an aggregate *function*. The value of an aggregate function is not just a single scalar value, but rather an entire set of such values, one such value for each distinct value of the field identified in the

---

*As this remark suggests, the BY clause permits the specification of multiple fields. It also permits specifications of the form "BY R.ALL."

BY clause. (In other words, the value of an aggregate function is an entire *column* of scalar values.) A query in which the target list involves an aggregate function is *conceptually* (we stress the "conceptually") evaluated in three stages, as follows.

1. First, the argument to the BY clause itself is evaluated, to yield an intermediate result table (TEMP1, say) consisting of a single column. In the example, table TEMP1 looks like this (it simply lists all values of the column S.SNO):

```
TEMP1   |sno |
        |----|
        |S1  |
        |S2  |
        |S3  |
        |S4  |
        |S5  |
        |----|
```

In general, table TEMP1 will contain all distinct values of the BY field. Note that *duplicates are eliminated* in the production of this first intermediate result (of course, duplicate elimination has no effect in the case at hand).

2. Next, the aggregate function is replaced by a set of simple aggregates, one for each of the values in TEMP1. For each of those TEMP1-values, a simple aggregate is constructed in which the BY clause from the aggregate function is replaced by a WHERE-predicate of the form

```
BY-variable = TEMP1-value
```

(this predicate is ANDed on to any WHERE-predicate already present in the aggregate). In the example, this step yields the following five simple aggregates:

```
COUNT ( SP.PNO WHERE SP.SNO = S.SNO AND S.SNO = "S1" )
COUNT ( SP.PNO WHERE SP.SNO = S.SNO AND S.SNO = "S2" )
COUNT ( SP.PNO WHERE SP.SNO = S.SNO AND S.SNO = "S3" )
COUNT ( SP.PNO WHERE SP.SNO = S.SNO AND S.SNO = "S4" )
COUNT ( SP.PNO WHERE SP.SNO = S.SNO AND S.SNO = "S5" )
```

From these five aggregates, another intermediate result table (table TEMP2, say) is constructed. Table TEMP2 consists of two columns, one ("by") listing the values of the BY variable and the other ("agg") listing the corresponding simple aggregate values. In the example, table TEMP2 looks like this:*

```
TEMP2  | by  | agg |
       | --------- |
       | S1  |   6 |
       | S2  |   2 |
       | S3  |   1 |
       | S4  |   3 |
       | S5  |   0 |
       | --------- |
```

3. Now the original query is altered to read as follows:

```
RETRIEVE UNIQUE ( S.ALL, X = TEMP2.agg )
WHERE     S.SNO = TEMP2.by
```

That is:

(a) A UNIQUE specification is inserted (unless one is already present);

(b) The aggregate function in the target list is replaced by a reference to the "agg" column of table TEMP2; and

(c) A WHERE-predicate is appended to the query (ANDed on to any WHERE-predicate already present), specifying an equality join condition between the BY field specified in the original query and the "by" column of table TEMP2.

   The altered query is then evaluated to yield the desired overall result.

Note that the effect of appending the join condition to the query is to make range variables that are mentioned in a BY clause known outside the aggregate function. In other words, such variables are *not* purely local to the aggregate function. Any other range variables referenced inside the aggregate function are, however, still purely local.

   Exercise for the reader: Try applying the foregoing algorithm to Example 4.5.1 to convince yourself that the final result in that example is indeed the one intuitively expected.

---

*The tabulation of TEMP2 is accurate as shown unless the WHERE clause in the original aggregate argument is prefixed by the keyword ONLY, as in, e.g.:

```
RETRIEVE ( S.ALL, X = COUNT ( SP.PNO BY S.SNO
                              ONLY WHERE SP.SNO = S.SNO ) )
```

In this latter case, rows for which the argument set is empty (i.e., rows for which the COUNT evaluates to zero) will not be included in TEMP2. In the example, therefore, the row for S5 would be eliminated at this step. For more information regarding the ONLY option, the reader is referred to the RTI manuals.

A very common mistake in the use of aggregate functions is to omit some necessary WHERE predicate. For example:

4.5.3   *Use of the BY Clause.*   For each supplier, get full supplier details, together with a count of the number of parts that supplier supplies. (Same as Example 4.5.2)

*** *BEWARE*: *INCORRECT FORMULATION* ***

```
RETRIEVE ( S.ALL, X = COUNT ( SP.PNO BY S.SNO ) )
```

This formulation does superficially look as if it might produce the desired result. But of course it does not. Let us go through the three evaluation steps:

1. First, evaluate the BY clause:

```
TEMP1   | sno |
        |-----|
        | S1  |
        | S2  |
        | S3  |
        | S4  |
        | S5  |
        |-----|
```

2. Next, replace the aggregate function by a set of simple aggregates, one for each of the values in TEMP1:

```
COUNT ( SP.PNO WHERE S.SNO = "S1" )
COUNT ( SP.PNO WHERE S.SNO = "S2" )
COUNT ( SP.PNO WHERE S.SNO = "S3" )
COUNT ( SP.PNO WHERE S.SNO = "S4" )
COUNT ( SP.PNO WHERE S.SNO = "S5" )
```

Given our usual sample data values, *each of these five simple aggregates evaluates to the same value, namely 12*. The WHERE clauses have no effect, because they include no reference to range variable SP; hence they do not restrict the set of SP.PNO values to be counted in any way.* Thus, table TEMP2 looks like this:

---

*More precisely, they have no effect because they include no reference to range variable SP *and* they evaluate to *true* in every case. As a counterexample, the simple aggregate

```
COUNT ( SP.PNO WHERE S.SNO = "S6" )
```

would evaluate to 0, not 12, because no supplier S6 exists.

```
TEMP2   |by   |agg  |
        |-----|-----|
        |S1   |   12|
        |S2   |   12|
        |S3   |   12|
        |S4   |   12|
        |S5   |   12|
        |-----------|
```

3. Last, the original query is altered to read as follows:

```
RETRIEVE UNIQUE ( S.ALL, X = TEMP2.agg )
WHERE     S.SNO = TEMP2.by
```

This query is then evaluated to yield the following:

```
|sno |sname |status|city   |x  |
|----------------------------------|
|S1  |Smith |   20|London |  12|
|S2  |Jones |   10|Paris  |  12|
|S3  |Blake |   30|Paris  |  12|
|S4  |Clark |   20|London |  12|
|S5  |Adams |   30|Athens |  12|
|----------------------------------|
```

which is certainly *not* the desired result.

Exercise for the reader: Explain why no WHERE clause was required in Example 4.5.1. (Hint: If there were a WHERE clause, what would it look like?)

For a given value of the BY-variable, an aggregate function behaves just like a simple aggregate, returning a simple scalar value. Thus, aggregate functions can appear wherever simple scalar variable references can appear. See the next three examples for a variety of illustrations of this point.

4.5.4   Aggregate Function in the WHERE Clause.   Get part numbers for all parts supplied by more than one supplier.

```
RETRIEVE ( SP.PNO )
WHERE     COUNT ( SP.SNO BY SP.PNO ) > 1
```

Result: |pno |
          |----|
          |P1 |
          |P2 |
          |P4 |
          |P5 |
          |----|

Exercise for the reader: Explain in detail how this query is evaluated.

4.5.5 Nested Aggregate Functions. Get the average of the total quantities in which each part is supplied.

```
RETRIEVE ( X = AVG ( SUM ( SP.QTY BY SP.PNO ) ) )
```

Result:
```
|x        |
|---------|
| 516.667 |
|---------|
```

4.5.6 Aggregate Functions in an Arithmetic Expression. For each supplier, get the supplier number and a count of the parts not supplied by that supplier.

```
RETRIEVE ( S.SNO, X = COUNT ( P.PNO ) -
                      COUNT ( SP.PNO BY S.SNO
                              WHERE SP.SNO = S.SNO ) )
```

The first COUNT returns the total number of parts, the second returns the number supplied by this supplier. Result:

```
|sno |x   |
|----------|
|S1  |   0|
|S2  |   4|
|S3  |   5|
|S4  |   3|
|S5  |   6|
|----------|
```

4.6 QUANTIFIED QUERIES

Note: *This section is probably best skipped on a first reading.*

In this section we explain the use of the ANY operator, which is QUEL's analog of the *existential quantifier* ("there exists," written simply EXISTS) of predicate logic. We begin by explaining the function of EXISTS in general terms, then describe the QUEL ANY operator specifically.

Consider the following expression, which is a predicate logic formulation of the query "Get supplier names for suppliers who supply part P2." *Note*: The colons in the expression can be read as "where" or "such that."

```
S.SNAME : EXISTS ( SP : S.SNO = SP.SNO AND
                        SP.PNO = "P2" )
```

Explanation: As already stated, EXISTS represents the existential quantifier of predicate logic. Let the symbol "x" designate some arbitrary variable. In logic, then, the *existentially quantified predicate*

```
EXISTS ( x : predicate-involving-x )
```

evaluates to *true* if and only if "predicate-involving-x" is *true* for some value of the variable x. For example, suppose the variable x can take as its value any arbitrary integer in the range 1 to 10. Then the predicate

```
EXISTS ( x : x < 5 )
```

("there exists some value x such that x is less than 5") evaluates to *true*. By contrast, the predicate

```
EXISTS ( x : x < 0 )
```

evaluates to *false*.

Turning now to the example at hand: To evaluate the query, we consider each value of S.SNAME in turn and see whether it causes the existence test to evaluate to *true*. Suppose the first such value is "Smith" (so that the corresponding SNO value is S1). Does there exist an SP record having SNO equal to S1 and PNO equal to P2? If the answer is yes, then "Smith" should be one of the values retrieved. Similarly for each of the other values of S.SNAME.

The normal QUEL formulation of this query is of course as follows:

```
RETRIEVE ( S.SNAME ) WHERE S.SNO = SP.SNO
                     AND    SP.PNO = "P2"
```

Comparing this with the predicate logic formulation, we can see that:

1. The keyword RETRIEVE and the parentheses surrounding the target list are essentially just noise;
2. The keyword WHERE corresponds to the colon separating the target list from the predicate;
3. The predicate

```
S.SNO = SP.SNO AND SP.PNO = "P2"
```

is merely QUEL syntax for the existentially quantified predicate

```
EXISTS ( SP : S.SNO = SP.SNO AND SP.PNO = "P2" )
```

In other words, *any range variable mentioned in the WHERE clause and not in the target list is implicitly considered to be existentially quantified.*

Thus the QUEL statement above can be paraphrased:

"Get supplier names such that *there exists a shipment record* with the same supplier number and with part number P2."

The aggregate function ANY can be used if desired to make the quantification more explicit:

```
RETRIEVE ( S.SNAME )
WHERE     ANY ( SP.SNO BY S.SNO
                WHERE  S.SNO = SP.SNO
                AND    SP.PNO = "P2" ) = 1
```

ANY returns the value 1 if its argument set is not empty, the value 0 otherwise. Thus ANY returns the value 1 if and only if the existence test is satisfied; to put this another way (and speaking rather loosely), "ANY (...) = 1" *corresponds to EXISTS,* "ANY(...) = 0" *corresponds to NOT EXISTS.*

A number of points arise in connexion with this example:

- In practice there is little point in using the "ANY(...) = 1" form, since such a query can always be expressed more simply without using ANY at all, as the example above illustrates. However, the "ANY(...) = 0" form *is* sometimes necessary, as we shall see below in Examples 4.6.1 and 4.6.2 below.

- The field over which we choose to compute the ANY function (field SP.SNO, in the example) is arbitrary; any field of the relevant table would suffice. At the time of writing, QUEL does not permit an ANY reference of the form "ANY(R.ALL...)."

- Note that the predicates ANY(...) = 0 and COUNT(...) = 0 are functionally identical. However, the ANY form is preferable from the standpoint of logic, in that it is a more "natural" formulation (it is closer to the natural language expression "there does not exist any"). As a result, it also has the potential for more efficient evaluation.

Although the single example discussed so far merely shows another way of formulating a query for a problem that we already know how to handle, in general ANY—at least in the form "ANY(...) = 0"—is an extremely useful feature of the QUEL language. We now consider a couple of examples of the "ANY(...) = 0" form.

4.6.1   *Query Using ANY (...) = 0.*   Get supplier names for suppliers who do not supply part P2.

```
RETRIEVE ( S.SNAME )
WHERE      ANY ( SP.SNO BY S.SNO
                 WHERE  S.SNO = SP.SNO
                 AND    SP.PNO = "P2" ) = 0

Result:    |sname |
           |------|
           |Adams |
           |------|
```

The query may be paraphrased:

"Get supplier names such that *there does not exist a shipment record* with the same supplier number and with part number P2."

Notice how easy it is to convert the formulation for the previous query (ANY version) into this formulation.

4.6.2   *Query Using ANY (. . .) = 0.*   Get supplier names for suppliers who supply all parts.

There are two quantifiers commonly encountered in predicate logic, EXISTS and *FORALL*. FORALL is the *universal* quantifier. In logic, the *universally quantified predicate*

```
FORALL ( x : predicate-involving-x )
```

evaluates to *true* if and only if "predicate-involving-x" is *true* for all values of the variable x. For example, if (again) the variable x can take as its value any arbitrary integer in the range 1 to 10, then the predicate

```
FORALL ( x : x < 100 )
```

("for all values x, x is less than 100") evaluates to *true*. By contrast, the predicate

```
FORALL ( x : x < 5 )
```

evaluates to *false*.

FORALL is fundamentally what is needed to express the query at hand; what we would like to say is something like "Retrieve supplier names where, FORALL parts, there EXISTS an SP record saying that the supplier supplies the part." Unfortunately QUEL does not directly support FORALL. However, any predicate involving FORALL can always be converted into an equivalent predicate involving EXISTS instead, by virtue of the following identity:

```
FORALL ( x : p ) ≡ NOT EXISTS ( x : NOT ( p ) )
```

Here "p" is any predicate involving the variable x. For example, suppose once again that x stands for some integer in the range 1 to 10. Then the predicate

```
FORALL ( x : x < 100 )
```

(which of course evaluates to *true*) is equivalent to the predicate

```
NOT EXISTS ( x : NOT ( x < 100 ) )
```

("there does not exist an x such that it is not the case that x is less than 100"—i.e., "there is no x such that x $> =$ 100"). Likewise, the predicate

```
FORALL ( x : x < 5 )
```

(which is *false*) is equivalent to the predicate

```
NOT EXISTS ( x : NOT ( x < 5 ) )
```

("there does not exist an x such that it is not the case that x is less than 5"—i.e., "there is no x such that x $> =$ 5").

As another example, suppose the variables x and y represent real numbers. Then the predicate

```
FORALL ( x : EXISTS ( y : y > x ) )
```

(which is *true*) is equivalent to the predicate

```
NOT EXISTS ( x : NOT EXISTS ( y : y > x ) )
```

("there is no real number x such that there is no real number y such that y is greater than x").*

Turning now to the problem at hand, we can convert the expression "Suppliers where FORALL parts there EXISTS an SP record saying that the supplier supplies the part," with predicate logic formulation—

```
S.SNAME : FORALL ( P : EXISTS ( SP : S.SNO = SP.SNO AND
                                     SP.PNO = P.PNO ) )
```

—into the equivalent expression "Suppliers where NOT EXISTS a part such that NOT EXISTS an SP record saying that the supplier supplies the part," with predicate logic formulation

```
S.SNAME : NOT EXISTS ( P : NOT EXISTS ( SP : S.SNO = SP.SNO AND
                                             SP.PNO = P.PNO ) )
```

Hence the QUEL formulation is:

```
RETRIEVE ( S.SNAME )
WHERE   ANY ( P.PNO BY S.SNO
                    WHERE ANY ( SP.PNO BY S.SNO, P.PNO
                                WHERE   S.SNO = SP.SNO
                                AND     SP.PNO = P.PNO ) = 0 ) = 0
```

```
Result:     | sname |
            |-------|
            | Smith |
            |-------|
```

---

*Incidentally, this example illustrates the important point that the order of quantifiers matters in expressions involving both types. The expression

```
FORALL ( x : EXISTS ( y : y > x ) )
```

is *true*. However, the expression

```
EXISTS ( y : FORALL ( x : y > x ) )
```

("there is a real number y such that, for all real numbers x, y is greater than x"—i.e., "there exists a number greater than all other numbers"), which is obtained from the first expression by inverting the order of the quantifiers, is *false*.

The query may be paraphrased: "Retrieve supplier names for suppliers such that there does not exist a part that they do not supply." In general, the easiest way to tackle complicated queries such as this one is probably to write them in a predicate logic form with FORALL quantifiers first, and then convert them, more or less mechanically, into a QUEL RETRIEVE statement involving "ANY(...) = 0" instead.

4.7 SUMMARY

We have now come to the end of this rather long chapter on the QUEL RETRIEVE statement. We have illustrated:

- the RETRIEVE clause itself, with its target list
- the use of INTO to save the result
- assignments in the target list, with introduced names
- scalar expressions and scalar functions
- the use of UNIQUE to eliminate duplicates
- the use of SORT BY (or UNIQUE) to order the result
- the WHERE clause, including:
  - comparison operators =, < >, >, > =, <, < =
  - join predicates
  - Boolean operators AND, OR, NOT
  - partial match retrieval
  - the special predicate IS [NOT] NULL
- aggregates and aggregate functions
- quantified queries

In the next chapter we will go on to consider the remaining QUEL data manipulation operations APPEND, REPLACE, and DELETE.

EXERCISES

All of the following exercises are based on the suppliers-parts-projects database (see the exercises in Chapter 3). In each one, you are asked to write a RETRIEVE statement for the indicated query. For convenience we repeat the structure of the database below:

```
S    ( SNO, SNAME, STATUS, CITY )
P    ( PNO, PNAME, COLOR, WEIGHT, CITY )
J    ( JNO, JNAME, CITY )
SPJ  ( SNO, PNO, JNO, QTY )
```

The exercises are arranged into groups, in approximate order of increasing difficulty within each group. You should try at least some of the easy ones in each group.

Single-Variable Queries

4.1 Get full details of all projects.

4.2 Get full details of all projects in London and save the result as a new table LJ.

4.3 Get supplier numbers for suppliers who supply project J1, in supplier number order.

4.4 Get all shipments where the quantity is in the range 300 to 750 inclusive.

4.5 Get a list of all part-color/part-city combinations, with duplicate color/city pairs eliminated.

4.6 Get all parts where the weight of the part in grams is less than 7000 (part weights are given in table P in pounds).

4.7 Get project numbers and cities where the city has an "o" as the second letter of its name.

Multi-Variable Queries

4.8 Get project names for projects supplied by supplier S5.

4.9 Get colors of parts supplied by supplier S1.

4.10 Get part numbers for parts supplied to any project in London.

4.11 Get project numbers for projects using at least one part available from supplier S1.

4.12 Get supplier numbers for suppliers supplying at least one part supplied by at least one supplier who supplies at least one red part.

4.13 Get supplier numbers for suppliers with a status lower than that of supplier S1.

4.14 Get all supplier-number/part-number/project-number triples such that the indicated supplier, part, and project are all colocated.

4.15 Get all supplier-number/part-number/project-number triples such that the indicated supplier, part, and project are not all colocated.

4.16 Get all supplier-number/part-number/project-number triples such that no two of the indicated supplier, part, and project are colocated.

4.17 Get part numbers for parts supplied by a supplier in London to a project in London.

4.18 Get all pairs of city names such that a supplier in the first city supplies a project in the second city.

4.19 Get part numbers for parts supplied to any project by a supplier in the same city as that project.

4.20 Get project numbers for projects supplied by at least one supplier not in the same city.

4.21 Get all pairs of part numbers such that some supplier supplies both the indicated parts.

Aggregates

4.22 Get the total number of projects supplied by supplier S1.

4.23 Get the total quantity of part P1 supplied by supplier S1.

4.24 Get project numbers for projects whose city is first in the alphabetic list of such cities.

Aggregate Functions

4.25 For each part being supplied to a project, get the part number, the project number, and the corresponding total quantity.

4.26 Get part numbers for parts for which the average shipment quantity is greater than 320.

4.27 Get part numbers for parts for which the average total shipment per project is greater than 320.

4.28 For each part, get full part details, together with the sum of all shipment quantities for that part.

4.29 Get project numbers for projects supplied with part P1 in an average quantity greater than the greatest quantity in which any part is supplied to project J1.

4.30 Get supplier numbers for suppliers supplying some project with part P1 in a quantity greater than the average quantity in which part P1 is supplied to that project.

Quantified Queries

4.31 Repeat Exercise 4.10 to use ANY in your solution.

4.32 Get project numbers for projects not supplied with any red part by any London supplier.

ANSWERS TO SELECTED EXERCISES

We assume throughout the answers below that the following RANGE statements are in effect:

```
RANGE OF SX IS S
RANGE OF SPJX IS SPJ
RANGE OF SPJY IS SPJ
```

The answers shown are not necessarily the only ones possible.

```
4.1   RETRIEVE ( J.ALL )

4.2   RETRIEVE INTO LJ ( J.ALL ) WHERE J.CITY = "London"

4.3   RETRIEVE ( SPJ.SNO )
      WHERE     SPJ.JNO = "J1"
      SORT BY   SNO

4.4   RETRIEVE ( SPJ.ALL )
      WHERE     SPJ.QTY >= 300
      AND       SPJ.QTY <= 750

4.5   RETRIEVE UNIQUE ( P.COLOR, P.CITY )

4.6   RETRIEVE ( P.ALL )
      WHERE     ( P.WEIGHT * 454 ) < 7000

4.7   RETRIEVE ( J.JNO, J.CITY )
      WHERE     J.CITY = "?o*"

4.8   RETRIEVE UNIQUE ( J.JNAME )
      WHERE     J.JNO = SPJ.JNO
      AND       SPJ.SNO = "S5"

4.9   RETRIEVE UNIQUE ( P.COLOR )
      WHERE     P.PNO = SPJ.PNO
      AND       SPJ.SNO = "S1"

4.10  RETRIEVE UNIQUE ( SPJ.PNO )
      WHERE     SPJ.JNO = J.JNO
      AND       J.CITY = "London"

4.11  RETRIEVE UNIQUE ( SPJ.JNO )
      WHERE     SPJ.PNO = SPJX.PNO
      AND       SPJX.SNO = "S1"

4.12  RETRIEVE UNIQUE ( SPJ.SNO )
      WHERE     SPJ.PNO = SPJX.PNO
      AND       SPJX.SNO = SPJY.SNO
      AND       SPJY.PNO = P.PNO
      AND       P.COLOR = "Red"

4.13  RETRIEVE UNIQUE ( S.SNO )
      WHERE     S.STATUS < SX.STATUS
      AND       SX.SNO = "S1"

4.14  RETRIEVE ( S.SNO, P.PNO, J.JNO )
      WHERE     S.CITY = P.CITY
      AND       P.CITY = J.CITY

4.15  RETRIEVE ( S.SNO, P.PNO, J.JNO )
      WHERE     S.CITY <> P.CITY
      OR        P.CITY <> J.CITY
      OR        J.CITY <> S.CITY

4.16  RETRIEVE ( S.SNO, P.PNO, J.JNO )
      WHERE     S.CITY <> P.CITY
      AND       P.CITY <> J.CITY
      AND       J.CITY <> S.CITY

4.17  RETRIEVE UNIQUE ( SPJ.PNO )
      WHERE     SPJ.SNO = S.SNO AND S.CITY = "London"
      AND       SPJ.JNO = J.JNO AND J.CITY = "London"
```

4.18 RETRIEVE UNIQUE (S.CITY, J.CITY)
　　　　WHERE　　S.SNO = SPJ.SNO AND SPJ.JNO = J.JNO

4.19 RETRIEVE UNIQUE (SPJ.PNO)
　　　　WHERE　　SPJ.SNO = S.SNO
　　　　AND　　　SPJ.JNO = J.JNO
　　　　AND　　　S.CITY = J.CITY

4.20 RETRIEVE UNIQUE (SPJ.JNO)
　　　　WHERE　　SPJ.SNO = S.SNO
　　　　AND　　　SPJ.JNO = J.JNO
　　　　AND　　　S.CITY <> J.CITY

4.21 RETRIEVE UNIQUE (LEFT = SPJ.PNO, RIGHT = SPJX.PNO)
　　　　WHERE　　SPJ.SNO = SPJX.SNO
　　　　AND　　　SPJ.PNO < SPJX.PNO

4.22 RETRIEVE (X = COUNTU (SPJ.JNO WHERE SPJ.SNO = "S1"))

4.23 RETRIEVE (Y = SUM (SPJ.QTY WHERE SPJ.SNO = "S1"
　　　　　　　　　　　　　　　　　AND　　SPJ.PNO = "P1"))

4.24 RETRIEVE UNIQUE (J.JNO)
　　　　WHERE　　J.CITY = MIN (J.CITY)

4.25 RETRIEVE (SPJ.PNO, SPJ.JNO,
　　　　　　　　　　Z = SUM (SPJ.QTY BY SPJ.PNO, SPJ.JNO))

4.26 RETRIEVE (SPJ.PNO)
　　　　WHERE　　AVG (SPJ.QTY BY SPJ.PNO, SPJ.JNO) > 320

4.27 RETRIEVE (SPJ.PNO)
　　　　WHERE　　AVG (SUM (SPJ.QTY BY SPJ.PNO, SPJ.JNO)
　　　　　　　　　　　　　　　　　BY SPJ.PNO) > 320

4.28 RETRIEVE (P.ALL, X = SUM (SPJ.QTY BY P.PNO
　　　　　　　　　　　　　　WHERE SPJ.PNO = P.PNO))

4.29 RETRIEVE UNIQUE (SPJ.JNO)
　　　　WHERE　　SPJ.PNO = "P1"
　　　　AND　　　AVG (SPJ.QTY BY SPJ.PNO, SPJ.JNO) >
　　　　　　　　MAX (SPJ.QTY WHERE SPJ.JNO = "J1")

4.30 RETRIEVE UNIQUE (SPJ.SNO)
　　　　WHERE　　SPJ.PNO = "P1"
　　　　AND　　　SPJ.QTY > AVG (SPJ.QTY BY SPJ.PNO, SPJ.JNO)

4.31 RETRIEVE UNIQUE (SPJ.PNO)
　　　　WHERE　　ANY (J.JNO BY SPJ.JNO
　　　　　　　　　　　WHERE SPJ.JNO = J.JNO
　　　　　　　　　　　AND　J.CITY = "London") = 1

4.32 RETRIEVE UNIQUE (J.JNO)
　　　　WHERE　　ANY (SPJ.JNO BY J.JNO
　　　　　　　　　　　WHERE SPJ.SNO = S.SNO AND S.CITY = "London"
　　　　　　　　　　　AND　SPJ.PNO = P.PNO AND P.COLOR = "Red"
　　　　　　　　　　　AND　SPJ.JNO = J.JNO) = 0

5

Data Manipulation II: Update Operations

5.1 INTRODUCTION

In the previous chapter we considered the QUEL RETRIEVE statement in considerable detail. Now we turn our attention to the update statements APPEND, REPLACE, and DELETE. Like the RETRIEVE statement, the three update statements operate on both base tables and views. However, for reasons that are beyond the scope of this chapter, *not all views are updatable*. If the user attempts to perform an update operation on a non-updatable view, INGRES will simply reject the operation (with some appropriate message to the user). For the purposes of the present chapter, therefore, let us assume that all tables to be updated are base tables, and defer the question of views (and of updating views, in particular) to Chapter 7.

Another preliminary remark: As we shall see in Chapter 8, INGRES allows the user to specify a variety of *integrity constraints* on the base tables in the database. Here is an example:

```
DEFINE INTEGRITY ON SP IS SP.QTY > 0
```

("shipment quantities must be greater than zero"). If such a constraint is specified, then INGRES will reject any attempt (via an APPEND or RE-PLACE statement) to introduce a QTY value that is not greater than zero. For the purposes of the present chapter once again, let us assume that no integrity constraints are in effect, and thus ignore the possibility of an update failing because of an integrity violation. The interaction between integrity constraints and update operations will be explored in Chapter 8.

The next three sections discuss the three update operations in detail. The syntax of those operations follows the same general pattern as that already shown for the RETRIEVE operation; for convenience, an outline of that general syntax is given for each operation at the beginning of the relevant section.

5.2   APPEND

The APPEND statement has the general form

```
APPEND TO table [ UNIQUE ] ( target-list ) [ WHERE predicate ]
```

The target list and optional WHERE clause portions of the statement are evaluated just as if they had been specified in a RETRIEVE, and the resulting rows (with duplicates eliminated if UNIQUE is specified) are then appended to "table." Existing rows in "table" (if any) remain undisturbed.

5.2.1   Single-Record APPEND.   Add part P7 (city Athens, weight 24, name and color at present unknown) to table P.

```
APPEND TO P ( PNO = "P7", CITY = "Athens", WEIGHT = 24 )
```

A new part record is created with the specified part number, city, and weight, and with blank values for the name and color fields (since no other value has been explicitly specified, and NOT NULL WITH DEFAULT applies—implicitly—to those fields). In general, the effect of omitting a value for some field in APPEND depends on the "default-spec" (see Chapter 3) for the field in question:

- WITH NULL: The field is set to null

- NOT NULL: The APPEND fails (the database remains unchanged)

- NOT NULL WITH DEFAULT (or "default-spec" omitted): The field is set to the appropriate default value (zero for numeric or money data types, blank or empty for other data types)

Note carefully that field names on the left of the equals signs in an APPEND target list must *not* be explicitly qualified. They must of course be field names from the table identified in the APPEND TO clause; they may be regarded as being implicitly qualified by that table name.

5.2.2 Multiple-Record APPEND. Suppose table NEWSP has the same fields (SNO, PNO, and QTY) as table SP. Copy all records of NEWSP for which the quantity is greater than 1000 into table SP.

```
APPEND TO SP ( SNO = NEWSP.SNO,
               PNO = NEWSP.PNO,
               QTY = NEWSP.QTY )
WHERE  NEWSP.QTY > 1000
```

Actually there is no need to specify "SNO =", "PNO =", or "QTY =" in the target list, since the obvious inherited names from the three expressions NEWSP.SNO, NEWSP.PNO, and NEWSP.QTY are precisely SNO, PNO, and QTY. In fact the statement could be simplified still further, as follows:

```
APPEND TO SP ( NEWSP.ALL )
WHERE  NEWSP.QTY > 1000
```

5.2.3 Multiple-Record APPEND. Suppose again that table NEWSP has the same fields (SNO, PNO, and QTY) as table SP. For each distinct part represented in NEWSP, add a record to table SP, with a dummy supplier number of S0 ("supplier zero"), a part number equal to the part number in question, and a quantity computed as the total quantity for that part in the NEWSP table.

```
APPEND TO SP ( SNO = "S0",
               PNO = NEWSP.PNO,
               QTY = SUM ( NEWSP.QTY BY NEWSP.PNO ) )
```

The purpose of this very contrived example is simply to show that the expressions on the right-hand side of the assignments in the target list can (as usual) be arbitrarily complex.

One important use of APPEND is in constructing the *union* of two (or more) tables. In general, the union of two sets is the set of all elements belonging to either or both of the original sets. Since a relation is a set (a set of rows), it is logically possible to define the union of two relations; the result will be a set consisting of all rows appearing in either or both of the original relations. However, if that result is itself to be another relation and not just a heterogeneous mixture of rows, the two original relations must be *union-compatible*—i.e., (loosely speaking) the rows in the two relations must be "the same shape." As far as QUEL is concerned, two tables *A* and *B* are union-compatible (and their union may therefore be computed) if and only if:

(a) They have the same number of columns, *m* say;

(b) There exists a one-to-one correspondence between the columns of *A* and the columns of *B* such that, for all pairs of corresponding columns *Ai* and *Bi* (i = 1,2,...,*m*), the data types of *Ai* and *Bi* are compatible (that is, they are both numeric or both strings or both date/times or both money).

The union of the two tables will then also be "the same shape" as *A* and *B*. Here is a simple (rather contrived) example.

5.2.4   *Using APPEND to Construct a Union*.   Construct a list of supplier and part names for suppliers and parts that are located in London.

```
RETRIEVE INTO TEMP ( NAME = S.SNAME ) WHERE S.CITY = "London"

APPEND TO TEMP ( NAME = P.PNAME ) WHERE P.CITY = "London"
```

```
Result:    | name  |
           | ----- |
           | Smith |
           | Clark |
           | Nut   |
           | Screw |
           | Cog   |
           | ----- |
```

A particularly important case of union occurs in connexion with what is called an *outer join*. As explained in Chapter 4, the ordinary join of two tables does not include a result row for any row in either of the two original tables that has no matching row in the other. For example, the ordinary equijoin of tables S and P over cities does not include any result row for supplier S5 or for part P3, because no parts are stored in Athens and no suppliers are located in Rome (see Example 4.3.1). In a sense, therefore, the ordinary join may be considered to *lose information* for such unmatched rows. Sometimes, however, it may be desirable to preserve such information. Consider the following example.

5.2.5   *Using Union to Construct an Outer Join*.   For each supplier, get the supplier number, name, status, and city, together with part numbers for all parts supplied by that supplier. If a given supplier supplies no parts at all, then show the information for that supplier in the result concatenated with a blank part number.

```
RETRIEVE INTO TEMP ( S.ALL, SP.PNO )
WHERE    S.SNO = SP.SNO

APPEND TO TEMP ( S.ALL, PNO = "bbbb" )
WHERE   ANY ( SP.PNO BY S.SNO WHERE SP.SNO = S.SNO ) = 0
```

Result (table TEMP):

sno	sname	status	city	pno
S1	Smith	20	London	P1
S1	Smith	20	London	P2
S1	Smith	20	London	P3
S1	Smith	20	London	P4
S1	Smith	20	London	P5
S1	Smith	20	London	P6
S2	Jones	10	Paris	P1
S2	Jones	10	Paris	P2
S3	Blake	30	Paris	P2
S4	Clark	20	London	P2
S4	Clark	20	London	P4
S4	Clark	20	London	P5
S5	Adams	30	Athens	bbbb

(We are using bbbb to represent a string of blanks.)

Explanation: The first twelve result rows as shown correspond to the RETRIEVE INTO, and represent the ordinary natural join of S and SP over supplier numbers (except that the QTY column is not included). The final result row corresponds to the APPEND, and preserves information for supplier S5, who does not supply any parts. The overall result is the *outer* natural join of S and SP over SNO—again, ignoring QTY. (The ordinary join, by contrast, is sometimes referred to as an *inner* join.)

Incidentally, the APPEND above could have been simplified to just

```
APPEND TO TEMP ( S.ALL )
WHERE   ANY ( SP.PNO BY S.SNO WHERE SP.SNO = S.SNO ) = 0
```

—i.e., the assignment PNO = ''bbbb'' could have been omitted from the target list; the normal rules for dealing with fields for which no values have been specified would have taken care of field TEMP.PNO appropriately.

One final comment on this topic: Outer join is extremely important in practice, and it is a pity that systems do not provide direct support for it (this is a criticism of relational products in general, not just of INGRES). It should not be necessary to have to indulge in circumlocutions of the kind illustrated in the example.

5.3   REPLACE

The REPLACE statement has the general form

```
REPLACE range-variable ( target-list ) [ WHERE predicate ]
```

The "range-variable" may have been explicitly declared in a RANGE statement, or it may be a simple table name (implicit range variable). All records in the table identified by "range-variable" that satisfy "predicate" have their field values REPLACEd in accordance with the assignments in the target list.

5.3.1   Single-Record REPLACE.   Change the color of part P2 to yellow, increase its weight by 5, and set its city to "unknown" (NULL).

```
REPLACE P ( COLOR  = "Yellow",
            WEIGHT = P.WEIGHT + 5,
            CITY   = NULL )
WHERE    P.PNO = "P2"
```

For each record to be REPLACEd (i.e., each record that satisfies the WHERE predicate, or all records if the WHERE clause is omitted), references on the right-hand sides of the assignments in the target list to fields within that record stand for the values of those fields before any of the assignments have been executed.

As with APPEND, field names on the left of the equals signs in a REPLACE target list must *not* be explicitly qualified. They may be regarded as being implicitly qualified by the range variable name that appears following the keyword REPLACE.

5.3.2   Multiple-Record REPLACE.   Double the status of all suppliers in London.

```
REPLACE S ( STATUS = 2 * S.STATUS )
WHERE    S.CITY = "London"
```

5.3.3   REPLACE Referring to Another Table.   Set the shipment quantity to zero for all suppliers in London.

```
REPLACE SP ( QTY = 0 )
WHERE    SP.SNO = S.SNO
AND      S.CITY = "London"
```

5.3.5   Updating One Table From Another.   Suppose table SP has an additional field, TOTWT, representing total shipment weight. Fill in the values for this field by multiplying the quantity for each shipment by the corresponding part weight.

```
REPLACE SP ( TOTWT = SP.QTY * P.WEIGHT )
WHERE    SP.PNO = P.PNO
```

Note: There are a couple of traps for the unwary in connexion with REPLACE (also DELETE—see Section 5.4). First, *don't* omit the WHERE clause unless you really mean to! Consider the following sequence of operations:

```
RETRIEVE ( S.ALL ) WHERE S.SNO = "S4"

REPLACE S ( STATUS = 25 )
```

The user might perhaps be forgiven for thinking that this sequence will update the status for supplier S4 only, but in fact it will update *all* supplier records.

Second, be careful over the use of range variables. Suppose SX is a range variable ranging over the supplier table. Then the operation

```
REPLACE S ( STATUS = 25 )
WHERE    SX.CITY = "London"
```

will either update *all* supplier records (if there exist any London suppliers) or *none* of them (otherwise). It will *not* update just the London suppliers.

5.4 DELETE

The DELETE statement has the general form

```
DELETE range-variable [ WHERE predicate ]
```

As with REPLACE, the "range-variable" may have been explicitly declared in a RANGE statement, or it may be a simple table name (implicit range variable). All records in the table identified by "range-variable" that satisfy "predicate" are DELETEd.

5.4.1 Single-Record DELETE.   Delete supplier S1.

```
DELETE S WHERE S.SNO = "S1"
```

5.4.2 Multiple-Record DELETE.   Delete all suppliers in Madrid.

```
DELETE S WHERE S.CITY = "Madrid"
```

5.4.3 *Multiple-Record DELETE.* Delete all shipments.

```
DELETE SP
```

SP is still a known table ("DELETE all records" is not a DESTROY), but it is now empty.

5.4.4 *DELETE Referring to Another Table.* Delete all shipments for suppliers in London.

```
DELETE SP
WHERE   SP.SNO = S.SNO
AND     S.CITY = "London"
```

5.4.5 *DELETE Referring to the Same Table.* Delete all suppliers whose status is lower than the average.

```
DELETE S
WHERE   S.STATUS < AVG ( S.STATUS )
```

INGRES will compute the average status value once and for all before any records are deleted.

5.5 CONCLUSION

This brings us to the end of our detailed discussion of the four data manipulation statements of QUEL, namely RETRIEVE, APPEND, REPLACE, and DELETE. Most of the complexity of those statements (what complexity there is) resides in the RETRIEVE statement; once you have a reasonable understanding of RETRIEVE, the other statements are fairly straightforward, as you can see. In practice, of course, RETRIEVE is usually pretty straightforward as well.

In conclusion, we point out that the fact that there are only four data manipulation operators in QUEL is one of the reasons for the ease of use of that language. And the fact that there *are* only four such operators is a consequence of the simplicity of the relational data structure. As we explained in Chapter 1, all data in a relational database is represented in exactly the same way, namely as values in column positions within rows of tables. Since there is only one way to represent anything, we need only one operator for each of the four basic manipulative functions (retrieve, insert, change, delete). By contrast, systems based on a more complex data structure fundamentally require $4n$ manipulative operators, where n is the number of ways that data can be represented in that system. In CODASYL-based systems, for example, where data can be represented either as records or as links between records, we typically find a STORE operator to create a record, plus a CONNECT operator to create a link; an ERASE operator to destroy a record plus a DISCONNECT operator to destroy a link; a MODIFY operator to change a record plus a RECONNECT operator to change a link; and so on. (Actually, CODASYL systems usually provide more than two ways of representing data and hence more than two sets of manipulative operators, but the record and link structures and operators are easily the most important.)

EXERCISES

As usual, all of the following exercises are based on the suppliers-parts-projects database:

```
S     ( SNO, SNAME, STATUS, CITY )
P     ( PNO, PNAME, COLOR, WEIGHT, CITY )
J     ( JNO, JNAME, CITY )
SPJ   ( SNO, PNO, JNO, QTY )
```

Write APPEND, REPLACE, or DELETE statements (as appropriate) for each of the following problems.

5.1 Change the color of all red parts to orange.

5.2 Delete all projects for which there are no shipments.

5.3 Increase the shipment quantity by 10 percent for all shipments by suppliers that supply a red part.

5.4 Delete all projects in Rome and all corresponding shipments.

5.5 Insert a new supplier (S10) into table S. The name and city are "White" and "New York," respectively; the status is not yet known.

5.6 Construct a new table (named LP) containing a list of part numbers for parts that are supplied either by a London supplier or to a London project.

5.7 Construct a new table containing a list of project numbers for projects that either are located in London or are supplied by a London supplier.

5.8 Add 10 to the status of all suppliers whose status is currently less than that of supplier S4.

5.9 Construct an ordered list of all cities in which at least one supplier, part, or project is located.

5.10 Construct the outer natural join of projects and shipments over project numbers.

5.11 Construct the outer natural join of parts and projects over cities.

5.12 Construct a table showing complete supplier, part, and project information (together with shipment quantity) for each shipment, together with "preserved" information for every supplier, part, and project that does not appear in the shipment table (see Example 5.2.6 for the meaning of "preserved" in this context).

5.13 Return to Exercise 3.2 in Chapter 3 if you have not already answered it.

ANSWERS TO SELECTED EXERCISES

The following solutions are not necessarily the only ones possible.

5.1
```
REPLACE P ( COLOR = "Orange" )
WHERE   P.COLOR = "Red"
```

5.2
```
DELETE J
WHERE   ANY ( SPJ.JNO BY J.JNO WHERE SPJ.JNO = J.JNO ) = 0
```

5.3
```
RANGE OF SPJX IS SPJ

REPLACE SPJ ( QTY = SPJ.QTY * 1.1 )
WHERE   SPJ.SNO = SPJX.SNO
AND     SPJX.PNO = P.PNO
AND     P.COLOR = "Red"
```

5.4
```
DELETE SPJ
WHERE   SPJ.JNO = J.JNO
AND     J.CITY = "Rome"

DELETE J
WHERE   J.CITY = "Rome"
```

5.5
```
APPEND TO S ( SNO = "S10",
              SNAME = "White",
              CITY = "New York" )
```

5.6 Trick question! The problem can be solved without using any of the standard update operators at all; all that is needed is a single RETRIEVE INTO operation, thus:

```
RETRIEVE INTO LP ( SPJ.PNO )
WHERE    SPJ.SNO = S.SNO AND S.CITY = "London"
OR       SPJ.JNO = J.JNO AND J.CITY = "London"
```

5.7
```
RETRIEVE INTO LJ1 ( J.JNO ) WHERE J.CITY = "London"

APPEND   TO LJ1 ( SPJ.JNO ) WHERE SPJ.SNO = S.SNO
                            AND   S.CITY = "London"

RETRIEVE INTO LJ2 UNIQUE ( LJ1.JNO )
```

Actually this problem can also be solved by means of a single RETRIEVE INTO operation, *provided* we can rely on the fact that every value of SPJ.JNO should also appear as a value of J.JNO (i.e., provided *referential integrity* can be guaranteed—see Appendix B):

```
RETRIEVE INTO LJ UNIQUE ( J.JNO )
WHERE    ( J.CITY = "London" )
OR       ( J.JNO = SPJ.JNO AND
           SPJ.SNO = S.SNO AND
           S.CITY = "London" )
```

5.8
```
RANGE OF SX IS S
RANGE OF SY IS S

REPLACE SX ( STATUS = SX.STATUS + 10 )
WHERE     SX.STATUS < SY.STATUS
AND       SY.SNO = "S4"
```

5.9
```
RETRIEVE INTO CC1 ( S.CITY )

APPEND   TO    CC1 ( P.CITY )

APPEND   TO    CC1 ( J.CITY )

RETRIEVE INTO CC2 UNIQUE ( CC1.CITY )
```

5.10
```
RETRIEVE INTO RES ( J.ALL, SPJ.SNO, SPJ.PNO, SPJ.QTY )
WHERE     J.JNO = SPJ.JNO

APPEND TO RES ( J.ALL )
WHERE  ANY ( SPJ.JNO BY J.JNO WHERE SPJ.JNO = J.JNO ) = 0
```

5.11
```
RETRIEVE INTO RES ( P.ALL, J.JNO, J.JNAME )
WHERE     P.CITY = J.CITY

APPEND TO RES ( P.ALL )
WHERE  ANY ( J.JNO BY P.CITY WHERE J.CITY = P.CITY ) = 0

APPEND TO RES ( J.ALL )
WHERE  ANY ( P.PNO BY J.CITY WHERE P.CITY = J.CITY ) = 0
```

5.12
```
RETRIEVE INTO RES
( S.SNO, S.SNAME, S.STATUS, SCITY = S.CITY,
  P.PNO, P.PNAME, P.COLOR, P.WEIGHT, PCITY = P.CITY,
  J.JNO, J.JNAME, JCITY = J.CITY,
  SPJ.QTY )
WHERE S.SNO = SPJ.SNO
AND   P.PNO = SPJ.PNO
AND   J.JNO = SPJ.JNO

APPEND TO RES
( S.SNO, S.SNAME, S.STATUS, SCITY = S.CITY )
WHERE ANY ( SPJ.SNO BY S.SNO WHERE SPJ.SNO = S.SNO ) = 0

APPEND TO RES
( P.PNO, P.PNAME, P.COLOR, P.WEIGHT, PCITY = P.CITY )
WHERE ANY ( SPJ.PNO BY P.PNO WHERE SPJ.PNO = P.PNO ) = 0

APPEND TO RES
( J.JNO, J.JNAME, JCITY  = J.CITY )
WHERE ANY ( SPJ.JNO BY J.JNO WHERE SPJ.JNO = J.JNO ) = 0
```

6

The Data Dictionary

6.1 INTRODUCTION

The INGRES Data Dictionary (dictionary for short) is a repository for information or *descriptors* concerning various objects that are of interest to the system itself. Examples of such objects are base tables, views, indexes, forms, reports, graphs, access rights, integrity constraints, and so on. Descriptor information is essential if the system is to be able to do its job properly. For example, the optimizer uses dictionary information about indexes (as well as other information) to choose an optimal access strategy, as explained in Chapter 2. Likewise, the authorization subsystem (see Chapter 8) uses dictionary information about access rights to protect the database from unauthorized access.

A significant advantage of a relational system like INGRES is that *the dictionary in such a system itself consists of relations or tables* (*system tables*, so called to distinguish them from ordinary user tables). As a result, users can interrogate the dictionary using the standard facilities of their normal query language, a very nice feature.

In INGRES specifically, the dictionary consists of some 20 or so system tables (for each INGRES database). It is not our purpose to give an exhaustive description of those 20 tables in this book; rather, we wish merely to give a basic—and deliberately somewhat simplified—introduction to the dictionary structure and content, in order to give some idea as to how the information in the dictionary can be helpful to the user as well as to the system. The only system tables we mention here are the following:

- RELATION

This dictionary table contains a row for every relation (base table or view) in the entire database. For each relation, it gives the relation name (RELID), the number of columns in the relation (RELATTS—so called because "attribute" is the formal relational term for a column), the number of rows in the relation (RELTUPS—so called because "tuple" is the formal relational term for a row), and many other items of information.

- ATTRIBUTE

As just explained, "attribute" is the formal relational term for a column of a relation. The ATTRIBUTE dictionary table contains a row for every column of every relation in the database. For each column, it gives the column name (ATTNAME), the name of the relation of which that column is a part (ATTRELID), the "format" (data type) and length of the column (ATTFRMT and ATTFRML), and many other things besides.

- INDEXES

This dictionary table contains a row for every index created by means of the INDEX operation (mentioned briefly in Chapter 1 and discussed in detail in Chapter 12). For each such index, it gives the name of the index (IRELIDI),* the name of the indexed relation (IRELIDP), the name(s) of the indexed column(s) (IDOM1 - IDOM6), and so on.

For example, the dictionary structure for the suppliers-and-parts database might be as indicated in Fig. 6.1 (in outline; of course, almost all the details have been omitted). For the sake of the example, we assume that the INDEX statement has been used to create two indexes XSC and XSN on the CITY and SNAME fields, respectively, of table S, and an index XSP on the composite field (SNO,PNO) of table SP.

---

*As this name suggests, indexes created by means of the INDEX operation are themselves regarded as relations ("index relations") in INGRES. However, index relations are subject to certain limitations. For instance, it is not possible to define a view over an index relation, or to build an index on an index relation via another INDEX operation.

```
relation   |relid  |relatts|reltups|  ...  |
           |-----------------------|- - -|
           |s      |     4 |     5 | ...   |
           |p      |     5 |     6 | ...   |
           |sp     |     3 |    12 | ...   |
           | ...   |  ...  |  ...  | ...   |
           |-----------------------|- - -|

attribute  |attrelid|attname|attfrmt|attfrml|   ...   |
           |-----------------------------------|- - -|
           |s       |sno    |text   |     5 | ...    |
           |s       |sname  |text   |    20 | ...    |
           |s       |status |integer|     2 | ...    |
           |s       |city   |text   |    15 | ...    |
           |p       |pno    |text   |     6 | ...    |
           |p       |pname  |text   |    20 | ...    |
           |p       |color  |text   |     6 | ...    |
           |p       |weight |integer|     2 | ...    |
           |p       |city   |text   |    15 | ...    |
           |sp      |sno    |text   |     5 | ...    |
           |sp      |pno    |text   |     6 | ...    |
           |sp      |qty    |integer|     4 | ...    |
           | ...    |  ...  |  ...  |  ...  | ...    |
           |-----------------------------------|- - -|

indexes    |irelidi|irelidp|idom1|idom2|idom3|  ...  |
           |-----------------------------------|- - -|
           |xsc    |s      |city |     |     | ...   |
           |xsn    |s      |sname|     |     | ...   |
           |xsp    |sp     |sno  |pno  |     | ...   |
           | ...   | ...   | ... | ... | ... | ...   |
           |-----------------------------------|- - -|
```

Fig. 6.1 Dictionary structure for the suppliers-and-parts database (outline)

6.2 QUERYING THE DICTIONARY

As indicated in Section 6.1, a nice feature of the dictionary in a relational system like INGRES is that it can be queried by means of ordinary retrieval operations, just as ordinary tables can. For example, to find out what tables contain an SNO column:

```
RANGE OF A IS ATTRIBUTE

RETRIEVE ( A.ATTRELID )
WHERE     A.ATTNAME = "sno"
```

Result:
```
|attrelid|
|--------|
|s       |
|sp      |
|--------|
```

(The range variable A is introduced purely to save writing.) Here is another example: What columns does table S have?

```
RETRIEVE ( A.ATTNAME )
WHERE     A.ATTRELID = "s"
```

Result:
```
|attname|
|-------|
|sno    |
|sname  |
|status |
|city   |
|-------|
```

And one more example: How many indexes have been created on table S?

```
RANGE OF X IS INDEXES

RETRIEVE ( N = COUNT ( X.IRELIDI WHERE X.IRELIDP = "s" ) )
```

A user who is not familiar with the structure of the database can use queries such as these to discover that structure. For example, a user who wishes to query the suppliers-and-parts database (say), but does not have any detailed knowledge as to exactly what tables exist in that database and exactly what columns they contain, can use dictionary queries to obtain that knowledge first, before going on to formulate the data queries per se.

The HELP statement

Certain dictionary queries are used so frequently in practice that INGRES provides a special shorthand for them, the HELP statement. HELP displays its result in a somewhat more readable form than the normal RETRIEVE statement does. For example, the statement

```
HELP  S
```

might result in the display shown in Fig. 6.2.

The various forms of HELP are summarized below.

HELP	lists all user tables in the database, giving name, owner, and table type (base table, view, or index)
HELP table	displays details of "table" (base table, view, or index)
HELP VIEW view	displays the definition of "view" (see Chapter 7)
HELP PERMIT table	lists the permits on base table "table" (see Chapter 8)
HELP INTEGRITY table	lists the integrity constraints on base table "table" (see Chapter 8)

```
Name:                      s
Owner:                     cjdate
Location:                  db_ingres
Type:                      user table
Row width:                 42
Number of rows:            5
Storage structure:         btree
Number of pages:           4
Overflow data pages:       0
Journaling:                enabled
Global Cache:              enabled
Permissions:               none
Integrities:               none
Optimizer statistics:      none
Column information:
                                          key
    column name    type    length    sequence

    sno            c          5        1
    sname          c         20
    status         i          2
    city           c         15


Secondary indices:

    index name    structure    keyed on

    xsc           isam         city
    xsn           isam         sname
```

Fig. 6.2 Sample HELP output

6.3 UPDATING THE DICTIONARY

We have seen how the dictionary can be queried by means of the QUEL
RETRIEVE and HELP statements. However, the dictionary *cannot* be updated using the QUEL APPEND, REPLACE, and DELETE statements
(and INGRES will reject any attempt to do so*). The reason is, of course,
that allowing such operations would potentially be very dangerous: It would
be far too easy to destroy information (inadvertently or otherwise) in the
dictionary so that INGRES would no longer be able to function correctly.
Suppose, for example, that the following were allowed:

```
RANGE OF A IS ATTRIBUTE

DELETE A
WHERE   A.ATTRELID = "s"
AND     A.ATTNAME = "sno"
```

---

*Actually this statement is slightly oversimplified. A user with "superuser" status
is allowed to update certain less than critical dictionary tables under certain circumstances. For details, see the RTI manuals.

Its effect would be to remove the row

```
( s, sno, text, 5, ... )
```

from the ATTRIBUTE table. *As far as INGRES is concerned, the SNO column in the S table would now no longer exist*—i.e., INGRES would no longer have any knowledge of that column. Thus, attempts to access data on the basis of values of that column—e.g.,

```
RETRIEVE ( S.CITY )
WHERE     S.SNO = "S4"
```

—would fail (the system would produce an error message, along the lines of "column CITY not in table S").

For such reasons, APPEND, REPLACE, and DELETE operations are (as already stated) not permitted against tables in the catalog. Instead, it is the *data definition* statements (CREATE, DESTROY, INDEX, etc.) that perform such updates. For example, the CREATE statement for table S causes (a) an entry to be made for S in the RELATION table and (b) a set of four entries, one for each of the four columns of the S table, to be made in the ATTRIBUTE table. (It also causes a number of other things to happen too, which are however of no concern to us here.) Thus CREATE is in some ways the analog of APPEND for the dictionary. Likewise, DESTROY can be regarded as the analog of DELETE, and MODIFY (see Chapter 12) can be regarded as an analog of REPLACE.

Aside: The dictionary also includes entries for the dictionary tables themselves, of course. However, those entries are not created by explicit CREATE operations. Instead, they are created automatically by INGRES itself as part of the system installation procedure. In effect, they are "hard-wired" into the system.

EXERCISES

6.1 Sketch the details of the dictionary for the suppliers-parts-projects database.

Now write RETRIEVE statements for the following dictionary queries (numbers 6.2–6.7).

6.2 Which tables include a CITY column?

6.3 How many columns are there in the shipments table?

6.4 How many rows are there in the parts table?

6.5 List the names of all tables that have at least one index.

6.6 List the names of all tables that have at least one index, together with the number of indexes in each case.

6.7 List the names of all tables that have more than one index.

6.8 Which of the foregoing could be more easily handled by means of the HELP statement?

ANSWERS TO SELECTED EXERCISES

For simplicity we assume throughout the solutions below that the following RANGE statements are in effect:

```
RANGE OF R IS RELATION
RANGE OF A IS ATTRIBUTE
RANGE OF X IS INDEXES
```

As usual the solutions are not necessarily unique.

6.2   RETRIEVE (A.ATTRELID)
       WHERE   A.ATTNAME = "city"

6.3   RETRIEVE (R.RELATTS)
       WHERE   R.RELID = "spj"
Or:

```
RETRIEVE ( N = COUNT ( A.ATTNAME
                       WHERE A.ATTRELID = "spj"  ) )
```

6.4   RETRIEVE (R.RELTUPS)
       WHERE   R.RELID = "p"

6.5   RETRIEVE UNIQUE (X.IRELIDP)

6.6   RETRIEVE (X.IRELIDP,
              N = COUNT (X.IRELIDI BY X.IRELIDP))

6.7   RETRIEVE UNIQUE (X.IRELIDP)
       WHERE   COUNT (X.IRELIDI BY X.IRELIDP) > 1

6.8   HELP would help with numbers 6.3 and 6.4 (only).

7

Views

7.1 INTRODUCTION

Recall from Chapter 1 that a view is a *virtual table*—that is, a table that does not exist in its own right but looks to the user as if it did. (By contrast, a base table is a *real* table, in the sense that, for each row of such a table, there really is some stored counterpart of that row in physical storage. See Chapter 12.) Views are not supported by their own, physically separate, distinguishable stored data. Instead, their *definition* in terms of other tables is stored in the INGRES dictionary. Here is an example:

```
DEFINE VIEW GOODSUPPS
      ( S.SNO, S.STATUS, S.CITY )
        WHERE  S.STATUS > 15
```

Note the similarity to the QUEL RETRIEVE statement. When a DEFINE VIEW is executed, however, no data retrieval is performed at that time; instead, the specified target list and WHERE clause (which between them constitute the actual definition of the view) are simply saved in the dictionary, under the specified view name. *To the user, however, it is now as if there really were a table in the database with the specified name.* In the example, it is as if there really were a table called GOODSUPPS, with rows and columns as shown in the unshaded portions (only) of Fig. 7.1 below.

111

```
goodsupps  |sno |sname |status|city    |
           |----|------|------------------|
           |S1  |Smith |    20|London  |
           |S2  |Jones |    10|Paris   |
           |S3  |Blake |    30|Paris   |
           |S4  |Clark |    20|London  |
           |S5  |Adams |    30|Athens  |
           |----|------|------------------|
```

Fig. 7.1 GOODSUPPS as a view of base table S (unshaded portions)

GOODSUPPS is in effect a "window" into the real table S. Furthermore, that window is *dynamic*: Changes to S will be automatically and instantaneously visible through that window (provided, of course, that those changes lie within the unshaded portion of S); likewise, changes to GOODSUPPS will automatically and instantaneously be applied to the real table S (see Section 7.3, later), and hence of course be visible through the window.

Now, depending on the sophistication of the user (and perhaps also on the application concerned), the user may or may not realize that GOODSUPPS really is a view; some users may be aware of that fact (and of the fact that there is a real table S underneath), others may genuinely believe that GOODSUPPS is a "real" table in its own right. Either way, it makes little difference; the point is, users may operate on GOODSUPPS just as if it were a real table (with certain exceptions, to be discussed later). For instance, here is an example of a RETRIEVE operation against GOODSUPPS:

```
RETRIEVE ( GOODSUPPS.ALL )
WHERE    GOODSUPPS.CITY <> "London"
```

As you can see, this RETRIEVE certainly looks just like a normal RETRIEVE on a conventional base table. INGRES handles such an operation by converting it into an equivalent operation on the underlying base table (or base tables, plural—see Section 7.2). In the example, the equivalent operation is

```
RETRIEVE ( S.SNO, S.STATUS, S.CITY )
WHERE    S.CITY <> "London"
AND      S.STATUS > 15
```

This new statement can now be executed in the usual way. The conversion is done by (in effect) *merging* the RETRIEVE issued by the user with the view definition stored in the dictionary. From the dictionary,

INGRES knows that references to the view GOODSUPPS are really references to base table S; it also knows that any retrieval from GOODSUPPS must be further qualified by the WHERE condition "STATUS > 15"; finally, it also knows that "ALL fields" (from view GOODSUPPS) really means "SNO, STATUS, and CITY" (from table S). Hence it is able to translate the original RETRIEVE on the virtual table GOODSUPPS into an equivalent RETRIEVE on the real table S—equivalent, in the sense that the effect of executing that RETRIEVE on the real table S is as if there really were a base table called GOODSUPPS and the original RETRIEVE were executed on that.

The conversion process just described is usually referred to as *query modification*. Of course, the operation being modified need not necessarily be a query (i.e., a retrieval). For example, the REPLACE operation

```
REPLACE GOODSUPPS ( CITY = "New York" )
WHERE    GOODSUPPS.CITY = "Paris"
```

will be modified to

```
REPLACE S ( CITY = "New York" )
WHERE    S.CITY = "Paris"
AND      S.STATUS > 15
```

APPEND and DELETE operations are handled analogously. (In general, that is. In the particular case of the view GOODSUPPS, however, APPEND operations are not permitted, for reasons to be discussed in Section 7.3. Any attempt to perform such an operation will be rejected by INGRES with an error message, along the lines of "table GOODSUPPS cannot be accessed for APPEND.")

7.2 VIEW DEFINITION

The general syntax of DEFINE VIEW is

```
DEFINE VIEW view ( target-list )
    [ WHERE predicate ]
```

A view definition cannot include either UNIQUE or a SORT BY specification;* apart from these limitations, however, any table that can be re-

---

*UNIQUE and SORT BY can be used in RETRIEVE operations against the view, of course.

trieved via a RETRIEVE statement can alternatively be defined as a view. Here are some examples.

```
1. DEFINE VIEW REDPARTS
        ( P.PNO, P.PNAME, WT = P.WEIGHT, P.CITY )
        WHERE P.COLOR = "Red"
```

The effect of this statement is to create a new view called REDPARTS, with four columns PNO, PNAME, WT, and CITY, corresponding respectively to the four columns PNO, PNAME, WEIGHT, and CITY of the underlying base table P. If the DEFINE VIEW does not explicitly specify a new name for some column of the view, then that column inherits a name from the underlying table in the obvious way (in the example, if the new name WT had not been specified for the "weight" column, then that column would have inherited the name WEIGHT). A new name *must* be specified explicitly if (a) there is no obvious inherited name for the column in question (i.e., if the column is derived from anything other than a simple column of the underlying table), or (b) if two or more columns of the view would otherwise have the same name. See the next two examples for illustrations of each of these two cases.

```
2. DEFINE VIEW PQ
        ( SP.PNO, TOTQTY = SUM ( SP.QTY BY SP.PNO ) )
```

In this example, there is no name that can be inherited for the "total quantity" column, since that column is derived from an aggregate function; hence a new column name *must* be specified explicitly, as shown. Notice that this view is not just a simple row-and-column subset of the underlying base table (unlike the views REDPARTS and GOODSUPPS shown earlier). It might be regarded instead as a kind of statistical summary or compression of that underlying table.

```
3. DEFINE VIEW CITYPAIRS
        ( SCITY = S.CITY, PCITY = P.CITY )
        WHERE S.SNO = SP.SNO
        AND    SP.PNO = P.PNO
```

The meaning of this particular view is that a pair of city names (x,y) will appear in the view if a supplier located in city x supplies a part stored in city y. For example, supplier S1 supplies part P1; supplier S1 is located in London and part P1 is stored in London; and so the pair (London,London) appears in the view. Notice that the definition of this view involves a join, so that this is an example of a view that is derived from multiple underlying tables. Compare Example 4.3.7 in Chapter 4.

```
4. DEFINE VIEW LREDPARTS
      ( REDPARTS.PNO, REDPARTS.WT )
        WHERE REDPARTS.CITY = "London"
```

It is perfectly possible to define a view in terms of other views, as this example illustrates.

Views are destroyed by means of the DESTROY statement—syntax:

```
DESTROY view
```

If view *V* is defined in terms of some underlying table *T* (where *T* can itself be a view in turn), and table *T* is destroyed, view *V* is automatically destroyed too.

7.3 DATA MANIPULATION OPERATIONS

We have already explained in outline (in Section 7.1) how operations on views are converted into equivalent operations on the underlying base table(s)—the process of *query modification*. In the case of RETRIEVE, that process is completely straightforward and works perfectly well, without any surprises for the user. In the case of update operations, however, it does *not* always work; as already stated in Chapter 5, *not all views are updatable*. We are now in a position to explain this state of affairs.

Note: Before going any further, we should stress the point that INGRES—like most other systems at the time of writing—does not in fact handle the updating of views in a totally systematic manner. In what follows, therefore, we first consider the question of view updating from a somewhat theoretical standpoint, then go on to discuss the more directly practical question of how INGRES actually behaves. The whole subject of updating views in general is discussed thoroughly (but rather formally) in the author's book *Relational Database: Selected Writings* (Addison-Wesley, 1986).

First, consider the two views GOODSUPPS and CITYPAIRS from Sections 7.1 and 7.2, respectively. For co. venience we repeat their definitions below:

```
DEFINE VIEW GOODSUPPS           | DEFINE VIEW CITYPAIRS
   ( S.SNO, S.STATUS, S.CITY )  |  ( SCITY = S.CITY, PCITY = P.CITY )
      WHERE  S.STATUS > 15      |     WHERE   S.SNO = SP.SNO
                                |     AND     SP.PNO = P.PNO
```

Of these two views, GOODSUPPS is logically updatable, while CITYPAIRS is logically not. It is instructive to examine why this is so. In the case of GOODSUPPS:

(a) We can APPEND a new row to the view—say the row (S6,40,Rome)—by actually appending the corresponding row (S6,bbbb,40,Rome) to the underlying base table. *Note*: As usual, we are using "bbbb" to represent a string of blanks.

(b) We can DELETE an existing row from the view—say the row (S1,20,London)—by actually deleting the corresponding row (S1,Smith,20,London) from the underlying base table.

(c) We can REPLACE the value of an existing field in the view—say the city field for supplier S1 (London), to change its value to Rome—by actually making that change to the corresponding field in the underlying base table.

We will refer to a view such as GOODSUPPS, which is derived from a single base table by simply eliminating certain rows and certain columns of that table *while preserving that table's primary key*, as a *key-preserving-subset* view. (Remember from Chapter 1 that the primary key is basically just a unique identifier.) Such views are inherently updatable, as the foregoing discussion indicates.

Now consider the view CITYPAIRS (which is certainly not a key-preserving-subset view). As explained earlier, one of the rows in that view is the row (London,London). Suppose it were possible to DELETE that row. What would such a DELETE signify?—i.e., what updates (DELETEs or otherwise) on the underlying data would such a DELETE correspond to? The only possible answer has to be "We don't know"; there is simply no way (in general) that we can go down to the underlying base tables and make an appropriate set of updates there. In fact, such an "appropriate set of updates" does not even exist; there is no set of updates (in general) that could be applied to the underlying data that would have *precisely* the effect of removing the row (London,London) from the view while leaving everything else in the view unchanged. In other words, *the original DELETE is an intrinsically unsupportable operation*. Similar arguments can be made to show that APPEND and REPLACE operations* are also intrinsically not supportable on this view.

Thus we see that some views are inherently updatable, whereas others are inherently not. *Note the word "inherently" here.* It is not just a question of some systems being able to support certain updates while others cannot. *No* system can consistently support updates on a view such as

---

*The truth of this observation notwithstanding, INGRES does in fact allow certain REPLACE operations against views such as CITYPAIRS!—with a "user beware" if the effect of such an operation is not quite what the user expects.

CITYPAIRS unaided (by "unaided" we mean "without help from some human user"). As a consequence of this fact, it is possible to classify views as indicated in the following Venn diagram (Fig. 7.2).

Note carefully from the diagram that although key-preserving-subset views such as GOODSUPPS are always theoretically updatable, *not all theoretically updatable views are key-preserving-subset views.* In other words, there are some views that *are* theoretically updatable that are *not* key-preserving-subset views. The trouble is, although we know that such views exist, we do not know precisely which ones they are; it is still (in part) a research problem to pin down precisely what it is that characterizes such views.

Now, INGRES unfortunately has no knowledge or understanding of

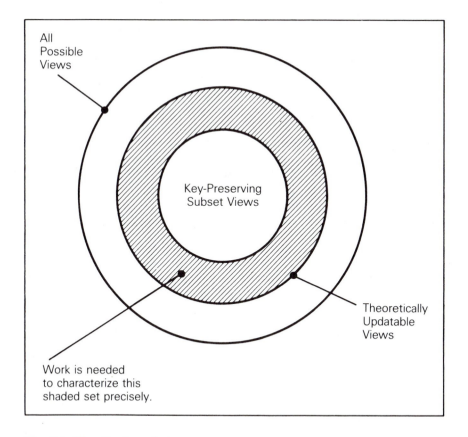

All
Possible
Views

Key-Preserving
Subset Views

Theoretically
Updatable
Views

Work is needed
to characterize this
shaded set precisely.

Fig. 7.2 Classification of views

primary keys. There is thus no chance of INGRES's view-updating mechanism operating in terms of key-preserving-subset views. Instead, it operates in terms of what we will call *row-and-column-subset* views. A row-and-column-subset view is a view that is derived from a single base table by simply eliminating certain rows and certain columns of that table. A row-and-column-subset view may or may not be a key-preserving-subset view. (More precisely, all key-preserving subset views are row-and-column subset views, but the converse is not true.) For the purposes of this chapter, the important point is the following:

In INGRES, only row-and-column subset views can be updated. (Actually even this statement is still not 100 percent accurate. We will make it more precise in a moment.) INGRES is not alone in this regard, by the way; very few products currently support update operations on views that are not row-and-column subsets, and *no* product currently supports update operations on all views that are theoretically updatable.

The fact that not all views are updatable is frequently expressed as "You cannot update a join." That statement is *not* an accurate characterization of the situation, nor indeed of the problem: There are some views that are not joins that are not updatable, and there are some views that are joins that are (theoretically) updatable—although not updatable in INGRES. But it is true that joins represent the "interesting case," in the sense that it would be very convenient to be able to update certain views whose definition involved a join. It should be clear from the foregoing discussion that such views may indeed be updatable at some future time; but we are concerned here only with what INGRES will currently allow. Let us now make it clear exactly what that is. In INGRES, a view that is to accept updates must be a row-and-column subset view;* in other words, the target list in the view definition must involve only a single range variable. Moreover:

(a) If case (c) does not apply (see below), but some field of the view is derived from something other than a simple column of an underlying base table (e.g., from an operational expression such as $A + B$), then APPEND operations are not allowed, and REPLACE operations are not allowed on that field. However, DELETE operations are allowed.

(b) If case (c) does not apply (see below), but the definition of the view includes a WHERE clause, then APPEND operations are not allowed, and REPLACE operations are not allowed on any field that is men-

---

*Except that certain REPLACEs are supported (in a somewhat ad hoc manner) on certain other kinds of view, as mentioned in the footnote on p. 116. In fairness, we should also mention the fact that INGRES does provide some limited additional support for "update of join" through its frontend subsystem QBF; see Chapter 16.

tioned in that WHERE clause. However, DELETE operations are allowed.

(c) If any field of the view is derived from an aggregate or aggregate function, then the view cannot be updated at all.

Let us examine the reasonableness of these restrictions. We consider each of the cases (a)-(c) in turn. For each case, we begin by considering an example of a view that illustrates the restriction.

Case (a): View field not derived from a simple column

```
DEFINE VIEW PINGRAMS
      ( P.PNO, GMWT = P.WEIGHT * 454 )
```

Assuming that table P is as given in Fig. 1.2 (Chapter 1), the set of rows visible through this view is as follows:

```
|pno |gmwt|
|--------|
|P1  |5448|
|P2  |7718|
|P3  |7718|
|P4  |6356|
|P5  |5448|
|P6  |8626|
|--------|
```

It should be clear that PINGRAMS cannot support APPEND operations, nor REPLACE operations on the field GMWT. (Each of those operations would require the system to be able to convert a gram weight back into pounds, without any knowledge as to how to perform such a conversion.) On the other hand, DELETE operations can be supported (e.g., deleting the row for part P1 from the view can be handled by deleting the row for part P1 from the underlying base table), and so can REPLACE operations on field PNO (such REPLACEs simply require a corresponding REPLACE on field PNO of the underlying base table).

Case (b): View involving a WHERE clause

```
DEFINE VIEW GOODSUPPS
      ( S.SNO, S.STATUS, S.CITY )
        WHERE S.STATUS > 15
```

DELETE operations on GOODSUPPS can obviously be handled. So too can REPLACE operations on fields SNO and CITY. However, INGRES will not permit a REPLACE on field STATUS, on the grounds that the new STATUS value might no longer satisfy the predicate "S.STATUS > 15"—

in which case the record no longer logically belongs to GOODSUPPS and should therefore not be visible through the view, a contradiction (of a kind). Of course, the system *could* check for such a condition and reject the REPLACE if necessary, but the fact is that currently it does not. For analogous reasons, INGRES will also not permit any APPENDs on such a view (again it *could* perform appropriate checks and reject the APPEND if necessary, but currently it does not).

Here are two more examples of case (b):

```
1. DEFINE VIEW BESTSUPPS ( S.ALL )
        WHERE S.STATUS = MAX ( S.STATUS )
```

A row-and-column-subset view can involve an aggregate operator *in the WHERE clause* and still be updatable. It is only if *a field of the view* is derived from such an operator—in other words, only if the operator appears within the DEFINE VIEW target list (case (c) below)—that the view is nonupdatable. In the case of view BESTSUPPS, APPENDs, DELETEs, and REPLACEs on field STATUS are not allowed, but REPLACEs on the other fields are legal.

```
2. DEFINE VIEW ACTIVES ( S.ALL )
        WHERE S.SNO = SP.SNO
```

A row-and-column-subset view can involve a join and still be updatable. It is only if multiple range variables appear in the DEFINE VIEW target list (in which case the view is not of the row-and-column-subset form, of course) that the view is not updatable. In the case of view ACTIVES, APPENDs and REPLACEs on field SNO are not allowed, but DELETEs and REPLACEs on the other fields are legal.

Case (c): View involving an aggregate or aggregate function

```
DEFINE VIEW TQ
      ( TOTQTY = SUM ( SP.QTY ) )
```

Sample value:

```
|totqty|
|------|
|  3100|
|------|
```

It should be obvious that none of REPLACE, APPEND, DELETE makes any sense on this view.

Here is another example of case (c), involving an aggregate function instead of just a simple aggregate:

```
DEFINE VIEW PQ
      ( SP.PNO, TOTQTY = SUM ( SP.QTY BY SP.PNO ) )
```

Sample values:

```
|pno |totqty|
|-----------|
|P1  |   600|
|P2  |  1000|
|P3  |   400|
|P4  |   500|
|P5  |   500|
|P6  |   100|
|-----------|
```

It is obvious that view PQ cannot support APPEND operations, nor REPLACE operations against field TOTQTY. DELETE operations, and REPLACE operations against field PNO, theoretically *could* be defined to DELETE or REPLACE all corresponding rows in table SP—for example, the operation

```
DELETE PQ
WHERE  PQ.PNO = "P1"
```

could be defined to translate into

```
DELETE SP
WHERE  SP.PNO = "P1"
```

—but such operations could equally well be expressed directly in terms of table SP anyway. And it is at least arguable that a user who is issuing such operations should probably be interested in exactly which real records are affected by those operations.

7.4 LOGICAL DATA INDEPENDENCE

We have not yet really explained what views are for. One of the things they are for is the provision of what is called *logical data independence*. The notion of *physical* data independence was introduced in Chapter 2: A system like INGRES is said to provide physical data independence because users and user programs are not dependent on the physical structure of the database. A system provides *logical* data independence if users and user programs are also independent of the *logical* structure of the database. There are two aspects to such independence, namely *growth* and *restructuring*.

Growth

As the database grows to incorporate new kinds of information, so the definition of the database must also grow accordingly. (*Note:* We discuss the question of growth in the database here only for completeness; it is important, but it has nothing to do with views as such.) There are two possible types of growth that can occur:

1. The expansion of an existing base table to include a new field (corresponding to the addition of new information concerning some existing type of object—for example, the addition of a COST field to the parts base table);

2. The inclusion of a new base table (corresponding to the addition of a new type of object—for example, the addition of a projects table to the suppliers-and-parts database).

Neither of these two kinds of change should have any effect on existing users at all.*

Restructuring

Occasionally it may become necessary to restructure the database in such a way that, although the overall information content remains the same, the placement of information within the database changes—i.e., the allocation of fields to tables is altered in some way. Before proceeding further, we make the point that such restructuring is generally undesirable; however, it may sometimes be unavoidable. For example, it may be necessary to split a table "vertically," so that commonly required columns can be stored on a faster device and less frequently required columns on a slower device. Let us consider this case in some detail. Suppose for the sake of the example that it becomes necessary (for some reason—the precise reason is not important here) to replace base table S by the following two base tables:

```
SX  ( SNO, SNAME, CITY )
SY  ( SNO, STATUS )
```

---

*Unless those users have been using RETRIEVE statements of the form "RETRIEVE (R.ALL)"; the meanings of such statements will obviously change if new fields are added to the table in question. Remember, however, that such statements cannot be used in EQUEL, only interactively.

Aside: Such a replacement can easily be performed as follows:

```
RETRIEVE INTO SX ( S.SNO, S.SNAME, S.CITY )
RETRIEVE INTO SY ( S.SNO, S,STATUS )
DESTROY S
```

The crucial point to observe in this example is that *the old table S is the (natural) join of the two new tables SX and SY* (over supplier numbers). For example, in table S we had the row (S1,Smith,20,London); in SX we now have the row (S1,Smith,London) and in SY the row (S1,20); join them together and we get the row (S1,Smith,20,London), as before. So we create a *view* that is exactly that join, and we name it S:

```
DEFINE VIEW S
    ( SX.SNO, SX.SNAME, SY.STATUS, SX.CITY )
      WHERE SX.SNO = SY.SNO
```

Any program that previously referred to base table S will now refer to view S instead. RETRIEVE operations will continue to work exactly as before (though they will require additional analysis during the optimization process and will incur additional execution-time overhead). However, update operations will no longer work, because (as explained in Section 7.3) INGRES will not allow updates against a view that is defined as a join.* In other words, a user performing update operations is not immune to this type of change, but instead must make some manual alterations to the update statements concerned.

Thus we have shown that INGRES does *not* provide complete protection against changes in the logical structure of the database (which is why such changes are not a good idea in the first place). But things may not be as bad as they seem, even if manual alterations are necessary. The basic point is, QUEL is a very high-level language. The number of statements that have to be changed is therefore usually small, and the meaning of those statements is usually readily apparent; as a result, the necessary changes are usually easy to make. It is *not* like having to change statements in a comparatively low-level language such as COBOL, where the meaning of a given statement is probably highly dependent on the dynamic flow of control through the program to the statement in question. So, even though it is true that manual corrections must be made, the amount of work involved may not be all that great in practice.

---

*Except as noted in footnote on page 116.

To return to the SX-SY example for a moment: Actually, the view S (defined as the join of SX and SY) is a good example of a join view that *is* theoretically updatable. If we assume that there is a one-to-one correspondence between SX and SY at all times (so that any supplier appearing in SX also appears in SY, and vice versa), then the effect of all possible update operations on view S is clearly defined in terms of SX and SY. (Exercise: Do you agree with this statement?) Thus the example illustrates not only why the ability to update join views would be a useful system feature, but also a case where such updating appears to be a feasible proposition.

7.5 ADVANTAGES OF VIEWS

We conclude this chapter with a brief summary of the advantages of views.

- They provide a certain amount of logical data independence in the face of restructuring in the database, as explained in the previous section.

- They allow the same data to be seen by different users in different ways (possibly even at the same time).

   This consideration is obviously important when there are many different categories of user all interacting with a single integrated database.

- The user's perception is simplified.

   It is obvious that the new mechanism allows users to focus on just the data that is of concern to them and to ignore the rest. What is perhaps not so obvious is that, for retrieval at least, that mechanism can also considerably simplify users' data manipulation operations. In particular, because the user can be provided with a view in which all underlying tables are joined together, the need for explicit operations to step from table to table can be greatly reduced. As an example, consider the view CITYPAIRS, and contrast (a) the RETRIEVE needed to find cities storing parts available from London via that view with (b) the RETRIEVE needed to obtain the same result directly from the underlying base tables. In effect, much of the complexity of the retrieval process has been moved out of the realm of data manipulation and into that of data definition (in fact, the distinction between the two realms is far from clearcut in relational languages like QUEL).

EXERCISES

7.1 Define relation SP of the suppliers-and-parts database as a view of relation SPJ of the suppliers-parts-projects database.

7.2 Create a view from the suppliers-parts-projects database consisting of all projects (project number and city fields only) that are supplied by supplier S1 or use part P1.

7.3 Is your solution to Exercise 7.2 an updatable view?

7.4 Create a view consisting of supplier numbers and part numbers for suppliers and parts that are not "colocated."

7.5 Given the view definition:

```
DEFINE VIEW SUMMARY
     ( SPJ.SNO, SPJ.PNO,
       MAXQ = MAX ( SPJ.QTY BY SPJ.SNO, SPJ.PNO ),
       MINQ = MIN ( SPJ.QTY BY SPJ.SNO, SPJ.PNO ),
       AVGQ = AVG ( SPJ.QTY BY SPJ.SNO, SPJ.PNO ) )
       WHERE  SUM ( SPJ.QTY BY SPJ.SNO, SPJ.PNO ) > 50
```

state which of the following operations are legal and, for those that are, give the translated equivalents:

(a) `RETRIEVE ( SUMMARY.ALL )`

(b) `RETRIEVE ( SUMMARY.ALL )`
     `WHERE SUMMARY.SNO <> "S1"`

(c) `RETRIEVE ( SUMMARY.ALL )`
     `WHERE SUMMARY.MAXQ > 250`

(d) `RETRIEVE ( XYZ = SUMMARY.MAXQ - SUMMARY.MINQ )`
     `WHERE SUMMARY.SNO = "S1"`
     `AND    SUMMARY.PNO = "P1"`

(e) `RETRIEVE ( SUMMARY.SNO,`
     `           XYZ = SUM ( SUMMARY.MAXQ BY SUMMARY.SNO ) )`

(f) `RETRIEVE ( S.SNO, SUMMARY.AVGQ )`
     `WHERE S.SNO = SUMMARY.SNO`

(g) `REPLACE SUMMARY ( SNO = "S2" )`
     `WHERE SUMMARY.SNO = "S1"`

(h) `REPLACE SUMMARY ( MAXQ = 1000 )`
     `WHERE SUMMARY.SNO = "S1"`

(i) `DELETE SUMMARY`
     `WHERE  SUMMARY.SNO = "S1"`

(j) `APPEND TO SUMMARY`
     `( SNO = "S6", PNO = "P7", MAXQ = 0, MINQ = 0, AVGQ = 0 )`

7.6 State the rules concerning the updatability of views in INGRES.

7.7 Suppose the database is restructured in such a way that tables A and B are replaced by their natural join C. To what extent can the view mechanism conceal that restructuring from existing users?

ANSWERS TO SELECTED EXERCISES

7.1 The problem here is: How should the field SP.QTY be defined? The sensible answer seems to be that, for a given (SNO,PNO) pair, SP.QTY should be the *sum* of all SPJ.QTY values, taken over all JNOs for that (SNO,PNO) pair:

```
DEFINE VIEW SP
          ( SPJ.SNO, SPJ.PNO,
            QTY = SUM ( SPJ.QTY BY SPJ.SNO, SPJ.PNO ) )
```

7.2 DEFINE VIEW JC (J.JNO, J.CITY)
            WHERE   J.JNO = SPJ.JNO
            AND   (SPJ.SNO = "S1" OR
                 SPJ.PNO = "P1")

7.3 APPEND operations are not allowed. REPLACE operations are allowed on field CITY but not on field JNO. DELETE operations are allowed.

7.4 DEFINE VIEW NONCOLOC (S.SNO, P.PNO)
            WHERE   S.CITY <> P.CITY

7.5 The RETRIEVEs are all legal, the other operations are all illegal. We give the translated equivalent for (e) only:

```
(e)  RETRIEVE ( SPJ.SNO,
               XYZ = SUM ( MAX ( SPJ.QTY BY SPJ.SNO, SPJ.PNO )
                           BY  SPJ.SNO ) )
     WHERE SUM ( SPJ.QTY BY SPJ.SNO, SPJ.PNO ) > 50
```

8

Security and Integrity

8.1 INTRODUCTION

The terms "security" and "integrity" are very frequently heard together in database contexts, though the two concepts are actually quite distinct. *Security* refers to the protection of the data against unauthorized disclosure, alteration, or destruction; *integrity* refers to the accuracy or validity of the data. In other words:

- Security involves ensuring that users are *allowed* to do the things they are trying to do.
- Integrity involves ensuring that the things they are trying to do are *correct*.

There are some similarities too, of course: In both cases, the system needs to be aware of certain *constraints* that users must not violate; in both cases those constraints must be specified to the system somehow, and must be maintained in the system dictionary; and in both cases the system must monitor user interactions in some way to ensure that the constraints are in fact observed. In this chapter we examine these ideas (as they apply to INGRES) in some detail. Sections 8.2–8.3 are concerned with security and Sections 8.4–8.5 with integrity.

127

8.2   SECURITY: AN OVERVIEW

From a security point of view, INGRES users can be divided into four categories: the system manager, database administrators, table creators, and what we will call "data manipulators." Overall, the system works as follows:

1. The *system manager* is the person responsible for installing the INGRES system. The system manager appoints database administrators (see paragraph 2 below) and authorizes users to access the INGRES system by entering the names of those users into the "database database" (DBDB). The DBDB is a special INGRES system database; it contains information regarding all databases and all users known to the system, including in particular an indication as to which users can access which databases. The DBDB can be logically considered part of the INGRES dictionary; it can be regarded as a special "private" database, with the system manager as its database administrator (again, see paragraph 2 below). In this capacity, the system manager has the normal database administrator powers over the DBDB (once again, see paragraph 2 below). The normal situation would be for the system administrator not to permit anyone else to update the DBDB, for reasons of system integrity and control. We will assume this normal situation throughout this book.

Aside: Of course, the foregoing paragraph should not be construed to mean that there really is a single person who is the system manager for all time (and remains so even if, e.g., he or she leaves the company). Rather, there is a single unchanging *sign-on ID* that is understood by INGRES to identify the system manager. Anyone who can sign on under that ID (and can pass the applicable password tests) will be treated as the system manager so long as he or she remains signed on. The passwords *can* of course be changed from time to time, and probably should be.

2. The system manager designates a specified user as a *database administrator* (DBA) by granting that user the authority to create new databases (i.e., the authority to execute the CREATEDB operation—see Chapter 13). The CREATEDB authority is recorded in the DBDB. A database administrator can create a new database at any time.

The CREATEDB operation includes a parameter to specify whether the new database is public (default) or private. If database D is defined as public, then anyone can access that database; in particular, anyone can create new tables in that database. If database D is private, then only the DBA for D, or users to whom the system manager has explicitly given the authority to access D, can access that database; in particular, only the DBA for D, or users explicitly authorized to access D, can create new tables in that database. Authorizing users to access a private database is done by making suitable entries in the DBDB.

3. Anyone who has access to a given database *D* can create new tables (that is, new *base* tables) in that database. If the table creator, *C* say, is not the DBA for *D*, then the table in question remains completely private to *C*; no one else can access it at all, not even the DBA for *D*. If the table creator is the DBA for *D*, then he or she may optionally authorize other users to access the table, by means of the DEFINE PERMIT operation (see Section 8.3). The user who creates a given table is considered to be the *owner* of that table.

4. Finally, a "data manipulator" user *U* (a) can perform all QUEL operations on tables created by *U*, without any restrictions (except as noted below); (b) can perform QUEL operations on other tables only where the DBA has explicitly authorized the operation in question via DEFINE PERMIT (again, see Section 8.3).

Note that only the creator of a table can execute DESTROY, INDEX, MODIFY, or DEFINE INTEGRITY operations for that table, and only the DBA can issue DEFINE PERMIT operations (and then only for tables created by the DBA).

The operating system files containing the stored database cannot be accessed other than via INGRES itself. In other words, it is not possible to bypass the INGRES security controls.

8.3 DEFINE PERMIT

Security constraints are stated in QUEL by means of the DEFINE PERMIT statement. Here is a simple example:

```
DEFINE PERMIT RETRIEVE ON P TO Joe WHERE P.CITY = "London"
```

(user Joe is allowed to see London parts only). Such constraints are enforced by *query modification* (the same mechanism that is used to implement views). In other words, user requests are modified before execution in such a way as to guarantee that they cannot possibly violate any security constraints. For example, suppose user Joe is allowed to see parts stored in London only (as above), and suppose user Joe issues the request:

```
RETRIEVE ( P.PNO, P.WEIGHT )
WHERE      P.COLOR = "Red"
```

INGRES will automatically modify the query to the form:

```
RETRIEVE ( P.PNO, P.WEIGHT )
WHERE       P.COLOR = "Red"
AND         P.CITY  = "London"
```

And of course this modified query cannot possibly violate the security constraint. Note, incidentally, that the modification process is "silent"—user Joe is not informed that the system has in fact executed a query that is somewhat different from his original request. The justification for the "silence" is that the fact that the request has been modified might itself be sensitive (user Joe might not even be allowed to know that there are any parts not stored in London).

As suggested above, the query modification process just outlined is actually identical to the technique used to implement views (see Chapter 7). So one advantage of the scheme is that it is very easy to implement—most of the necessary code exists in the system already. On the other hand, a disadvantage is that not all security constraints can be handled in this simple fashion. As a trivial counterexample, suppose user Joe is not allowed to access table P at all. Then there is no simple "modified" form of the RETRIEVE shown above that can preserve the illusion that table P does not exist. Instead, an explicit error message—"You are not allowed to access this table"—must necessarily be generated.

The general syntax of DEFINE PERMIT is as follows:

```
DEFINE PERMIT operation(s)
       ON     table [ ( field [, field ] ... ) ]
       TO     user
     [ AT     terminal(s) ]
     [ FROM   time1  TO  time2 ]
     [ ON     day1   TO  day2  ]
     [ WHERE  predicate ]
```

The legal "operations" are RETRIEVE, APPEND, REPLACE, DELETE, and ALL. The specified "table" must be a base table, not a view. Observe that it is possible not only to limit a given user's access to a given table to some specific set of operations on some specific row-and-column subset of that table, but also to insist that all such access be made from some specific terminal(s) and/or at some specific times and/or on some specific days of the week. Here is an example:

```
DEFINE PERMIT RETRIEVE, REPLACE
       ON     S ( SNAME, CITY )
       TO     Judy
       AT     TTA4
       FROM   9:00 TO 17:30
       ON     SAT  TO SUN
       WHERE  S.STATUS < 50
       AND    S.SNO = SP.PNO
       AND    SP.PNO = P.PNO
       AND    P.COLOR = "Red"
```

DEFINE PERMIT (like everything else in QUEL) is of course an executable statement and can be executed at any time.

We present several further examples in order to illustrate a number of additional points.

```
1. DEFINE PERMIT ALL ON S TO ALL
```

The first ALL here stands for "all operations," the second for "all users."

2. Suppose the following constraints are specified:

```
DEFINE PERMIT RETRIEVE ON S TO Joe

DEFINE PERMIT REPLACE ON S TO Joe
              WHERE S.CITY = "Paris"
```

User Joe can perform RETRIEVE operations on supplier records unconditionally; however, he can perform REPLACE operations on such records only if the CITY field has the value "Paris."

3. Notice the difference between the following two cases:

```
(a) DEFINE PERMIT RETRIEVE ON S ( SNO, STATUS ) TO Judy

(b) DEFINE PERMIT RETRIEVE ON S ( SNO          ) TO Judy
    DEFINE PERMIT RETRIEVE ON S (       STATUS ) TO Judy
```

In case (a), user Judy can retrieve supplier numbers and corresponding status values from table S via a single RETRIEVE operation; that is, she can discover the status for any given supplier. In case (b), she can again retrieve supplier numbers and status values from table S, *but not in the same RETRIEVE operation*; that is, she *cannot* discover the status for any given supplier.

4. INGRES provides a special system variable or "symbolic constant" called USERNAME to allow constraints to be formulated that are dependent on the user issuing the QUEL request. For example:

```
DEFINE PERMIT RETRIEVE ON P TO ALL
         WHERE   P.PNO = SP.PNO
         AND     SP.SNO = S.SNO
         AND     S.SNAME = USERNAME
```

The value of USERNAME is the INGRES-known name for the user executing the statement that invokes the USERNAME reference. In the example, therefore, it does not represent the user who issues the DEFINE PERMIT, but rather any user who attempts to execute some data manipulation operation on table P. For example, if user Joe issues the statement

```
RETRIEVE ( P.ALL )
```

then INGRES will effectively convert that statement into

```
RETRIEVE ( P.ALL )
WHERE       P.PNO = SP.PNO
AND         SP.SNO = S.SNO
AND         S.SNAME = "Joe"
```

In other words, a given user will only be allowed to access part records for parts supplied by that user as a supplier.

Security constraints are kept in the INGRES dictionary under numeric identifiers (0, 1, 2, etc.). Those identifiers can be discovered by querying the dictionary (a special form of HELP is provided to assist in this process, though the conventional QUEL RETRIEVE statement can also be used; see Chapter 6). Thus, to delete a given constraint on table S, say, it is first necessary to discover the applicable identifier. The statement

```
HELP PERMIT S
```

will return a list of all security constraints on table S, together with their numeric identifiers. Suppose the constraint in question has identifier 27. Then the statement

```
DESTROY PERMIT S 27
```

will remove the constraint from the system.

8.4 INTEGRITY: AN OVERVIEW

As explained in Section 8.1, the term "integrity" refers to the accuracy or correctness of the data in the database. In order to maintain a given database in a correct state, the system needs to be aware of the *integrity constraints* that apply to that database. An integrity constraint can be regarded as a *predicate* that all correct states of the database are required to satisfy. A simple example of such a predicate might be

```
S.STATUS > 0
```

("status values must be greater than zero"). If this constraint were in effect, the system would have to monitor all APPEND operations on table S and all REPLACE operations on field S.STATUS to ensure that the constraint is never violated. INGRES's technique for performing that monitoring is explained in Section 8.5.

Integrity constraints can conveniently be classified into several distinct kinds:

- *Data type constraints*: Values of a given field are required to be of some specified data type. For example, if field SP.QTY is defined to be one of the numeric data types (e.g., I4), then INGRES will reject any attempt to assign a character string value to that field. See Chapter 3 for a discussion of INGRES data types.

- *Single-variable constraints*: The database is required to satisfy some specified predicate p, where p involves a single range variable. The predicate shown above (S.STATUS > 0) is a simple example of such a predicate. Single-variable constraints are discussed in Section 8.5. *Note*: The specification NOT NULL (WITH DEFAULT or otherwise) for a particular field in the CREATE statement (see Chapter 3) can be regarded as special-case syntax for a particular kind of single-variable constraint.

- *Multi-variable constraints*: The database is required to satisfy some specified predicate p, where p involves multiple range variables. INGRES does not currently support multi-variable constraints, except for the important special case of UNIQUE. The INGRES UNIQUE specification (part of the MODIFY statement—see Chapter 12) can be regarded as special-case syntax for a particular kind of multi-variable constraint.*

---

*"Referential" integrity constraints (see Appendix B) are another (extremely important) special case—unfortunately one that the INGRES DBMS does not currently support.

In INGRES, only the creator of a table can specify integrity constraints for that table.

8.5 DEFINE INTEGRITY

Integrity constraints are stated in QUEL by means of the DEFINE INTEGRITY statement. Here is a simple example:

```
DEFINE INTEGRITY ON S IS S.STATUS > 0
```

("status values must be greater than zero"—the QUEL version of the constraint shown in Section 8.4). Like security constraints, integrity constraints are enforced in INGRES by query modification; that is, user requests are modified before execution in such a way as to guarantee that they cannot possibly violate any constraints. (*Note*: The only user requests that can possibly need such modification are APPEND and REPLACE operations.) For example, suppose the above integrity constraint is in force, and suppose user Joe issues the request:

```
REPLACE S ( STATUS = S.STATUS - 25 )
WHERE    S.CITY = "Paris"
```

INGRES will automatically modify the operation to the form:

```
REPLACE S ( STATUS = S.STATUS - 25 )
WHERE    S.CITY = "Paris"
AND      ( S.STATUS - 25 ) > 0
```

And of course this modified operation cannot possibly violate the specified constraint. As in the case of security (see Section 8.3), the modification process is "silent"—user Joe is not informed that the system has in fact executed an operation that is somewhat different from his original request. Notice, incidentally, that the effect of the modification will be that some of the target records will be updated and some not (in general).

The general syntax of DEFINE INTEGRITY is as follows:

```
DEFINE INTEGRITY ON range-variable IS predicate
```

where "range-variable" (a) identifies a base table, not a view, and (b) is the only range variable referenced in "predicate" (so that "predicate" is definitely single-variable, as INGRES requires). INGRES checks the database to ensure that all existing rows in the indicated base table do currently satisfy "predicate"; if so, the constraint is accepted and enforced from this point on, otherwise it is rejected with an error message. As mentioned in Section 8.4, only the creator of a table is allowed to execute DEFINE INTEGRITY statements for that table.

Integrity constraints, like security constraints, are kept in the INGRES dictionary under numeric identifiers (0, 1, 2, etc.), which can be discovered by means of the HELP INTEGRITY statement (or by means of a conventional QUEL RETRIEVE statement; see Chapter 6). Thus, for example, to delete a given integrity constraint on table S, say, we might proceed as follows. First, the statement

```
HELP INTEGRITY S
```

will return a list of all integrity constraints on table S, together with their numeric identifiers. Suppose the constraint in question has identifier 18. Then the statement

```
DESTROY INTEGRITY S 18
```

will remove the constraint from the system.

We conclude this section by remarking that INGRES does provide some limited additional support for integrity functions through certain of its frontend subsystems (QBF, VIFRED, and ABF). See Part III of this book.

EXERCISES

8.1 Suppose you are the DBA for some database *D*, and you create a table STATS in *D* with definition as follows:

```
CREATE STATS
       ( USERID   = TEXT(12),
         SEX      = TEXT(1),
         DEPNDNTS = I2,
         OCCUPTN  = TEXT(20),
         SALARY   = I4,
         TAX      = I4,
         AUDITS   = I2  )
```

Write QUEL statements to give:
(a) User Ford RETRIEVE access to the entire table.
(b) User Smith APPEND and DELETE access to the entire table.
(c) Each user RETRIEVE access to that user's own record (only).
(d) User Nash RETRIEVE·access to the entire table and REPLACE access to the SALARY and TAX fields (only).

(e) User Todd RETRIEVE access to the USERID, SALARY, and TAX fields (only).

(f) User Ward RETRIEVE access as for Todd and REPLACE access to the SAL-ARY and TAX fields (only).

(g) User Pope full access (RETRIEVE, REPLACE, APPEND, DELETE) to records for preachers (only).

(h) User Jones RETRIEVE access as for Todd and REPLACE access to the TAX and AUDITS fields (only).

8.2 Write DEFINE INTEGRITY statements (where possible) for the following constraints on the suppliers-parts-projects database:

(a) The only legal part colors are red, blue, and green.

(b) All red parts weigh less than 50 pounds.

(c) Every supplier number appearing in a shipment record must also appear in some supplier record.

(d) All red parts, and only red parts, are stored in London.

(e) All red parts are stored in London, all green parts are stored in Paris, and all blue parts are stored in either Paris or Rome.

(f) Every project must be located in a city in which there is at least one supplier.

(g) The highest-status supplier must not be located in the same city as the lowest-status supplier.

ANSWERS TO SELECTED EXERCISES

8.1 (a) `DEFINE PERMIT RETRIEVE ON STATS TO FORD`

(b) `DEFINE PERMIT APPEND, DELETE ON STATS TO SMITH`

(c) `DEFINE PERMIT RETRIEVE ON STATS TO USERNAME`
`            WHERE STATS.USERID = USERNAME`

(d) `DEFINE PERMIT RETRIEVE ON STATS TO NASH`

`DEFINE PERMIT REPLACE ON STATS ( SALARY, TAX ) TO NASH`

(e) `DEFINE PERMIT RETRIEVE ON STATS ( USERID, SALARY, TAX )`
`                                         TO TODD`

(f) `DEFINE PERMIT RETRIEVE ON STATS ( USERID, SALARY, TAX )`
`                                         TO WARD`

`DEFINE PERMIT REPLACE ON STATS ( SALARY, TAX ) TO WARD`

(g) `DEFINE PERMIT ALL ON STATS TO POPE`
`            WHERE   STATS.OCCUPTN = "Preacher"`

(h) `DEFINE PERMIT RETRIEVE ON STATS ( USERID, SALARY, TAX )`
`                                         TO JONES`

`DEFINE PERMIT REPLACE ON STATS ( TAX, AUDITS ) TO JONES`

8.2 (a) `DEFINE INTEGRITY ON P IS`
`            P.COLOR = "Red" OR`
`            P.COLOR = "Blue" OR`
`            P.COLOR = "Green"`

(b) ```
DEFINE INTEGRITY ON P IS
        P.COLOR <> "Red" OR P.WEIGHT < 50
```

(c) Cannot be done (it is a multi-variable constraint; in fact, it is an example of a referential constraint). See Appendix B.

(d) ```
DEFINE INTEGRITY ON P IS
        ( P.COLOR = "Red" AND P.CITY = "London" ) OR
        ( P.COLOR <> "Red" AND P.CITY <> "London" )
```

(e) ```
DEFINE INTEGRITY ON P IS
        (P.COLOR <> "Red" OR P.CITY = "London") OR
        (P.COLOR <> "Green" OR P.CITY = "Paris") OR
        (P.COLOR <> "Blue" OR (P.CITY = "London" OR
                                 P.CITY = "Rome"))
```

(f) Cannot be done (it is a multi-variable constraint).

(g) Cannot be done (it is a multi-variable constraint).
```

9

Transaction Processing

9.1 INTRODUCTION

The concept of transaction processing is an extremely important one in modern database management systems. In this chapter, we explain in some detail what exactly a transaction is and what is meant by the term "transaction processing" (or "transaction management"). In particular, we discuss the problems of recovery and concurrency control that the transaction concept is intended to solve. Also, of course, we examine the relevant aspects of INGRES and QUEL in some detail. Note, however, that much of the chapter is very general and could apply with little change to many other systems—with the exception of Section 9.3 on savepoints; very few products other than INGRES currently support such a feature, so far as this writer is aware. Sections 9.2–9.3 are concerned with recovery and Sections 9.4–9.6 are concerned with concurrency.

9.2 WHAT IS A TRANSACTION?

A transaction (as we use the term) is a *logical unit of work*. Consider the following example. Suppose for the sake of the example that table P, the parts table, includes an additional field TOTQTY representing the total shipment quantity for the part in question. In other words, the value of

139

TOTQTY for any given part is equal to the sum of all SP.QTY values, taken over all SP records for that part. Now consider the following sequence of operations, the intent of which is to add a new shipment (S5,P1,1000) to the database:

```
BEGIN TRANSACTION

APPEND TO SP ( SNO = "S5", PNO = "P1", QTY = 1000 )

REPLACE P ( TOTQTY = P.TOTQTY + 1000 ) WHERE P.PNO = "P1"

END TRANSACTION
```

The APPEND adds the new shipment to the SP table, the REPLACE updates the TOTQTY field for part P1 appropriately.

The point of the example is that what is presumably intended to be a single, atomic operation—"Create a new shipment"—in fact involves *two* updates to the database. What is more, the database is not even consistent between the two updates; it temporarily violates the requirement that the value of TOTQTY for part P1 is supposed to be equal to the sum of all SP.QTY values for part P1. Thus a transaction, or logical unit of work, is not necessarily just one QUEL operation; rather, it is a *sequence* of several such operations (in general) that transforms a consistent state of the database into another consistent state, without necessarily preserving consistency at all intermediate points.

Now, it is clear that what must *not* be allowed to happen in the example is for one of the two updates to be executed and the other not (because then the database would be left in an inconsistent state). Ideally, of course, we would like a cast-iron guarantee that both updates will be executed. Unfortunately, it is impossible to provide any such guarantee: There is always a chance that things will go wrong, and go wrong moreover at the worst possible moment. For example, a system crash might occur between the two updates, or an I/O error might occur on the second of them, or the user might just get tired and decide to go home. . . . But a system that supports *transaction processing* does provide the next best thing to such a guarantee. Specifically, it guarantees that if the transaction executes some updates and then a failure occurs (for whatever reason) before the transaction reaches its normal termination, *then those updates will be undone*. Thus the transaction *either* executes in its entirety *or* is totally canceled (i.e., made as if it never executed at all). In this way a sequence of operations that is fundamentally not atomic internally can be made to look as if it really were atomic from an external point of view.

The INGRES component that provides this atomicity (or semblance of atomicity) is known as the *transaction manager*, and the QUEL statements BEGIN TRANSACTION, END TRANSACTION, and ABORT are the key to the way it works:

- BEGIN TRANSACTION signals the beginning of a new transaction (obviously).

- END TRANSACTION signals *successful* end-of-transaction: It tells the transaction manager that a logical unit of work has been successfully completed, the database is (or should be) in a consistent state again, and all of the updates made by that unit of work can now be "committed" or made permanent. Prior to END TRANSACTION, any updates made by the transaction should be regarded as *tentative only*— tentative in the sense that, if something subsequently goes wrong, *those updates may be undone*. Updates remain tentative until one of two things happens:

  - An END TRANSACTION is executed, which "commits" all tentative updates and makes them permanent; or

  - An ABORT is executed, which undoes all tentative updates. Once committed, an update is guaranteed never to be undone (this is the definition of "committed").

- ABORT, by contrast, signals *unsuccessful* end-of-transaction: It tells the transaction manager that something has gone wrong, the database might be in an inconsistent state, and all of the updates made by the logical unit of work so far must be aborted or undone.

In the example, therefore, we first issue BEGIN TRANSACTION to inform INGRES that we are about to embark on a sequence of related operations that are to be treated as an atomic unit. We issue END TRANSACTION after we get through those operations (i.e., the two updates) successfully; the effect of that END TRANSACTION is to commit the changes in the database and make them permanent. If anything goes wrong, however—i.e., if either update fails for any reason—then we should issue ABORT instead, to undo any changes made prior to the point of failure.

At this juncture the reader may be wondering how it is possible to undo an update. The answer is that updates are not actually "done" in the first place until END TRANSACTION—i.e., they are not physically written out to the database until that time. If the transaction does not terminate with END TRANSACTION, the updates are simply never written out to the database at all.* Note carefully that this last point implies that if you issue a BEGIN TRANSACTION, you *must* eventually issue a corresponding END TRANSACTION or your updates will have no lasting effect. It also

---

*More accurately: An update *may* be physically written to the database prior to END TRANSACTION, but if so, then a record is also written to the INGRES journal giving the old (nonupdated) version of the data. That journal record can be used to undo the update if the transaction fails to terminate successfully.

implies that if a system crash occurs, then all transactions that were running at the time of the crash will effectively be aborted, because none of their updates will be written to the database (the effect of a system crash is thus logically to cause an ABORT for all such transactions).

One final remark: Our explanations so far have been entirely in terms of what INGRES calls a *multi-statement transaction* (MST). INGRES actually supports two kinds of transaction, multi-statement transactions and *single*-statement transactions (SSTs). An MST is a sequence of one or more QUEL operations enclosed within a BEGIN TRANSACTION–END TRANSACTION pair (like the example at the beginning of this section). An SST is any single QUEL operation not so enclosed. (Note that even a single QUEL operation can involve multiple updates to the database, so the question of atomicity can still arise.) An MST can include any QUEL operations except the following:

```
ABORT
BEGIN TRANSACTION
END TRANSACTION
```

The fact that BEGIN TRANSACTION cannot appear means that transactions cannot be nested (see Exercise 9.1 at the end of this chapter). It follows that ABORT and END TRANSACTION cannot appear either (*within* an MST; of course they can and do appear to mark *termination* of an MST).

9.3 SAVEPOINTS

The savepoint facility allows a multi-statement transaction (MST) to be *partially* aborted (on user command). The SAVEPOINT statement allows the user to establish a named "savepoint" within an MST. Subsequently, a special form of the ABORT statement—"ABORT TO savepoint"—allows the user to undo all updates performed since the specified savepoint, while at the same time preserving updates performed prior to that point. Note that "ABORT TO savepoint" (unlike the ordinary ABORT statement) does not terminate the transaction.

Here is an example (somewhat contrived):

```
BEGIN TRANSACTION                    /* time t1, say */
APPEND TO S ( SNO = "S6" )           /* time t2     */
SAVEPOINT ALPHA                      /* time t3     */
APPEND TO S ( SNO = "S7" )           /* time t4     */
SAVEPOINT BETA                       /* time t5     */
APPEND TO S ( SNO = "S8" )           /* time t6     */
ABORT TO BETA                        /* time t7     */
```

```
APPEND TO S ( SNO = "S9" )               /* time t8      */

ABORT TO ALPHA                           /* time t9      */

END TRANSACTION                          /* time t10     */
```

By time t6, suppliers S6, S7, and S8 have logically been added to the suppliers table S. At time t7, however, supplier S8 is logically removed again. At time t8 supplier S9 is added; however, at time t9, suppliers S7 and S9 are both removed. Thus the only update that is committed at time t10 is the first one, and supplier S6 is the only supplier to be permanently added to the database. Note, therefore, that the SAVEPOINT operation does *not* commit any updates; it merely establishes a possible target for future "ABORT TO . . ." operations.

Note too in the example that the ABORT TO ALPHA at time t9 means that BETA is no longer a known savepoint (because it was established after ALPHA was established). Any subsequent attempt to ABORT TO BETA would fail (unless a new savepoint called BETA had been established again after the ABORT TO ALPHA).

The savepoint facility can be useful in certain kinds of "what if" processing.

9.4 THREE CONCURRENCY PROBLEMS

INGRES is a *shared system*; that is, it is a system that allows any number of transactions to access the same database at the same time. Any such system requires some kind of *concurrency control mechanism* to ensure that concurrent transactions do not interfere with each other's operation, and of course INGRES does include such a mechanism, namely *locking*. For the benefit of readers who may not be familiar with the problems that can occur in the absence of such a mechanism—in other words, with the problems that such a mechanism must be able to solve—this section is devoted to an outline explanation of those problems. We defer specific discussion of the INGRES facilities to Sections 9.5 and 9.6. Readers who are already familiar with the basic ideas of concurrency control may wish to turn straight to those sections.

There are essentially three ways in which things can go wrong—three ways, that is, in which a transaction, though correct in itself, can nevertheless produce the wrong answer because of interference on the part of some other transaction* (in the absence of suitable controls, of course). The three problems are:

---

*Note that the interfering transaction may also be correct in itself. It is the *interleaving* of operations from the two transactions that can cause an overall incorrect result.

1. The *lost update* problem,
2. The *uncommitted dependency* problem, and
3. The *inconsistent analysis* problem.

We consider each in turn.

The Lost Update Problem

Consider the situation illustrated in Fig. 9.1. That figure is intended to be read as follows: Transaction A retrieves some record R at time t1; transaction B retrieves that same record R at time t2; transaction A updates the record (on the basis of the values seen at time t1) at time t3; and transaction B updates the same record (on the basis of the values seen at time t2, which are the same as those seen at time t1) at time t4. Transaction A's update is lost at time t4, because transaction B overwrites it without even looking at it.

The Uncommitted Dependency Problem

The uncommitted dependency problem arises if one transaction is allowed to retrieve (or, worse, update) a record that has been updated by another transaction and has not yet been committed by that other transaction. For if it has not yet been committed, there is always a possibility that it never will be committed but will be undone instead—in which case the first transaction will have seen some data that now no longer exists (and in a sense "never" existed). Consider Figs. 9.2 and 9.3.

Transaction A	time	Transaction B
—		—
—		—
RETRIEVE R	t1	—
—		—
—	t2	RETRIEVE R
—		—
REPLACE R	t3	—
—		—
—	t4	REPLACE R
—		—

Fig. 9.1 Transaction A loses an update at time t4

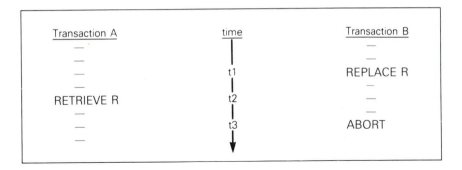

Fig. 9.2 Transaction A becomes dependent on an uncommitted change at time t2

In the first example (Fig. 9.2), transaction A sees an uncommitted update (or uncommitted change) at time t2. That update is then undone at time t3. Transaction A is therefore operating on a false assumption—namely, the assumption that record R has the value seen at time t2, whereas in fact it has whatever value it had prior to time t1. As a result, transaction A may well produce incorrect output. Note, incidentally, that the ABORT of transaction B may be due to no fault of B's—for example, B may have failed because of a system crash. (And transaction A may already have terminated by that time, in which case the crash would not cause an ABORT for A.)

The second example (Fig. 9.3) is even worse. Not only does transaction A become dependent on an uncommitted change at time t2, but it actually

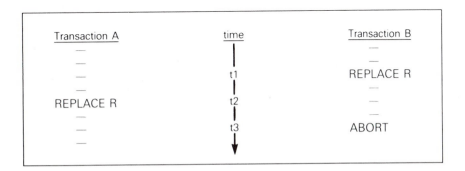

Fig. 9.3 Transaction A updates an uncommitted change at time t2, and loses that update at time t3

loses an update at time t3—because the ABORT at time t3 causes record R to be restored to its value prior to time t1. This is another version of the lost update problem.

The Inconsistent Analysis Problem

Consider Fig. 9.4, which shows two transactions A and B operating on account (ACC) records: Transaction A is summing account balances, transaction B is transferring an amount 10 from account 3 to account 1. The result produced by A (110) is obviously incorrect; if A were to go on to

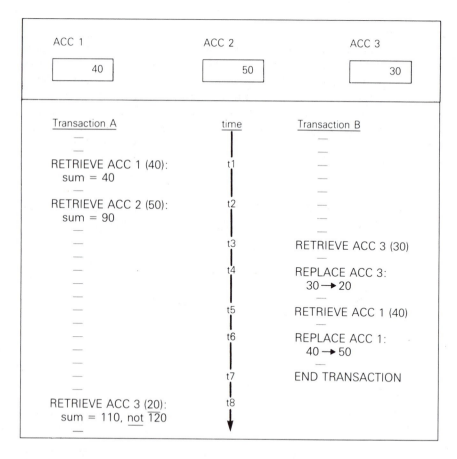

Fig. 9.4 Transaction A performs an inconsistent analysis

write that result back into the database, it would actually leave the database in an inconsistent state. We say that A has seen an inconsistent state of the database and has therefore performed an inconsistent analysis. Note the difference between this example and the previous one: There is no question here of A being dependent on an uncommitted change, since B commits all its updates before A sees ACC 3.

9.5 HOW INGRES SOLVES THE THREE CONCURRENCY PROBLEMS

As mentioned at the beginning of the previous section, the INGRES concurrency control mechanism—like that of most other systems currently available—is based on a technique known as *locking*. The basic idea of locking is simple: When a transaction needs an assurance that some object that it is interested in—typically a database record—will not change in some unpredictable manner while its back is turned (as it were), it *acquires a lock* on that object. The effect of the lock is to lock other transactions out of the object, and in particular to prevent them from changing it. The first transaction is thus able to carry out its processing in the certain knowledge that the object in question will remain in a stable state for as long as that transaction wishes it to.

We now proceed to give a more detailed (but still very much simplified) explanation of the way locking works in INGRES specifically. We start by making some simplifying assumptions:

1. We assume that the unit of locking—i.e., the unit of data that is subject to the locking mechanism—is the individual database record (i.e., a row of a base table, or more precisely the stored form of such a row). In practice, for implementation reasons, INGRES does not actually lock the individual record but rather the page (see Chapter 12) or table that contains that record.* However, that fact does not materially affect the discussions that follow. The reader is referred to the RTI manuals for more details.

2. We discuss only two kinds of lock, namely exclusive locks (abbreviated "X locks") and shared locks (abbreviated "S locks"). Other types of lock exist in some systems (in fact, INGRES itself supports additional types internally), but X and S are the only ones that are of interest to the user. *Note*: S and X locks are sometimes referred to as read and write locks, respectively.

3. We consider record-level operations only (i.e., operations that retrieve

---

*For certain utility operations, in fact, it locks the entire database.

or update a single record). For locking purposes, set-level operations (i.e., multiple-record retrievals or updates) can be regarded just as a shorthand for an appropriate series of record-level operations.

4. We ignore the INGRES "lockmode" option—or, more precisely, we assume that the INGRES system defaults apply for that option. For more information regarding the lockmode option, the reader is referred to the RTI manuals.

We now proceed with our detailed explanation.

1. First, if transaction A holds an exclusive (X) lock on record R, then a request from transaction B for a lock of either type on R will cause B to go into a wait state. B will wait until A's lock is released.

2. Next, if transaction A holds a shared (S) lock on record R, then: (a) a request from transaction B for an X lock on R will cause B to go into a wait state (and B will wait until A's lock is released); (b) a request from transaction B for an S lock on R will be granted (that is, B will now also hold an S lock on R).

These first two points can conveniently be summarized by means of a *compatibility matrix* (Fig. 9.5). The matrix is interpreted as follows: Consider some record R; suppose transaction A currently has a lock on R as indicated by the entries in the column headings (dash = no lock); and suppose some distinct transaction B issues a request for a lock on R as indicated by the entries down the left-hand side (for completeness we again include the "no lock" case). An N indicates a *conflict* (B's request cannot be satisfied and B goes into a wait state), a Y indicates compatibility (B's request is satisfied). The matrix is obviously symmetric.

To continue with our explanation:

3. Transaction requests for record locks are always implicit. When a transaction successfully retrieves a record, it automatically acquires an S

	X	S	—
X	N	N	Y
S	N	Y	Y
—	Y	Y	Y

Fig. 9.5 Lock type compatibility matrix

lock on that record. When a transaction successfully updates a record (where "update" means APPEND, REPLACE, or DELETE), it automatically acquires an X lock on that record (if it already holds an S lock on the record, as it may do in a retrieve/update sequence, then the update promotes the S lock to X level).

4. All locks are held until the end of the transaction.

Now we are in a position to see how INGRES solves the three problems described in the previous section. Again we consider them one at a time.

The Lost Update Problem

Figure 9.6 is a modified version of Fig. 9.1, showing what would happen to the interleaved execution of that figure under the locking mechanism of INGRES. As you can see, transaction A's REPLACE at time t3 is not accepted, because it is an implicit request for an X lock on R, and such a request conflicts with the S lock already held by transaction B; so A goes into a wait state. For analogous reasons, B goes into a wait state at time t4. Now both transactions are unable to proceed, so there is no question of any update being lost. INGRES thus solves the lost update problem by reducing it to another problem!—but at least it does solve the original prob-

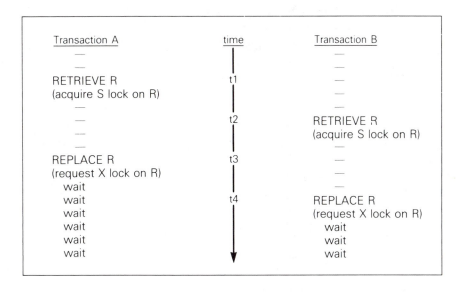

Fig. 9.6 No update is lost, but deadlock occurs at time t4

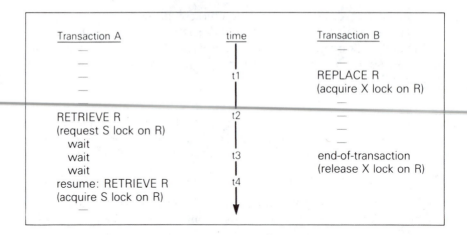

Fig. 9.7 Transaction A is prevented from seeing an uncommitted change at time t2

lem. The new problem is called *deadlock*. To see how INGRES deals with the deadlock problem, see Section 9.6.

The Uncommitted Dependency Problem

Figures 9.7 and 9.8 are, respectively, modified versions of Figs. 9.2 and 9.3, showing what would happen to the interleaved executions of those figures

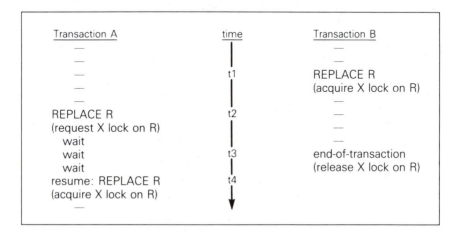

Fig. 9.8 Transaction A is prevented from updating an uncommitted change at time t2

under the locking mechanism of INGRES. As you can see, transaction A's operation at time t2 (RETRIEVE in Fig. 9.7, REPLACE in Fig. 9.8) is not accepted in either case, because it is an implicit request for a lock on R, and such a request conflicts with the X lock already held by B; so A goes into a wait state. It remains in that wait state until B reaches end-of-transaction (END TRANSACTION or ABORT), when B's lock is released and A is able to proceed; and at that point A sees a *committed* value (either the

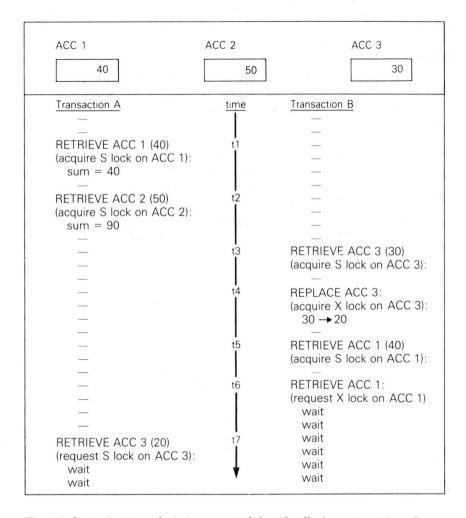

Fig. 9.9 Inconsistent analysis is prevented, but deadlock occurs at time t7

pre-B value, if B terminates with ABORT, or the post-B value otherwise). Either way, A is no longer dependent on an uncommitted update.

The Inconsistent Analysis Problem

Figure 9.9 (see page 151) is a modified version of Fig. 9.4, showing what would happen to the interleaved execution of that figure under the locking mechanism of INGRES. As you can see, transaction B's REPLACE at time t6 is not accepted, because it is an implicit request for an X lock on ACC 1, and such a request conflicts with the S lock already held by A; so B goes into a wait state. Likewise, transaction A's RETRIEVE at time t7 is also not accepted, because it is an implicit request for an S lock on ACC 3, and such a request conflicts with the X lock already held by B; so A goes into a wait state also. Thus (again) INGRES solves the original problem (the inconsistent analysis problem, in this case) by forcing a deadlock. As already mentioned, deadlock is discussed in the next section.

9.6   DEADLOCK

We have seen how locking can be used to solve the three basic problems of concurrency. Unfortunately, however, we have also seen that locking introduces problems of its own, principally the problem of deadlock. Section 9.5 gave two examples of deadlock. Figure 9.10 below shows a slightly more generalized version of the problem. *Note*: The LOCK operation in that figure is intended to represent any operation that requests a lock—e.g., any

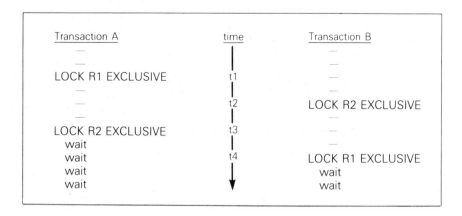

Fig. 9.10 An example of deadlock

QUEL data manipulation operation. For simplicity we assume that all locks are exclusive (X locks).

Deadlock is a situation in which two or more transactions are in a simultaneous wait state, each one waiting for one of the others to release a lock before it can proceed. Figure 9.10 shows a deadlock involving two transactions, but deadlocks involving three, four, . . . transactions are also possible, at least in theory. In practice, however, deadlocks almost never involve more than two transactions.

If a deadlock occurs, INGRES will detect it and break it. Breaking a deadlock involves choosing one of the deadlocked transactions as the *victim* and automatically aborting it (thus undoing all its updates and releasing all its locks, and hence allowing some other transaction to proceed). An error message is returned to the victim. In general, therefore, *any operation that requests a lock*—in particular, any QUEL data manipulation operation— may be rejected with an error message indicating that the transaction has just been selected as the victim in a deadlock situation and has been aborted. The problem of deadlock is thus a significant one so far as the user is concerned, because the user must be ready to deal with it if it arises. Dealing with it will normally mean starting the transaction again from the beginning.

9.7 SUMMARY

In this chapter we have introduced the topic of transaction management, both in general terms and as it is handled in INGRES specifically. A transaction is a logical unit of work—also (as can be seen from the discussions of Sections 9.2–9.6) a unit of recovery and a unit of concurrency. Transaction management is the task of supervising the execution of transactions in such a way that each transaction can be considered as an all-or-nothing proposition, even given the possibility of arbitrary failures on the part of either individual transactions or the system itself, and given also the fact that multiple independent transactions may be executing concurrently and accessing the same data. In fact, the overall function of the system might well be defined as *the reliable execution of transactions.*

In INGRES specifically, transactions are of two kinds, multi-statement transactions (MSTs) and single-statement transactions (SSTs). An MST is a sequence of QUEL operations, bracketed by BEGIN TRANSACTION and END TRANSACTION (or BEGIN TRANSACTION and ABORT). An SST is a QUEL operation not thus bracketed. INGRES guarantees the atomicity of transactions, as explained in Section 9.2. MSTs can also include savepoints and can perform partial aborts to such savepoints, as described in Section 9.3.

Concurrency control in INGRES is based on locking. Basically, every record a transaction accesses is locked with an S lock; if the transaction goes on to update the record, then that S lock will be promoted to X level. All locks are held until end-of-transaction. This simple protocol solves the three basic problems of concurrency, but also introduces the possibility of deadlock; hence users must be prepared to deal with that eventuality. Deadlock is signaled by an error message that may potentially be returned after any QUEL operation that requests a lock.

EXERCISES

9.1 Why cannot transactions be nested?

9.2 The following list represents the sequence of events in an interleaved execution of a set of transactions T1, T2, . . . , T12. A, B, C, . . . represent individual record occurrences.

```
time t0        . . . . . . . . . .
time t1   (T1)   : BEGIN TRANSACTION
time t2   (T1)   : RETRIEVE A
time t3   (T2)   : BEGIN TRANSACTION
time t4   (T2)   : RETRIEVE B
   -      (T1)   : RETRIEVE C
   -      (T4)   : BEGIN TRANSACTION
   -      (T4)   : RETRIEVE D
   -      (T5)   : BEGIN TRANSACTION
   -      (T5)   : RETRIEVE A
   -      (T2)   : RETRIEVE E
   -      (T2)   : REPLACE E
   -      (T3)   : BEGIN TRANSACTION
   -      (T3)   : RETRIEVE F
   -      (T2)   : RETRIEVE F
   -      (T5)   : REPLACE A
   -      (T1)   : END TRANSACTION
   -      (T6)   : BEGIN TRANSACTION
   -      (T6)   : RETRIEVE A
   -      (T5)   : ABORT
   -      (T6)   : RETRIEVE C
   -      (T6)   : REPLACE C
   -      (T7)   : BEGIN TRANSACTION
   -      (T7)   : RETRIEVE G
   -      (T8)   : BEGIN TRANSACTION
   -      (T8)   : RETRIEVE H
   -      (T9)   : BEGIN TRANSACTION
   -      (T9)   : RETRIEVE G
```

```
   -      (T9)    : REPLACE G
   -      (T8)    : RETRIEVE E
   -      (T7)    : END TRANSACTION
   -      (T9)    : RETRIEVE H
   -      (T3)    : RETRIEVE G
   -      (T10)   : BEGIN TRANSACTION
   -      (T10)   : RETRIEVE A
   -      (T9)    : REPLACE H
   -      (T6)    : END TRANSACTION
   -      (T11)   : BEGIN TRANSACTION
   -      (T11)   : RETRIEVE C
   -      (T12)   : BEGIN TRANSACTION
   -      (T12)   : RETRIEVE D
   -      (T12)   : RETRIEVE C
   -      (T2)    : REPLACE F
   -      (T11)   : REPLACE C
   -      (T12)   : RETRIEVE A
   -      (T10)   : REPLACE A
   -      (T12)   : REPLACE D
   -      (T4)    : RETRIEVE G
time tn        .........
```

Are there any deadlocks at time *tn*?

ANSWERS TO SELECTED EXERCISES

9.1 The ability to nest transactions (if it were supported) would conflict with the objective of transaction atomicity. For consider what would happen if transaction B were nested inside transaction A, and the following sequence of events occurred:

```
BEGIN TRANSACTION (transaction A)

REPLACE R1 (transaction A)

    BEGIN TRANSACTION (transaction B)

    REPLACE R2 (transaction B)

    END TRANSACTION (transaction B)

ABORT (transaction A)
```

If record R2 is restored to its pre-A value at this point, then B's END TRANS-ACTION, which was supposed to commit B's updates, in fact did not commit those updates at all. Conversely, if B's END TRANSACTION did commit those updates, then record R2 cannot be restored to its pre-A value, and hence A's ABORT cannot be honored. Thus transaction nesting is a contradiction in terms.

9.2 At time t*n* *no* transactions are doing any useful work at all! There is one dead-lock, involving transactions T2, T3, T9, and T8; in addition, T4 is waiting for T9, T12 is waiting for T4, and T10 and T11 are both waiting for T12. We can represent the situation by means of a graph (the *Wait-For Graph*), in which the nodes represent transactions and a directed edge from node T*i* to node T*j* indicates that T*i* is waiting for T*j*. Edges are labeled with the name of the record and level of lock they are waiting for.

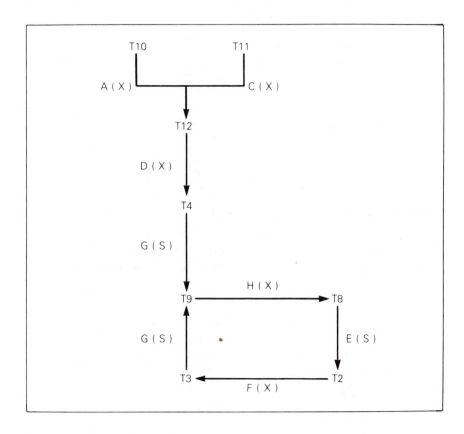

Fig. 9.11 The Wait-For graph

10

Embedded QUEL

10.1 INTRODUCTION

In Chapter 1 we explained that QUEL was used in INGRES both as an interactive query language and as a database programming language. Up to this point, however, we have more or less ignored the programming aspects of QUEL and have tacitly assumed (where it made any difference) that the language was being used interactively. In this chapter we turn our attention to those programming aspects specifically and discuss the principal ideas behind "Embedded QUEL" or (as it is usually called) EQUEL.

The fundamental principle underlying EQUEL, which we may refer to as *the dual-mode principle*, is that *any QUEL statement that can be used at the terminal can also be used in an application program*. Of course, as pointed out in Chapter 1, there are various differences of detail between a given interactive QUEL statement and its corresponding embedded form, and RETRIEVE statements in particular require significantly extended treatment in the programming environment (see Sections 10.4 and 10.5); but the principle is nevertheless broadly true. (Its converse is not, incidentally; that is, there are a number of EQUEL statements that are programming statements only and cannot be used interactively, as we shall see.)

Note clearly that the dual-mode principle applies to the entire QUEL language, not just to the data manipulation operations. It is true that the data manipulation operations are far and away the most frequently used in a programming context, but there is nothing wrong in embedding (for example) CREATE and DESTROY statements in a program, if it makes sense to do so for the application at hand.

The programming languages currently supported by INGRES—the so-called "host languages"—are Ada, BASIC, C, COBOL, FORTRAN, Pascal, and PL/I. In Section 10.2 we consider the mechanics of embedding QUEL in a host language. Then in Sections 10.3–10.5 we present the major ideas behind the embedding of data manipulation statements specifically. Finally, in Section 10.6, we present a brief introduction to EQUEL/FORMS. *Note*: For reasons of definiteness, all of our coding examples are given in terms of COBOL. Of course, the ideas translate into other host languages without significant change.

One final introductory remark: In order to keep the size of this book within reasonable bounds, the treatment of the material in this chapter is somewhat less exhaustive than that of the last few chapters. Many details are deliberately omitted. Section 10.6 in particular is intentionally very sketchy.

10.2 PRELIMINARIES

Before we can begin to discuss the EQUEL statements per se, it is necessary to cover a number of preliminary details. Most of those details are illustrated by the sample program shown (in outline) in Fig. 10.1. The effect of that program is to retrieve the status and city for some specified supplier, to display those values as output, and then to delete the supplier if the status is less than some specified value.

Points arising:

1. Host language programs that include EQUEL statements must be processed by the appropriate EQUEL preprocessor before they are submitted to the regular host language processor. Every line of source code to be processed by that preprocessor—not only EQUEL statements per se but also declarations of host variables that are referenced within those EQUEL statements—must begin with two number signs (##) in columns 1 and 2.

2. The EQUEL preprocessor will replace executable EQUEL statements, such as RETRIEVE and DELETE, by host language calls to the EQUEL run-time system. (At execution time, the run-time system will then execute the EQUEL statements as explained in Section 2.2, "Query Processing.") The special statement

```
## DECLARE
```

```
DATA DIVISION .
WORKING-STORAGE SECTION .

##   DECLARE

##   01  GIVENSNO  PIC X(5) .
##   01  RANK      PIC S9(5) USAGE DISPLAY .
##   01  CITY      PIC X(15) .

PROCEDURE DIVISION .

##   INGRES "s_sp_p"

##   BEGIN TRANSACTION

     MOVE "S4" TO GIVENSNO .

##   RETRIEVE ( RANK = S.STATUS, CITY = S.#CITY )
##   WHERE     S.SNO = GIVENSNO
##   {

     DISPLAY "Rank and city for supplier ", GIVENSNO,
             "are ", RANK, "and ", CITY .

##   }

     IF RANK < 25 THEN
##       DELETE S WHERE S.SNO = GIVENSNO .

##   END TRANSACTION

##   EXIT
```

Fig. 10.1 An EQUEL/COBOL program (example—most COBOL details omitted)

(required for COBOL only) causes the preprocessor to include a set of
COBOL declarations that are needed to support those calls.

3. Executable EQUEL statements can appear wherever an executable host
statement can appear.

4. Executable EQUEL statements can include references to host variables.
Host variables must of course be used as the target variables for
RETRIEVE operations. They can also be used to represent any or all of the
following:

- Range variable names
- Tables and field names
- Values within expressions and predicates
- Complete expressions and predicates

In the case of RETRIEVE targets, the host variables can be of any appropriate data type (see, e.g., RANK and CITY in Fig. 10.1). In the other cases, they must be of type character string. Here is an example of the use of a host variable to represent a field name:

```
##   01  FIELD  PIC X(12) .

     . . . . . . . . . . . . . . . . . .

     MOVE "STATUS" TO FIELD .

##   REPLACE S ( CITY = "London" ) WHERE S.FIELD > 25
```

And here is an example of the use of a host variable to represent an entire predicate:

```
##   01  PRED  PIC X(50) .

     . . . . . . . . . . . . . . . . . .

     MOVE "S.STATUS > 25" TO PRED .

##   REPLACE S ( CITY = "London" ) WHERE PRED
```

All host variable names appearing within an EQUEL statement must identify scalar (elementary) data items, not groups or structures. Subscripted and qualified names are allowed.

5. An EQUEL program can access only one database at a time. The database must be "opened" via the statement

```
##   INGRES database
```

before it can be processed, and "closed" via the statement

```
##   EXIT
```

when processing is complete. (The program can then continue with more processing by opening another database, if desired.)

6. For reasons of simplicity and generality, we will assume that all EQUEL programs include explicit BEGIN TRANSACTION and END TRANSACTION statements, as in the example.

7. After any EQUEL statement has been executed, feedback information can be obtained via the special EQUEL operation INQUIRE_EQUEL. For example:

```
## INQUIRE_EQUEL ( Z = ERRORNO )
```

The "error number" for the most recently executed EQUEL statement is returned in host variable Z. An error number of zero indicates successful execution, a nonzero value indicates that some exception has occurred. See the RTI manuals for details.

Here is another example of the use of INQUIRE_EQUEL:

```
## INQUIRE_EQUEL ( N = ROWCOUNT )
```

The number of rows retrieved (or replaced or . . .) in the most recently executed EQUEL RETRIEVE (or REPLACE or . . .) is returned in host variable N.

8. Host variables must have a data type compatible with the INGRES data type of fields they are to be compared with or assigned to or from, where applicable.*

9. Note that host variables and database fields can have the same name. For instance, the symbol "CITY" is used in the example of Fig. 10.1 to identify both a COBOL variable and a database field. *All appearances of such a symbol are taken by EQUEL as references to the value of the host variable.* When it is necessary to prevent EQUEL from taking such an interpretation, the user must "dereference" the symbol by prefixing it with a number sign (#). By way of example, note the appearance of "#CITY" in the RETRIEVE target list in Fig. 10.1. If the # sign had been omitted, as follows—

```
## RETRIEVE ( RANK = S.STATUS, CITY = S.CITY )
## WHERE     S.SNO = GIVENSNO
```

—then EQUEL would have taken the reference "CITY" in the expression S.CITY to mean the *value* of the host variable CITY. Suppose that value were "London." Then EQUEL would have effectively tried to execute the statement

```
## RETRIEVE ( RANK = S.STATUS, CITY = S.LONDON )
## WHERE     S.SNO = GIVENSNO
```

which would cause a run-time error.

---

*This rule can be circumvented to some extent by means of the INGRES type conversion functions (FLOAT4, ASCII, etc.). See Appendix C.

10. One particular context in which dereferencing is very often required is the SORT BY clause. Consider the following example:

```
##   RETRIEVE ( SUPP = S.SNO, RANK = S.STATUS )
##   WHERE      S.#CITY = CITY
##   SORT BY   #RANK
```

The result table generated by the RETRIEVE is considered to have column names RANK and CITY (taken from the host-variable names appearing on the left-hand sides of the assignments in the target list). To sort that result by status values, therefore, it is necessary to specify "BY #RANK"—not "BY RANK", because EQUEL would take "BY RANK" to mean "BY x," where x is whatever the value of the variable RANK was before the RETRIEVE was executed.

11. *The REPEAT option*: If a particular EQUEL data manipulation statement is to be executed repeatedly, it is probably a good idea (for performance reasons) to specify the REPEAT option for that statement. For example:

```
PERFORM GET-VALUES THROUGH END-VALUES
         UNTIL no more input SNO values .

GET-VALUES .

    get next SNO value from the terminal into GIVENSNO

##   REPEAT RETRIEVE ( RANK = S.STATUS, CITY = S.#CITY )
##          WHERE      S.SNO = @GIVENSNO
##   {

    DISPLAY "Rank and city for supplier ", GIVENSNO,
            "are ", RANK, "and ", CITY .

##   }

END-VALUES.
```

The first time the RETRIEVE statement is executed, INGRES (as usual) builds a query plan for it, as explained in Chapter 2. The query plan consists essentially of the optimized internal code needed to implement the original RETRIEVE. The effect of the REPEAT option is to cause INGRES to *save* that query plan for subsequent executions. Thus subsequent iterations round the PERFORM loop in the example do not cause the query plan to be built again.*

---

*This feature can produce very considerable run-time performance improvements, especially if the program remains resident in main memory for a significant length of time. Techniques are available (details beyond the scope of this text) for structuring applications in such a way as to exploit this feature to the maximum in a production environment.

When specifying the REPEAT option for a given EQUEL request, the programmer must also indicate which host variables represent *parameters* to that request—i.e., which host variables in the request will take on different values on each execution. Such variables must be flagged with an "at sign" prefix (@); see GIVENSNO in the WHERE clause above for an example. Parameters can appear only in positions where *constants* are allowed. Thus, for example, a parameter cannot be used to designate a receiving variable in a target list.

The REPEAT option and parameters (flagged with @ signs) can be used with RETRIEVE, APPEND, REPLACE, and DELETE statements.

12. Null values (as usual) require special treatment. For example, if there is a chance that the value of some expression to be retrieved might be null, the user should supply an *indicator variable* for that expression in the target list clause (as well as the normal target variable), as illustrated in the following example (where we assume that part weights can be null):

```
## RETRIEVE ( WT:WTIND = P.WEIGHT )
## WHERE        P.PNO = GIVENPNO
## {
       IF WTIND = -1 THEN
          DISPLAY "Weight of part ", GIVENPNO, "is null" .
             . . . . .
## }
```

If the expression to be retrieved is null and an indicator variable has been specified, then that indicator variable will be set to –1 (minus one) and the ordinary target variable will remain unchanged. Indicator variables are specified as shown—i.e., following the corresponding ordinary target variable and separated from that target variable by a colon. They should be defined as data type I2.

Note: Indicator variables should not be used in a WHERE clause. For example, the following code will *not* retrieve part numbers for parts where the weight is null (what will it do?):

```
   MOVE -1 TO WTIND .
## RETRIEVE ( PART = P.PNO )
## WHERE      P.WEIGHT = WT:WTIND
```

The correct way to retrieve part numbers where the weight is null is:

```
## RETRIEVE ( PART = P.PNO )
## WHERE      P.WEIGHT IS NULL
```

Indicator variables can be used on the right-hand side of an assignment in a target list in APPEND or REPLACE. For example,

```
        MOVE -1 TO WTIND
  ##    REPLACE P ( WEIGHT = WT:WTIND )
  ##    WHERE    P.CITY = "London"
```

will set the weight for all London parts to null. So also of course will the statement

```
  ##    REPLACE P ( WEIGHT = NULL )
  ##    WHERE    P.CITY = "London"
```

For brevity and simplicity, we will ignore indicator variables and the possibility of null values in the examples and exercises in this book from this point on.

So much for the preliminaries. In the rest of this chapter we concentrate on the data manipulation operations RETRIEVE, APPEND, REPLACE, and DELETE specifically. As already indicated, most of those operations can be handled in a fairly straightforward fashion (i.e., with only minor changes to their syntax). RETRIEVE statements require special treatment, however. The problem is that executing a RETRIEVE statement causes a *table* to be retrieved—a table that, in general, contains multiple records— and languages like COBOL are simply not well equipped to handle more than one record at a time. It is therefore necessary to provide some kind of bridge between the set-at-a-time level of EQUEL and the record-at-a-time level of such host languages. EQUEL provides two such bridges:

(a) The RETRIEVE loop (discussed in Section 10.4);

(b) Cursors (discussed in Section 10.5).

We defer detailed discussion of these facilities to the indicated sections, and consider first (in Section 10.3) the more straightforward statements APPEND, REPLACE, and DELETE.

10.3 APPEND, REPLACE, AND DELETE

There is actually not a great deal to be said about the EQUEL versions of these statements. For completeness, however, we give a simple example of each one.

10.3.1 APPEND.   Add a new part (part number, name, and weight given by host variables PNO, PNAME, and WT, respectively; color and city un-known) to table P.

```
  ##    APPEND TO P ( #PNO = PNO, #PNAME = PNAME, WEIGHT = WT )
```

Note the dereferencing for PNO and PNAME (not needed for WEIGHT).

10.3.2   REPLACE.   Increase the status of all London suppliers by the amount given by the host variable RAISE.

```
##   REPLACE S ( STATUS = S.STATUS + RAISE )
##   WHERE   S.CITY = "London"
```

10.3.3   DELETE. Delete all shipments for suppliers whose city is given by the host variable CITY.

```
##   DELETE SP
##   WHERE   SP.SNO = S.SNO
##   AND     S.#CITY = CITY
```

Again, note the dereferencing.

10.4   RETRIEVE

The general syntax of RETRIEVE statements in EQUEL (other than the "RETRIEVE INTO table" form, which does not retrieve any data into the program) is as suggested by the example in Fig. 10.1:

```
##     RETRIEVE [ UNIQUE ] ( target-list )
##   [ WHERE predicate ]
##   [ SORT BY field(s) ]
##     {
         statements
##     }
```

The statements between the two braces are executed once for each record in the result table generated by the RETRIEVE (unless an ENDRETRIEVE statement is encountered—see below). Thus the statements between the braces represent the body of a loop, and the overall syntactic construct is usually referred to as a RETRIEVE-loop for that reason. When all records have been processed, execution continues with the statement following the closing brace. Note that no database operation can be executed from within the body of the loop.

It is possible to leave the loop "early"—i.e., before all records have been processed—by means of the ENDRETRIEVE statement (*not* by a host language GO TO statement). For example:

```
   *    Find the three highest status suppliers
        MOVE 0 TO N
   ##   RETRIEVE ( X = S.SNO, Y = S.STATUS )
   ##   SORT BY  #Y:DESCENDING
   ##   {
           ADD 1 TO N
           IF N > 3
   ##          ENDRETRIEVE .
           print X and Y
   ##   }
```

ENDRETRIEVE passes control directly to the statement following the closing brace.

10.5 CURSOR OPERATIONS

The EQUEL cursor operations provide an alternative (and in some respects
more flexible) manner of handling the retrieval of whole sets of records
from within a language like COBOL that does not provide set-level operations directly.* A cursor is a new kind of QUEL object, one that applies
to EQUEL only (because interactive QUEL has no need of it). It consists
essentially of a kind of *pointer* that can be used to run through a set of
records, pointing to each of the records in the set in turn and thus providing
addressability to those records one at a time.

The use of cursors is illustrated in outline in the example of Fig. 10.2,
which is intended to retrieve supplier details (SNO, SNAME, and STATUS)
for all suppliers in the city given by the host variable Y.

Explanation:

1. The DECLARE CURSOR statement defines a cursor called X, with an
associated query as specified by the RETRIEVE appearing within that
DECLARE. The RETRIEVE is not executed at this point; DECLARE
CURSOR is a purely declarative statement.

---

*The fact that cursors are available means that it is never actually necessary to use
the RETRIEVE-loop construct described in Section 10.4; anything that can be done
via RETRIEVE-loops can also be done by means of cursor operations (though not
so succinctly). Given that RETRIEVE-loops thus provide strictly less functionality
than cursors, the reader may be wondering why EQUEL supports both. In fact,
there are two reasons. First, earlier versions of EQUEL supported RETRIEVE-
loops only; cursors were a later addition to the language. Second, because
RETRIEVE-loops are not allowed to include any further database operations, they
can on occasion be implemented more efficiently—i.e., they can provide better performance—than an equivalent cursor-based loop.

```
## DECLARE CURSOR X FOR
##         RETRIEVE ( S.SNO, S.SNAME, S.STATUS )
##         WHERE     S.CITY = Y

## OPEN CURSOR X

   PERFORM BEGIN-RET-LOOP THROUGH END-RET-LOOP
           UNTIL no more records to come .

BEGIN-RET-LOOP .
##    RETRIEVE CURSOR X ( ALPHA, BETA, GAMMA )
##    INQUIRE_EQUEL ( EOS = ENDQUERY )
      IF EOS = no more records THEN ...
      ELSE process ALPHA, BETA, GAMMA
END-RET-LOOP .

## CLOSE CURSOR X
```

Fig. 10.2 Example of the use of a cursor (EQUEL)

2. The RETRIEVE *is* executed when the cursor is opened (via OPEN CURSOR), in the procedural part of the program.

3. The RETRIEVE CURSOR statement is then used to retrieve records of the result table one at a time. That statement must specify a list of *n* host variables, where *n* is the number of expressions in the target list in the cursor declaration. Each time the RETRIEVE CURSOR is executed, the current value of the *i*th expression from the cursor declaration target list is assigned to the *i*th variable named in the RETRIEVE CURSOR (i = 1 to *n*). In the example, therefore, the supplier number is assigned to ALPHA, the supplier name to BETA, and the status to GAMMA.

4. The INQUIRE_EQUEL statement sets the host variable EOS to an INGRES-specified value ($+100$) if there are no records remaining in the result table. That variable can then be used to cause exit from the loop on the next attempt at iteration.

5. Since there will normally be multiple records in the result table, the RETRIEVE CURSOR will normally appear within a program loop. The loop will normally be repeated so long as there are more records still to come in the result table.

6. On exit from the loop, cursor X is closed (deactivated) via an appropriate CLOSE CURSOR statement.

Now let us consider cursors and cursor operations in more detail. First, a cursor is declared by means of a DECLARE CURSOR statement, which takes the general form

```
##   DECLARE CURSOR cursor FOR [ REPEAT ]
##          RETRIEVE [ UNIQUE ] ( target-list )
##          [ WHERE predicate ]
##          [ SORT BY field(s) ]
##          [ FOR [ DEFERRED | DIRECT ] UPDATE
##                            [ OF ( field [, field ] ... ) ] ]
```

For an example, see Fig. 10.2. As previously stated, the DECLARE CURSOR statement is declarative, not executable; it declares a cursor with the specified name and having the specified query permanently associated with it. The specified query can include host variable references. Note, however, that there is no need to specify receiving variables in the target list (unless a result field is derived from something other than a simple field of the RETRIEVEd-from table—same rules as for the "RETRIEVE INTO table" form of the regular RETRIEVE statement); receiving variables will be specified in the RETRIEVE CURSOR statement. The REPEAT option is as described in Section 10.2.

If the cursor will be used in REPLACE CURSOR or DELETE CURSOR statements (see later in this section), then the declaration must include a FOR UPDATE clause. In the case of REPLACE CURSOR, that clause must specify all fields that will be replaced via this cursor in any REPLACE CURSOR statement. If the cursor will not be used in any REPLACE/DELETE CURSOR statements (and only if not), then the declaration may optionally include a SORT BY specification (and/or UNIQUE specification), as in a conventional RETRIEVE statement, to control the order in which result rows are retrieved via RETRIEVE CURSOR. Note, therefore, that it is not possible to retrieve a set of records via a cursor in some specified order *and* update (REPLACE or DELETE) some of those records via that same cursor at the same time.

For an explanation of DEFERRED vs. DIRECT update, see later in this section.

Five executable statements are provided specifically for operating on cursors: OPEN and CLOSE, and the cursor forms of RETRIEVE, REPLACE, and DELETE. There is no cursor form of APPEND.

1. The statement

```
##   OPEN CURSOR cursor
```

opens or *activates* the specified cursor (which must not already be open). In effect, the query associated with that cursor is executed (using the current values for any host variables referenced within that query); a set of records is thus identified and becomes the *active set* for the cursor. The cursor also identifies a *position* within that set, namely the position just before the first record in the set. (Active sets are always considered to have an ordering, so that the concept of position has meaning. The ordering is that defined by SORT BY [or UNIQUE], if specified, or a system-determined ordering otherwise.)

2. The statement

```
##   RETRIEVE CURSOR cursor ( variable [, variable ] ... )
```

(where the identified cursor must be open) advances that cursor to the next record in the active set and then assigns values from that record to host variables as explained earlier. The INQUIRE_EQUEL statement can be used to detect the situation in which there is no next record in the active set, as explained earlier.

Note, incidentally, that "retrieve the next record" is the *only* cursor movement operation. It is not possible to move a cursor, e.g., "forward three positions" or "backward two positions" or "directly to the *i*th record" (etc.).

3. The statement

```
##   REPLACE CURSOR cursor ( target-list )
```

replaces fields within the record on which the specified cursor is currently positioned in accordance with the specified target list. For example:

```
##   REPLACE CURSOR X ( STATUS = STATUS + RAISE )
```

In this example, cursor X must be currently positioned on a supplier record, or the operation will be rejected. *Note that the reference to STATUS on the right-hand side of the assignment in the target list is NOT qualified by the range variable S. References to range variables (explicit or implicit) are not allowed in a REPLACE CURSOR target list.* Thus, for example, the following is *** *INCORRECT* ***:

```
##   REPLACE CURSOR X ( STATUS = S.STATUS + RAISE )
```

Instead, any reference to a field name in an expression (such as the reference to STATUS in the expression "STATUS + RAISE") is automatically taken to be a reference to the value of that field in the record on which the designated cursor is currently positioned.

REPLACE CURSOR is not permitted if the RETRIEVE in the cursor declaration involves UNIQUE or SORT BY, or if the target list and WHERE clause in that RETRIEVE would define a nonupdatable view if they were part of a DEFINE VIEW statement (see Section 7.3 in Chapter 7). Also, as explained earlier, the DECLARE CURSOR statement for the cursor in question must include a FOR UPDATE clause naming all the fields that appear as targets within a target list in any REPLACE CURSOR statement for that cursor. The FOR UPDATE clause can optionally specify either DEFERRED or DIRECT (DEFERRED is the default):

- DEFERRED means that the update is not actually done until the cursor is closed.

- DIRECT means that the update is done when the cursor moves away from the record (i.e., at the time of the next RETRIEVE or CLOSE, whichever occurs first).

DIRECT is faster, but might possibly give rise to inconsistencies. For example, if part records are being processed in part weight order, and the program changes a part weight, then the record might change position in the ordering and subsequently be seen again through the same cursor.

4. The statement

```
##   DELETE CURSOR cursor
```

deletes the record on which the specified cursor is currently positioned. For example:

```
##   DELETE CURSOR X
```

Cursor X must be currently positioned on a record, or the operation will be rejected.

DELETE CURSOR is not permitted if the RETRIEVE in the cursor declaration involves UNIQUE or SORT BY, or if the target list and WHERE clause in that RETRIEVE would define a nonupdatable view if they were part of a DEFINE VIEW statement (again, see Section 7.3 in Chapter 7). Also, as explained earlier, the DECLARE CURSOR statement for the cursor in question must include a FOR UPDATE clause for the DELETE CURSOR operation to be accepted (see REPLACE above for further discussion).

5. The statement

```
##   CLOSE CURSOR cursor
```

closes or *deactivates* the specified cursor (which must currently be open). The cursor now has no corresponding active set. However, it can subsequently be opened again, in which case it will acquire another active set—probably not exactly the same set as before, especially if the values of host variables referenced in the cursor declaration have changed in the meantime. Note that changing the values of those host variables while the cursor is open has no effect on the active set.

We conclude this section with a note on the interaction between cursors and the transaction processing statements (BEGIN TRANSACTION, END TRANSACTION, etc.). Briefly:

- BEGIN TRANSACTION and SAVEPOINT operations can be executed only when no cursors are open.

- END TRANSACTION and ABORT operations (either total or the partial "ABORT TO savepoint" form) close all open cursors.

The rationale for these rules is as follows:

(a) A set of related cursor operations corresponds logically to a single, atomic, set-level RETRIEVE (possibly with some associated updates);

(b) It does not make any sense for such an atomic operation to straddle a savepoint or transaction boundary.

10.6 EQUEL/FORMS

We conclude this chapter with a very brief introduction to the facilities of EQUEL/FORMS. As explained in Chapter 2, EQUEL/FORMS is to the INGRES Forms Management System what EQUEL is to the INGRES DBMS; i.e., EQUEL/FORMS provides a set of operations that allow application programs to manipulate forms, just as EQUEL provides a set of operations that allow them to manipulate stored data. Thus EQUEL/FORMS handles interactions with the terminal, just as EQUEL handles interactions with the database. See Fig. 10.3.

Normally a program that is using EQUEL/FORMS to communicate with the terminal will also be using EQUEL to communicate with the database. Normally, that is, but not necessarily; it is quite possible, at least in theory, to develop an application that uses forms (and EQUEL/FORMS) without ever touching the database at all.

The forms used in an EQUEL/FORMS application must be defined by means of the INGRES Visual-Forms-Editor (VIFRED). It is therefore not really possible to appreciate the capabilities of EQUEL/FORMS without

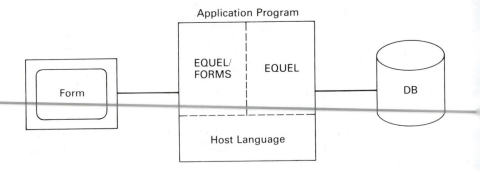

Fig. 10.3 EQUEL and EQUEL/FORMS

first having some appreciation of the capabilities of VIFRED; and a discussion of VIFRED per se would be out of place at this point in the book. For that reason we content ourselves here with merely scratching the surface of the capabilities of EQUEL/FORMS. For more detail, the reader is referred to the RTI manuals.

In Fig. 10.4 we show a very simple program (in outline) that uses some of the basic EQUEL/FORMS functions. The purpose of the program is merely to display all the part records from the database, one at a time, in part number order, using the simple display form shown as Fig. 2.2 in Section 2.3 (Chapter 2). We assume that the name of that form is PARTFORM, and that the end-user has a menu of operations at his or her disposal containing just two options—"Next" (display the next record) and "Quit" (stop displaying records).

Note: The example is not intended to be particularly realistic. To be specific, it is not very efficient—INITIALIZE, for example, is a comparatively expensive operation, and should ideally not be performed within the body of a loop as shown. The purpose of the example is merely to illustrate certain typical EQUEL/FORMS operations.

Explanation:

1. Any program using EQUEL/FORMS must include the statement

       ## FORMS

as the first EQUEL/FORMS operation, and the statement

       ## ENDFORMS

```
##    INGRES "s_sp_p"
##    FORMS
##    FORMINIT partform
##    RETRIEVE ( XPNO    = P.PNO,
##                XPNAME  = P.PNAME,
##                XCOLOR  = P.COLOR,
##                XWEIGHT = P.WEIGHT,
##                XCITY   = P.CITY )
##    SORT BY #XPNO
##    {
##        DISPLAY partform READ
##        INITIALIZE ( FPNO    = XPNO,
##                      FPNAME  = XPNAME,
##                      FCOLOR  = XCOLOR,
##                      FWEIGHT = XWEIGHT,
##                      FCITY   = XCITY )
##        ACTIVATE MENUITEM "Next"
##        {
##            BREAKDISPLAY
##        }
##        ACTIVATE MENUITEM "Quit"
##        {
##            ENDRETRIEVE
##        }
##        FINALIZE
##    }
##    ENDFORMS
##    EXIT
```

Fig. 10.4 A simple EQUEL/FORMS program (outline)

as the last. These statements perform certain housekeeping functions, the details of which are beyond the scope of this book.

2. The statement

```
##    FORMINIT partform
```

retrieves the definition of the form called PARTFORM from the dictionary for the S_SP_P database.

3. The major part of the program consists of a single EQUEL RETRIEVE-loop. The RETRIEVE itself causes past records to be retrieved and fields of those records to be assigned to the host variables XPNO, XPNAME, XCOLOR, XWEIGHT, and XCITY in accordance with the assignments in the RETRIEVE target list. The body of the RETRIEVE-loop in turn consists of a single EQUEL/FORMS DISPLAY statement; that DISPLAY statement will be executed once for each record retrieved by the RETRIEVE statement.

4. The DISPLAY statement—or at least the limited form of that statement that we discuss here—has the general structure:

```
##   DISPLAY form option
##   INITIALIZE ( target-list )
##      ACTIVATE condition value
##      {
            .....
##      }
##      ACTIVATE ...
         ...
##   FINALIZE
```

In other words, there is a DISPLAY clause, an INITIALIZE clause with a number of embedded ACTIVATE subclauses, and a FINALIZE clause. The effect of the statement is to display the specified "form" (PARTFORM in the example) in accordance with the specified "option" (READ in the example; READ means that the displayed form is read-only from the end-user's point of view—i.e., the end-user cannot change any value in the displayed form).

5. The INITIALIZE clause defines the values to be displayed in the form, via another target list. In the example we have assumed that the fields of the form (*not to be confused with fields in the database or host variables*) have the names FPNO, FPNAME, FCOLOR, FWEIGHT, and FCITY; the target list assigns values to these form fields from the host variables XPNO, XPNAME, XCOLOR, XWEIGHT, and XCITY, respectively.

6. The ACTIVATE subclauses specify what to do when the end-user selects an item from the menu of available operations. In the example there are two possible menu items, "Next" and "Quit," so there are two ACTIVATE subclauses, each with an associated set of actions enclosed in braces. The action for the menu item "Next" (in our simple example) consists of a single operation—namely,

```
##   BREAKDISPLAY
```

—which causes the EQUEL/FORMS system to stop displaying the current form; the body of the RETRIEVE-loop is then executed again for the next part record. The action for the menu item "Quit" also consists of a single operation—namely,

```
##   ENDRETRIEVE
```

—which causes termination of the entire RETRIEVE-loop.

7. The FINALIZE clause is executed (in general) if the end-user hits the "Escape" key at the terminal and there are no menu options displayed. In our simple example, the FINALIZE clause has no effect; typically, however, it might be used (for example) to transfer values entered into the form

by the end-user back to fields in the database (and hence to support end-user database updates).

This concludes the explanation of our simple example. We stress once again the point that the example is *extremely* simple. In practice, the facilities of EQUEL/FORMS are much more sophisticated than our rather trivial example suggests. Indeed, they are very powerful; they can reduce the programming complexities traditionally associated with forms-based applications very greatly. To paraphrase the RTI manual: "The flow of control in such applications can branch and fork in many unexpected ways. The EQUEL/FORMS constructs consolidate the loop control, interrupt-handling, condition checking, and other program controls required for effective forms-based application programming . . . leaving the irksome low-level details to be handled by [the system]."

We bring this chapter to a close with a short list of some of the major EQUEL/FORMS statements, in the hope that the names of those statements will give some hint, in and of themselves, as to their function and thus to the overall scope of EQUEL/FORMS.

DISPLAY	BREAKDISPLAY	MESSAGE
INITIALIZE	PUTFORM	SCROLL
FINALIZE	GETFORM	PROMPT
ACTIVATE	VALIDATE	PUTROW
RESUME	REDISPLAY	GETROW
RESUME FIELD	CLEAR FIELD	DELETEROW
ENDDISPLAY	CLEAR SCREEN	INSERTROW

EXERCISES

10.1 Using the suppliers-parts-projects database, write an EQUEL program to list all supplier records, in supplier number order. Each supplier record should be immediately followed in the listing by all project records for projects supplied by that supplier, in project number order. Give both RETRIEVE-loop and cursor solutions.

10.2 Revise your answer to Exercise 10.1 to do the following in addition: (a) Increase the status by 50 percent for any supplier who supplies more than two projects; (b) delete any supplier who does not supply any projects at all.

10.3 (Harder.) Given the tables

```
CREATE P
     ( PNO         = ... ,
       DESCRIPTION = ... )

CREATE PARTSTRUC
     ( MAJOR_PNO   = ... ,
       MINOR_PNO   = ... ,
       QTY         = ... )
```

where PARTSTRUC shows which parts (MAJOR_PNO) contain which other parts (MINOR_PNO) as first-level components, write an EQUEL program to list all component parts of a given part, to all levels (the "parts explosion" problem). The following sample values may help you visualize this problem:

```
|major_pno|minor_pno|qty|
|-----------------------|
| P1       | P2       |  2 |
| P1       | P4       |  4 |
| P5       | P3       |  1 |
| P3       | P6       |  3 |
| P6       | P1       |  9 |
| P5       | P6       |  8 |
| P2       | P4       |  3 |
|-----------------------|
```

ANSWERS TO SELECTED EXERCISES

10.1 (a) RETRIEVE-loop version:
The difficulty with this problem is that it requires an *outer join* of tables S and SPJ. The program must therefore construct that outer join first before it can apply a RETRIEVE-loop to it, as follows. (The solution may therefore not be very efficient, because it effectively requires the same data to be scanned multiple times. Direct QUEL support for an outer join operator, which is desirable anyway for usability reasons, might alleviate this problem.)

```
##   RETRIEVE INTO TEMP ( S.ALL, J.JNO, J.JNAME, Z = J.CITY )
##   WHERE     S.SNO = SPJ.SNO AND SPJ.JNO = J.JNO

##   APPEND TO TEMP ( S.ALL )
##   WHERE   ANY ( J.JNO BY S.SNO WHERE S.SNO = SPJ.SNO
##                               AND   SPJ.JNO = J.JNO ) = 0

##   RETRIEVE ( ZSNO = TEMP.SNO, ZSNAME = TEMP.SNAME,
##              ZSTATUS = TEMP.STATUS, ZSCITY = TEMP.CITY,
##              ZJNO = TEMP.JNO, ZJNAME = TEMP.JNAME,
##              ZJCITY = TEMP.Z )
##   SORT BY #ZSNO, #ZJNO
##   {
         IF ZSNO different from previous iteration
            print ZSNO, ZSNAME, ZSTATUS, ZSCITY .
         print ZJNO, ZJNAME, ZJCITY .
##   }
```

10.1 (b) Cursor version:
Two solutions are possible, one involving two cursors and one involving only one. We show the two-cursor solution only (the one-cursor solution is analogous to the RETRIEVE-loop solution already shown).

```
## DECLARE CURSOR X FOR
##          RETRIEVE ( S.SNO, S.SNAME, S.STATUS, S.CITY )
##          SORT BY #SNO

## DECLARE CURSOR Y FOR
##          RETRIEVE ( J.JNO, J.JNAME, J.CITY )
##          WHERE    J.JNO = SPJ.JNO
##          AND      SPJ.SNO = XSNO )
##          SORT BY #JNO
```

When cursor Y is opened, host variable XSNO will contain a supplier number value (fetched via cursor X). The logic is essentially as shown in the following pseudocode (ignoring the INQUIRE_EQUEL statements that would be needed in practice in order to control loop termination):

```
## OPEN CURSOR X
   PERFORM UNTIL no more S records accessible via X
##     RETRIEVE CURSOR X ( XSNO, XSNAME, XSTATUS, XCITY )
       print XSNO, XSNAME, XSTATUS, XCITY
##     OPEN CURSOR Y
       PERFORM UNTIL no more J records accessible via Y
##         RETRIEVE CURSOR Y ( YJNO, YJNAME, YCITY )
           print YJNO, YJNAME, YCITY
       END-PERFORM
##     CLOSE CURSOR Y
   END-PERFORM
## CLOSE CURSOR X
```

10.2 First, the RETRIEVE-loop solution to Exercise 10.1 does not permit any database operations within the loop; thus we are forced into using a cursor approach. Second, the one-cursor solution operates on a copy of the real data; thus we are forced into using the two-cursor version. Third, the cursor declarations include a SORT BY clause, and therefore REPLACE CURSOR and DELETE CURSOR operations are not allowed! The relevant EQUEL statements are therefore

```
## REPLACE S ( STATUS = S.STATUS * 1.5 )
## WHERE    S.SNO = XSNO

## DELETE   S
## WHERE    S.SNO = XSNO
```

10.3 This is a good example of a problem that QUEL (or EQUEL) in its current form does not handle well. The basic difficulty is as follows: We need to "explode" the given part to *n* levels, where the value of *n* is unknown at the time of writing the program. If it were possible, the most straightforward way of performing such an *n*-level "explosion" would be by means of a recursive program, in which each recursive invocation creates a new cursor, as follows. *Note*: We use PL/I for this example instead of COBOL, because PL/I provides direct support for recursion. As usual, we omit certain details (such as the INQUIRE_EQUEL statements).

```
## BEGIN TRANSACTION
   GET LIST ( GIVENPNO ) ;
   CALL RECURSION ( GIVENPNO ) ;
## END TRANSACTION
   RETURN ;

   RECURSION: PROC ( UPPER_PNO ) RECURSIVE ;
##     DCL UPPER_PNO ... ;
##     DCL LOWER_PNO ... ;
##     RANGE OF PS IS PARTSTRUC
##     DECLARE "reopenable" CURSOR C FOR
##             RETRIEVE ( PS.MINOR_PNO )
##             WHERE     PS.MAJOR_PNO = UPPER_PNO
       print UPPER_PNO ;
##     OPEN CURSOR C
       DO WHILE ( record found ) ;
##         RETRIEVE CURSOR C ( LOWER_PNO )
           CALL RECURSION ( LOWER_PNO ) ;
       END ;
##     CLOSE CURSOR C
   END /* of RECURSION */ ;
```

We have assumed that the (fictitious) specification "reopenable" means that it is legal to issue "OPEN CURSOR C" for a cursor C that is already open, and that the effect of such an OPEN CURSOR is to create a new *instance* of the cursor for the specified RETRIEVE (using the current values of any host variables referenced in that RETRIEVE). We have further assumed that references to C in RETRIEVE CURSOR (etc.) are references to the "current" instance of C, and that CLOSE CURSOR destroys that instance and reinstates the previous instance as "current." In other words, we have assumed that a reopenable cursor forms a *stack*, with OPEN CURSOR and CLOSE CURSOR serving as the "push" and "pop" operators for that stack.

Unfortunately, those assumptions are purely hypothetical today. There is no such thing as a reopenable cursor in EQUEL today (indeed, an attempt to issue "OPEN CURSOR C" for a cursor C that is already open will fail). The foregoing code is illegal. But the example makes it clear that "reopenable cursors" would be a very desirable extension.

Since the foregoing procedure does not work, we give a sketch of one possible (but very inefficient) procedure that does.

```
## BEGIN TRANSACTION
   GET LIST ( GIVENPNO ) ;
   CALL RECURSION ( GIVENPNO ) ;
## END TRANSACTION
   RETURN ;

   RECURSION: PROC ( UPPER_PNO ) RECURSIVE ;
##     DCL UPPER_PNO ... ;
##     DCL LOWER_PNO ... INITIAL ( 'bbbbbb' ) ;
##     RANGE OF PS IS PARTSTRUC
##     DECLARE CURSOR C IS
##             RETRIEVE ( PS.MINOR_PNO )
##             WHERE     PS.MAJOR_PNO = UPPER_PNO
##             AND       PS.MINOR_PNO > LOWER_PNO
##             SORT BY #MINOR_PNO
```

```
          DO forever ;
             print UPPER_PNO ;
##           OPEN CURSOR C
##           RETRIEVE CURSOR C ( LOWER_PNO )
             IF no record found
             THEN RETURN ;
             ELSE DO ;
##                   CLOSE CURSOR C
                     CALL RECURSION ( LOWER_PNO ) ;
                   END ;
          END ;
        END /* of RECURSION */ ;
```

Note in this solution that the same cursor is used on every invocation of RE-CURSION. (By contrast, new instances of UPPER_PNO and LOWER_PNO are created dynamically each time RECURSION is invoked; those instances are destroyed at completion of that invocation.) Because of this fact, we have to use a trick—

```
... AND PS.MINOR_PNO > LOWER_PNO SORT BY #MINOR_PNO
```

—so that, on each invocation of RECURSION, we ignore all immediate components (LOWER_PNOs) of the current UPPER_PNO that have already been processed.

11

INGRES/SQL

11.1 INTRODUCTION

As explained in Chapter 1, INGRES supports two distinct relational languages, QUEL and SQL ("Structured Query Language"; the acronym is usually pronounced "sequel"). The two languages provide almost exactly the same functionality (actually QUEL has a slight edge over SQL in certain areas). The reason that both are supported is that (a) QUEL was the language first defined for INGRES, back in the days of the original University INGRES prototype, but (b) SQL was adopted in 1986 by the American National Standards Institute (ANSI) as an official standard for relational systems. So far as this writer is aware, no system at the time of writing supports exactly the pure ANSI standard version of SQL—every system has its own particular version or dialect. In this chapter we examine the facilities of the INGRES dialect, INGRES/SQL, specifically. (INGRES/SQL is actually very close to the ANSI standard version of SQL, but does include a number of INGRES-specific extensions.)

The treatment of SQL in this chapter is deliberately less detailed than that of QUEL over the last few chapters. The reader is assumed to have read those chapters and thus to be reasonably familiar with QUEL. For purposes of reference we begin with a list of the major statements of SQL (excluding certain statements that apply to embedded SQL or "ESQL" only, to be discussed in Section 11.5), with their corresponding QUEL equivalents. *Note*: Not all of those QUEL equivalents have yet been discussed in this book.

SQL statements	*QUEL equivalents*

Data definition operations:

~~CREATE TABLE~~	CREATE
CREATE TABLE AS	~~RETRIEVE INTO~~
DROP [TABLE]	DESTROY

Data manipulation operations:

SELECT	RETRIEVE
INSERT	APPEND
UPDATE	REPLACE
DELETE	DELETE

View definition operations:

CREATE VIEW AS	DEFINE VIEW
DROP [VIEW]	DESTROY

Security and integrity operations:

(*) CREATE PERMIT	DEFINE PERMIT
(*) HELP PERMIT	HELP PERMIT
(*) DROP PERMIT	DESTROY PERMIT
(*) CREATE INTEGRITY	DEFINE INTEGRITY
(*) HELP INTEGRITY	HELP INTEGRITY
(*) DROP INTEGRITY	DESTROY INTEGRITY

Transaction processing operations:

(*) COMMIT [WORK]	END TRANSACTION
(*) SAVEPOINT	SAVEPOINT
(*) ROLLBACK [WORK]	ABORT
(*) ROLLBACK TO savepoint	ABORT TO savepoint

Note: There is no explicit SQL counterpart to the QUEL operation BEGIN TRANSACTION. Instead, an implicit "begin transaction" occurs automatically whenever a SQL operation is executed and no transaction is currently in progress. Note that, as a consequence, all transactions are MSTs in SQL.

Storage structure definition operations:

```
MODIFY                      MODIFY
CREATE INDEX                INDEX
DROP [ INDEX ]              DESTROY
RELOCATE                    RELOCATE
```

Miscellaneous operations:

```
      COPY                  COPY
(*)   HELP                  HELP
      SAVE                  SAVE
      SET                   SET
```

Of the SQL statements listed above, those marked with an asterisk (*) are virtually identical to their QUEL counterparts and are not discussed further in this book. (*Note*: The storage structure definition statements and the miscellaneous operations RELOCATE, COPY, SAVE, and SET are also virtually identical in the two languages but have not yet been discussed at all.)

The structure of the chapter is as follows. Following this introductory section, Section 11.2 discusses data definition, for both base tables and views. Then Sections 11.3 and 11.4 discuss data manipulation; Section 11.3 deals with retrieval and Section 11.4 with update. It is in the area of data retrieval (the SELECT statement) that SQL is most obviously different from QUEL, which accounts for the fact that Section 11.3 is far and away the longest section of the chapter. Finally, Section 11.5 presents a brief overview of ESQL (including ESQL/FORMS), and Section 11.6 discusses the Embedded SQL cursor operations.

11.2 DATA DEFINITION

CREATE TABLE: Format 1

The SQL statement for creating base tables is CREATE TABLE. It comes in two formats. Format 1 is very similar to the CREATE statement in QUEL:

```
CREATE TABLE base-table
      ( column-definition [ , column-definition ] ... )
      [ WITH JOURNALING ]
```

where a "column-definition," in turn, takes the form:

```
column data-type [ default-spec ]
```

The optional "default-spec" is identical to its counterpart in QUEL (see Chapter 3), except that omitting the specification in SQL is equivalent to specifying WITH NULL rather than NOT NULL WITH DEFAULT as in QUEL. (We would therefore recommend always specifying NOT NULL— WITH DEFAULT or otherwise—explicitly, for reasons explained in Chapter 3.) The specification WITH JOURNALING is explained in Chapter 13.

The SQL data types and their QUEL equivalents are as follows:

SQL data types	*QUEL equivalents*
CHAR(n)	CHAR(n)
VARCHAR(n)	VARCHAR(n)
INTEGER1	I1
INTEGER2 or SMALLINT	I2
INTEGER4 or INTEGER	I4
FLOAT4	F4
FLOAT8 or FLOAT	F8
DATE	DATE
MONEY	MONEY

Aside: SQL also supports a data type VCHAR(n), the counterpart of the QUEL data type TEXT(n).

Here is an example (a SQL CREATE TABLE statement for the suppliers base table S):

```
CREATE TABLE S
      ( SNO    CHAR(5)  NOT NULL,
        SNAME  CHAR(20) NOT NULL WITH DEFAULT,
        STATUS SMALLINT NOT NULL WITH DEFAULT,
        CITY   CHAR(15) NOT NULL WITH DEFAULT )
        WITH JOURNALING
```

CREATE TABLE: Format 2

Format 2 of CREATE TABLE corresponds to the RETRIEVE INTO statement in QUEL:

```
CREATE TABLE base-table
    [ ( column-name [, column-name ] ... ) ]
      AS select-operation
```

where "select-operation" is basically a regular SQL SELECT statement (see Section 11.3). The select-operation is executed, and the resulting table is saved under the specified name. Here is an example:

```
CREATE TABLE TEMP ( SNO, STATUS )
     AS SELECT S.SNO, S.STATUS
        FROM    S
        WHERE   S.CITY = 'Paris'
        AND     S.STATUS > 20
```

(a SQL version of Example 4.2.6 from Chapter 4). Note that string constants are enclosed in single quotes in SQL, instead of double quotes as in QUEL.* For the sake of the example, we have explicitly specified the names of the columns (SNO and STATUS) of the newly created table; in general, such explicit specification is required only if a column is derived from something other than a simple column of (one of) the FROM-table(s), and/or two of the result columns would otherwise have the same name. Note, however, that in these latter cases explicit names must be specified for *all* result columns, even if some of those columns have an obvious inherited name.

CREATE VIEW

Views are created in SQL by means of the CREATE VIEW statement. CREATE VIEW is syntactically very similar to Format 2 of CREATE TABLE:

```
CREATE VIEW view
     [ ( column-name [, column-name ] ... ) ]
       AS select-operation
```

where "select-operation" is as for CREATE TABLE (Format 2), except that DISTINCT and UNION are not allowed. Here is an example:

```
CREATE VIEW GOODSUPPS ( SNO, STATUS, CITY )
     AS SELECT S.SNO, S.STATUS, S.CITY
        FROM    S
        WHERE   S.STATUS > 15
```

(a SQL version of the first example in Chapter 7). Once again we have specified the names of the columns (SNO, STATUS, CITY) of the result explicitly; once again, however, such explicit specification is required in general only if a column is derived from something other than a simple column of (one of) the FROM-table(s), and/or two of the result columns

---

*SQL also supports an additional kind of string constant, the hexadecimal constant, written as a string of pairs of hexadecimal digits (representing character encodings) enclosed in single quotes and preceded by the letter X.

would otherwise have the same name. (Note again that in these latter cases explicit names must be specified for *all* columns, even if some of those columns have an obvious inherited name.)

DROP

The SQL analog of DESTROY in QUEL is the DROP statement:

```
DROP [ TABLE ¦ VIEW ] table
```

where "table" is a base table or a view, as applicable. (It can be either if the optional TABLE or VIEW keyword is omitted.)

11.3   RETRIEVAL OPERATIONS

Retrieval is specified in SQL by means of the SELECT statement. The general form of that statement—ignoring for the moment the possibility of UNION, which is illustrated in Examples 11.3.22–11.3.23—is as follows:

```
    SELECT [ DISTINCT ] target-list
    FROM   table [, table ] ...
[ WHERE  predicate ]
[ GROUP  BY field(s) ]
[ HAVING predicate ]
[ ORDER  BY field(s) ]
```

We illustrate the use of SELECT by means of a series of examples, paying particular attention as we go to those aspects of SQL that differ significantly from their QUEL counterpart. Also, we give the number of the corresponding QUEL example from Chapter 4, where applicable.

Simple Queries

11.3.1   Simple Retrieval.   Get part numbers for all parts supplied. (Example 4.2.1)

```
SELECT SP.PNO
FROM   SP
```

As usual, the target list consists of a series of assignments,* from which the left-hand side and equals sign can be omitted (the usual case in practice) if there is an obvious inherited name for the result column in question and/or there is no need to reference that result column elsewhere in the statement. Also, INGRES allows the table-name qualifier to be omitted from target-list elements (also from elements of the WHERE clause—see Example 11.3.3 below), in the common special case where no ambiguity results from such omission. For example:

```
SELECT PNO
FROM   SP
```

However, it is never wrong to qualify names in a target list (or in a WHERE clause), and in this book we will generally do so for reasons of explicitness. See, e.g., Example 11.3.5 for a case in which such qualification is positively required.

Duplicate elimination is specified via the keyword DISTINCT (the SQL analog of UNIQUE in QUEL):

```
SELECT DISTINCT SP.PNO
FROM   SP
```

Another general point: The symbol "SP" in the target list here does not really refer to table SP—rather, it refers to an implicitly defined *range variable* called SP, whose range is table SP (compare the discussion of the analogous point in QUEL, under Example 4.2.8). As in QUEL, range variables can always be defined explicitly if necessary or desired. They are defined by means of the FROM clause. For example:

```
SELECT SPX.PNO
FROM   SP SPX
```

---

*The assignment "name = expression" can equivalently be written "expression AS name" in SQL. For example:

```
SELECT SP.PNO AS ZETA
FROM   SP
```

instead of

```
SELECT ZETA = SP.PNO
FROM   SP
```

This is the SQL analog of the pair of QUEL statements:

```
RANGE OF SPX IS SP

RETRIEVE ( SPX.PNO )
```

11.3.2   Simple Retrieval ("SELECT *").   Get full details of all suppliers. (Example 4.2.3)

```
SELECT *
FROM   S
```

The SELECT clause "SELECT *" (or "SELECT S.*") here corresponds to the RETRIEVE clause "RETRIEVE (S.ALL)" in QUEL.

11.3.3   Qualified Retrieval.   Get supplier numbers for suppliers in Paris with status > 20. (Example 4.2.4)

```
SELECT S.SNO
FROM   S
WHERE  S.CITY = 'Paris'
AND    S.STATUS > 20
```

Or, with all name qualifications omitted:

```
SELECT SNO
FROM   S
WHERE  CITY = 'Paris'
AND    STATUS > 20
```

As in QUEL, the WHERE clause in SQL is basically a Boolean combination of comparisons. Every comparison format in QUEL has some reasonably direct analog in SQL. However, SQL also has a number of additional forms, which are sketched briefly below:

- The comparison

```
y [ NOT ] BETWEEN x AND z
```

is shorthand for the comparison

```
[ NOT ] ( x <= y AND y <= z )
```

- The comparison

```
y [ NOT ] IN ( x, ..., z )
```

is shorthand for the comparison

```
[ NOT ] ( y = x OR ... OR y = z )
```

- The comparison

```
x [ NOT ] LIKE SQL-pattern
```

is the SQL analog of the QUEL partial-match comparison

```
[ NOT ] ( x = QUEL-pattern )
```

except that the roles of the special characters "?" and "*" in the QUEL-pattern are played by the characters "_" (underscore) and "%" in the SQL-pattern, and the special QUEL-pattern "[. . .]" has no equivalent SQL-pattern.

- The comparison

```
x [ NOT ] IN ( subquery )
```

is explained later (see Examples 11.3.8–11.3.10)

- The comparison

```
[ NOT ] EXISTS ( subquery )
```

is also explained later (see Examples 11.3.18–11.3.21)

11.3.4 Retrieval with Ordering. Get supplier numbers and status for suppliers in Paris, in descending order of status. (Example 4.2.5)

```
SELECT S.SNO, S.STATUS
FROM   S
WHERE  S.CITY = 'Paris'
ORDER  BY STATUS DESC
```

ORDER BY is the SQL analog of SORT BY in QUEL; ASC and DESC are the SQL analogs of :A and :D, with ASC as the default.

Join Queries

11.3.5 Retrieval Involving a Join. Get all supplier-number/part-number combinations such that the supplier and part in question are colocated. (Example 4.3.4)

```
SELECT  S.SNO, P.PNO
FROM    S, P
WHERE   S.CITY = P.CITY
```

Notice that the FROM clause names the two tables to be joined.

11.3.6 Retrieval Involving a Join. Get supplier names for suppliers who supply at least one red part. (Example 4.3.6)

```
SELECT  DISTINCT S.SNAME
FROM    S, SP, P
WHERE   S.SNO = SP.SNO
AND     SP.PNO = P.PNO
AND     P.COLOR = 'Red'
```

Again, notice that the FROM clause identifies all the tables involved in the join, even though the SELECT clause retrieves fields from one of those tables only.

11.3.7 Joining a Table with Itself. Get all pairs of supplier numbers such that the two suppliers concerned are colocated. (Example 4.3.8)

```
SELECT X = FIRST.SNO, Y = SECOND.SNO
FROM    S FIRST, S SECOND
WHERE   FIRST.CITY = SECOND.CITY
AND     FIRST.SNO < SECOND.SNO
```

The "X =" and "Y =" can be omitted, if desired.

Subqueries

In this subsection we discuss "subqueries" or *nested SELECTs*. Loosely speaking, a subquery is a SELECT-FROM-WHERE expression that is nested inside another such expression. Subqueries are typically used to represent the set of values to be searched via an IN comparison, as the following example illustrates.

11.3.8 Simple Subquery. Get supplier names for suppliers who supply part P2.

```
SELECT  S.SNAME
FROM    S
WHERE   S.SNO IN
      ( SELECT SP.SNO
        FROM    SP
        WHERE   SP.PNO = 'P2' )
```

Explanation: The system evaluates the overall query by evaluating the nested subquery first. That subquery returns the set of supplier *numbers* for suppliers who supply part P2, namely the set (S1,S2,S3,S4). The original query is thus logically equivalent to the following simpler query:

```
SELECT  S.SNAME
FROM    S
WHERE   S.SNO IN
      ( 'S1', 'S2', 'S3', 'S4' )
```

Hence the result is the set (Smith, Jones, Blake, Clark).

Note that the original problem—"Get supplier names for suppliers who supply part P2"—can equally well be expressed as a join query, as follows:

```
SELECT  DISTINCT S.SNAME
FROM    S, SP
WHERE   S.SNO = SP.SNO
AND     SP.PNO = 'P2'
```

The two formulations—one using a subquery, one using a join—are equally correct. It is basically just a matter of taste as to which formulation a given user might prefer.

11.3.9 Subquery with Multiple Levels of Nesting.   Get supplier names for suppliers who supply at least one red part. (Example 4.3.6; see also Example 11.3.7 for an equivalent join version)

```
SELECT  S.SNAME
FROM    S
WHERE   S.SNO IN
      ( SELECT SP.SNO
        FROM    SP
        WHERE   SP.PNO IN
              ( SELECT P.PNO
                FROM    P
                WHERE   P.COLOR = 'Red' ) )
```

11.3.10 Correlated Subquery.   Get supplier names for suppliers who supply part P2 (same as Example 11.3.8).

We show another solution to this problem in order to illustrate another point.

```
SELECT  S.SNAME
FROM    S
WHERE   'P2' IN
        ( SELECT  SP.PNO
          FROM    SP
          WHERE   SP.SNO = S.SNO )
```

Explanation: This example differs from the preceding ones in that the inner subquery cannot be evaluated once and for all before the outer query is evaluated, because that inner subquery depends on a *variable*, namely S.SNO, whose value changes as the system examines different rows of table S. Conceptually, therefore, evaluation proceeds as follows:

(a) The system examines the first row of table S; let us assume this is the row for S1. The variable S.SNO thus currently has the value "S1", so the system evaluates the inner subquery

```
( SELECT  SP.PNO
  FROM    SP
  WHERE   SP.SNO = 'S1' )
```

to obtain the set (P1,P2,P3,P4,P5,P6). Now it can complete its processing for S1; it will select the SNAME value for S1, namely Smith, if and only if "P2" is in this set (which of course it is).

(b) The system then moves on to repeat this kind of processing for the next supplier, and so on, until all rows of table S have been dealt with.

A subquery such as the one in this example is said to be a *correlated* subquery. A correlated subquery is one whose value depends upon some variable that receives its value in some outer query (or outer subquery); such a subquery therefore has to be evaluated repeatedly (once for each value of the variable in question), instead of once and for all.

Incidentally, this example illustrates another significant syntactic difference between SQL and QUEL—namely that, in SQL, range variables defined outside a given subquery can be referenced within that subquery without any need for a BY clause or similar syntactic device to force such variables to be recognized as "global." In the example, the range variable S in the correlated subquery is not considered to be local to the subquery, but instead is the same S that appears (and is defined) in the outer query.

Several further examples of correlated subqueries appear later in this chapter (see the next two subsections).

Aggregates and Aggregate Functions

Like QUEL, SQL provides the operators COUNT, SUM, etc., to operate on the collection of values in some column of some table. The official SQL term for these operators is *set functions*. The available set functions, with their QUEL equivalents, are summarized below:

SQL functions	*QUEL equivalents*
COUNT	COUNT
COUNT (*)	COUNT (any field)
COUNT (DISTINCT ...)	COUNTU
SUM	SUM
SUM (DISTINCT ...)	SUMU
AVG	AVG
AVG (DISTINCT ...)	AVGU
MAX	MAX
MIN	MIN

Note 1: The SQL set function reference COUNT(*) applied to table T is equivalent to the QUEL aggregate reference COUNT(T.F), where F is any field of table T that does not accept null values. Alternatively, it is equivalent to the QUEL aggregate reference COUNT(T.ALL). Unlike the other SQL functions, COUNT(*) treats null values in its argument just like nonnull values.

Note 2: The SQL EXISTS operator is also considered to be a set function, but it differs from those above in that it returns a truth value, not a numeric or string value. It is somewhat analogous to the ANY operator in QUEL. See the next subsection.

Note 3: The SQL functions SUM, AVG, MAX, and MIN differ from their QUEL counterparts in that they return the null value if their argument evaluates to an empty set.

11.3.11 Function in the SELECT Clause. Get the total number of suppliers. (Example 4.4.1)

```
SELECT N = COUNT ( * )
FROM    S
```

The special function COUNT(*) is used for counting *whole rows*.

Note: The "N =" can be omitted, if desired, since it is not referenced elsewhere within the statement. For explicitness, however, we will usually (not always) include such result column names in our examples.

Here is another query that would return the same result:

```
SELECT N = COUNT ( S.SNO )
FROM    S
```

Any other field of table S—say field S.CITY—could be substituted for field S.SNO here without changing the overall effect (providing nulls are not allowed for the field in question). By contrast, the following version would *not* return the same result (in general):

```
SELECT N = COUNT ( DISTINCT S.CITY )
FROM    S
```

11.3.12 Function in the SELECT Clause, with a Predicate.   Get the total quantity of part P2 supplied. (Example 4.4.3)

```
SELECT SQ = SUM ( SP.QTY )
FROM    SP
WHERE   SP.PNO = 'P2'
```

11.3.13 Function in a Subquery.   Get supplier numbers for suppliers with status value less than the current maximum status value in the S table. (Example 4.4.4)

```
SELECT S.SNO
FROM    S
WHERE   S.STATUS <
        ( SELECT MAX ( S.STATUS )
          FROM    S )
```

The S in the subquery here is a different S from that in the outer query, *because it is redefined* (via the inner FROM clause). Notice, incidentally, that it is legal to use a scalar comparison operator such as " < " with a subquery if that subquery is guaranteed to return a single value (as it obviously is in this example).

11.3.14 Function in Correlated Subquery.   Get supplier information for all suppliers whose status is greater than or equal to the average for their particular city.

```
SELECT SX.*
FROM    S SX
WHERE   SX.STATUS >=
        ( SELECT AVG ( SY.STATUS )
          FROM    S SY
          WHERE   SY.CITY = SX.CITY )
```

It is not possible to include the average status for each city in this result. (Exercise for the reader: Why not? *Hint*: It *is* possible in QUEL. What exactly is it about the QUEL formulation that cannot be emulated in SQL?)

11.3.15   Use of GROUP BY.   For each part supplied, get the part number and the total shipment quantity for that part. (Example 4.5.1)

```
SELECT  SP.PNO, SPQ = SUM ( SP.QTY )
FROM    SP
GROUP   BY SP.PNO
```

Explanation: GROUP BY is the SQL analog of the BY clause in QUEL (speaking *very* approximately). Conceptually, GROUP BY rearranges the table designated by the FROM clause into partitions or groups, such that within any one group all rows have the same value for the GROUP BY field(s). In the example, table SP is grouped so that one group contains all the rows for part P1, another contains all the rows for part P2, and so on. The SELECT clause is then applied to each group of the partitioned table (rather than to each row of the original table). Each expression in the SE-LECT clause must be *single-valued per group*; i.e., it can be one of the GROUP BY fields (or an arithmetic expression involving such a field), or a constant, or a function such as SUM that operates on all values of a given field within a group and reduces those values to a single value.

11.3.16   Use of WHERE with GROUP BY.   For each supplier, get the supplier number and city and a count of the number of parts supplied by that supplier. (Modified version of Example 4.5.2)

```
SELECT  S.SNO, S.CITY, N = COUNT ( SP.PNO )
FROM    S, SP
WHERE   S.SNO = SP.SNO
GROUP   BY S.SNO, S.CITY
```

Rows that do not satisfy the WHERE clause are eliminated before any grouping is done. In the example, therefore, the result does not contain a row for supplier S5, because supplier S5 does not currently supply any parts. Note that (by contrast) the QUEL version (Example 4.5.2) does produce a result row for supplier S5.*

11.3.17   Use of HAVING.   Get part numbers for all parts supplied by more than one supplier. (Example 4.5.4)

---

*Unless the QUEL aggregate includes the ONLY option. See the discussion of Example 4.5.2.

```
SELECT  SP.PNO
FROM    SP
GROUP   BY SP.PNO
HAVING  COUNT ( SP.SNO ) > 1
```

HAVING is to groups what WHERE is to rows (if HAVING is specified, GROUP BY should also have been specified).* In other words, HAVING is used to eliminate groups, just as WHERE is used to eliminate rows. Expressions in a HAVING clause must be single-valued per group. Exercise: What is the QUEL equivalent of the HAVING clause?

Quantified Queries

In this subsection we explain the use of the SQL EXISTS operator, which is the SQL analog of the ANY operator of QUEL (loosely speaking).

11.3.18 Query Using EXISTS. Get supplier names for suppliers who supply part P2. (Same as Example 11.3.9)

```
SELECT  S.SNAME
FROM    S
WHERE   EXISTS
        ( SELECT  *
          FROM    SP
          WHERE   SP.SNO = S.SNO
          AND     SP.PNO = 'P2' )
```

Explanation: The expression "EXISTS (SELECT * FROM . . .)" evaluates to *true* if and only if the result of evaluating the subquery represented by the "SELECT * FROM. . . . " is not empty—in other words, if and only if there exists a record in the FROM table of the subquery satisfying the WHERE condition of that subquery. (In practice, that subquery will always be of the correlated variety.) In the example at hand, the expression evaluates to *true* precisely for those suppliers that supply part P2—whence the desired result.

Although this first example merely shows another way of formulating a query for a problem that we already know how to handle in SQL (using either join or IN), in general EXISTS is one of the most important features of the entire SQL language. In fact, any query that can be expressed using IN can alternatively be formulated using EXISTS; note, however, that the converse is not true (see, e.g., Example 11.3.20 below).

---

*Actually it is possible—though very unusual—to omit the GROUP BY, in which case the entire table is treated as a single group.

11.3.19   Query Using NOT EXISTS.   Get supplier names for suppliers who do not supply part P2. (Example 4.6.1)

```
SELECT  S.SNAME
FROM    S
WHERE   NOT EXISTS
      ( SELECT *
        FROM    SP
        WHERE   SP.SNO = S.SNO
        AND     SP.PNO = 'P2' )
```

(Exercise: Give an alternative formulation of this query involving NOT IN.)

The parenthesized subquery in an EXISTS expression does not necessarily have to involve the "SELECT *" form of SELECT; it may, for example, be of the form "SELECT field FROM. . . ." In practice, however, it almost always will be of the "SELECT *" form, as our examples have already suggested.

11.3.20   Query Using NOT EXISTS.   Get supplier names for suppliers who supply all parts. (Example 4.6.2)

```
SELECT  S.SNAME
FROM    S
WHERE   NOT EXISTS
      ( SELECT *
        FROM    P
        WHERE   NOT EXISTS
              ( SELECT *
                FROM    SP
                WHERE   SP.SNO = S.SNO
                AND     SP.PNO = P.PNO ) )
```

Exercise: Try converting this rather complex SQL statement back into a precise English sentence.

11.3.21   Query Using NOT EXISTS.   Get supplier numbers for suppliers who supply at least all those parts supplied by supplier S2.

```
SELECT  DISTINCT SPX.SNO
FROM    SP SPX
WHERE   NOT EXISTS
      ( SELECT *
        FROM    SP SPY
        WHERE   SPY.SNO = 'S2'
        AND     NOT EXISTS
              ( SELECT *
                FROM    SP SPZ
                WHERE   SPZ.SNO = SPX.SNO
                AND     SPZ.PNO = SPY.PNO ) )
```

Exercise: Again, try converting this SQL statement back into a precise English sentence.

UNION

Unlike QUEL, SQL includes direct support for a UNION operator.

11.3.22 Query Involving UNION. Construct a list of supplier and part names for suppliers and parts that are located in London. (Example 5.2.4)

```
SELECT NAME = S.SNAME
FROM    S
WHERE   S.CITY = 'London'

UNION

SELECT NAME = P.PNAME
FROM    P
WHERE   P.CITY = 'London'
```

Duplicate rows are always eliminated from the result of a UNION.

11.3.23 Using Union to Construct an Outer Join. For each supplier, get the supplier number, name, status, and city, together with part numbers for all parts supplied by that supplier. If a given supplier supplies no parts at all, then show the information for that supplier in the result concatenated with a blank part number. (Example 5.2.6)

```
SELECT S.*, SP.PNO
FROM    S, SP
WHERE   S.SNO = SP.SNO

UNION

SELECT S.*, 'bbbb'
FROM    S
WHERE   NOT EXISTS
      ( SELECT *
        FROM    SP
        WHERE   SP.SNO = S.SNO )
```

We have now covered all of the features of the SQL SELECT statement that we intend to illustrate in this book. To conclude the section, we present a very contrived example that shows how many (by no means all) of those features can be used together in a single query. We also give a conceptual algorithm for the evaluation of SQL queries in general.

11.3.24 A Comprehensive Example. For all red and blue parts such that the total quantity supplied is greater than 350 (excluding from the total all shipments for which the quantity is less than or equal to 200), get the part number, the weight in grams, the color, and the maximum quantity supplied of that part; and order the result by descending part number within ascending values of that maximum quantity.

```
SELECT  P.PNO,
        W = 'Weight in grams =',
        X = P.WEIGHT * 454,
        P.COLOR,
        Y = 'Max shipped quantity =',
        Z = MAX ( SP.QTY )
FROM    P, SP
WHERE   P.PNO = SP.PNO
AND     P.COLOR IN ( 'Red', 'Blue' )
AND     SP.QTY > 200
GROUP   BY P.PNO, P.WEIGHT, P.COLOR
HAVING  SUM ( SP.QTY ) > 350
ORDER   BY Z, P.PNO DESC
```

Result:

```
|pno |w                   |x    |color |y                        |z   |
|--------------------------------------------------------------------|
|P1  |Weight in grams =|  5448|Red   |Max shipped quantity = |300|
|P5  |Weight in grams =|  5448|Blue  |Max shipped quantity = |400|
|P3  |Weight in grams =|  7718|Blue  |Max shipped quantity = |400|
|--------------------------------------------------------------------|
```

Explanation: The clauses of a SELECT statement are applied in the order suggested by that in which they are written—with the exception of the SELECT clause itself, which is applied between the HAVING clause (if any) and the ORDER BY clause (if any). In the example, therefore, we can imagine the result being constructed as follows.

1. *FROM*. The FROM clause is evaluated to yield a new table that is the Cartesian product of tables P and SP.

2. *WHERE*. The result of Step 1 is reduced by the elimination of all rows that do not satisfy the WHERE clause. In the example, rows not satisfying the predicate

```
P.PNO = SP.PNO AND P.COLOR IN ('Red','Blue') AND SP.QTY > 200
```

are eliminated.

3. *GROUP BY*. The result of Step 2 is grouped by values of the field(s) named in the GROUP BY clause. In the example, those fields are P.PNO, P.WEIGHT, and P.COLOR. *Note:* In theory P.PNO alone would be sufficient as the grouping field, since P.WEIGHT and P.COLOR are themselves single-valued per part number. However, SQL is not aware of this latter fact, and will raise an error condition if P.WEIGHT and P.COLOR are omitted from the GROUP BY clause, because they are *included* in the SELECT clause. (The basic problem here is that SQL does not support primary keys. See Appendix B.)

4. *HAVING*. Groups not satisfying the condition

```
SUM ( SP.QTY ) > 350
```

are eliminated from the result of Step 3.

5. *SELECT*. Each group in the result of Step 4 generates a single result row, as follows. First, the part number, weight, color, and maximum quantity are extracted from the group. Second, the weight is converted to grams. Third, the two string constants "Weight in grams =" and "Max shipped quantity =" are inserted at the appropriate points in the row.

6. *ORDER BY*. The result of Step 5 is ordered in accordance with the specifications of the ORDER BY clause to yield the final result.

It is of course true that the query shown above is quite complex—but think how much work it is doing. A conventional program to do the same job in a language such as COBOL could easily be fourteen pages long, instead of just fourteen lines as above, and the work involved in getting that program operational would be significantly greater than that needed to construct the SQL version shown. In practice, of course, most queries will be much simpler than this one anyway.

11.4 UPDATE OPERATIONS

The SQL update operations are INSERT, UPDATE, and DELETE, with syntax as follows:*

```
    INSERT INTO table ( field [, field ] ... )
           VALUES ( constant [, constant ] ... )
```
Or:

```
    INSERT INTO table ( field [, field ] ... )
           select-operation

    UPDATE table
    SET    field = expression [, field = expression ] ...
  [ WHERE  predicate ]

    DELETE FROM table
  [ WHERE  predicate ]
```

---

*The term "update" unfortunately has two distinct meanings in SQL: It is used generically to refer to all three operations as a class, and also specifically to refer to the UPDATE operation per se. We will distinguish between the two meanings in this book by always using lower case when the generic meaning is intended and upper case when the specific meaning is intended.

INSERT

11.4.1 Single-Record INSERT. Add part P7 (city Athens, weight 24, name and color at present unknown) to table P. (Example 5.2.1)

```
INSERT INTO P ( PNO, CITY, WEIGHT )
VALUES ( 'P7', 'Athens', 24 )
```

A new part record is created with the specified part number, city, and weight, and with null values for the name and color fields (assuming that WITH NULL was specified—explicitly or implicitly—for those fields). In general, the effect of omitting a value for some field in INSERT depends on the "default-spec" (see Chapter 3) for the field in question, exactly as with APPEND in QUEL.

11.4.2 Multiple-Record INSERT. Suppose table NEWSP has the same fields (SNO, PNO, and QTY) as table SP. Copy all records of NEWSP for which the quantity is greater than 1000 into table SP. (Example 5.2.2)

```
INSERT INTO SP ( SNO, PNO, QTY )
       SELECT NEWSP.SNO, NEWSP.PNO, NEWSP.QTY
       FROM   NEWSP
       WHERE  NEWSP.QTY > 1000
```

In this second format of INSERT ("INSERT . . . SELECT"), the "select-operation" must not include UNION.

UPDATE

11.4.3 Single-Record UPDATE. Change the color of part P2 to yellow, increase its weight by 5, and set its city to "unknown" (NULL). (Example 5.3.1)

```
UPDATE P
SET    COLOR = 'Yellow', WEIGHT = P.WEIGHT + 5, CITY = NULL
WHERE  P.PNO = 'P2'
```

11.4.4 Multiple-Record UPDATE. Double the status of all suppliers in London. (Example 5.3.2)

```
UPDATE S
SET    STATUS = 2 * S.STATUS
WHERE  S.CITY = 'London'
```

11.4.5 UPDATE Referring to Another Table. Set the shipment quantity to zero for all suppliers in London. (Example 5.3.3)

```
UPDATE SP
SET    QTY = 0
WHERE  SP.SNO IN
      ( SELECT S.SNO
        FROM   S
        WHERE  S.CITY = 'London' )
```

11.4.6 UPDATE Referring to the Same Table. Set the status to zero for all suppliers in the same city as supplier S1 or supplier S2.

```
UPDATE S
SET    STATUS = 0
WHERE  S.CITY IN
      ( SELECT S.CITY
        FROM   S
        WHERE  S.SNO IN ( 'S1', 'S2' ) )
```

DELETE

11.4.7 Single-Record DELETE. Delete supplier S1. (Example 5.4.1)

```
DELETE
FROM   S
WHERE  S.SNO = 'S1'
```

11.4.8 Multiple-Record DELETE. Delete all suppliers in Madrid. (Example 5.4.2)

```
DELETE
FROM   S
WHERE  S.CITY = 'Madrid'
```

11.4.9 DELETE Referring to Another Table. Delete all shipments for suppliers in London. (Example 5.4.4)

```
DELETE
FROM   SP
WHERE  SP.SNO IN
      ( SELECT S.SNO
        FROM   S
        WHERE  S.CITY = 'London' )
```

11.4.10 DELETE Referring to the Same Table. Delete all suppliers whose status is lower than the average. (Example 5.4.5)

```
DELETE
FROM    S
WHERE   S.STATUS <
     ( SELECT AVG ( S.STATUS )
       FROM    S )
```

11.5 EMBEDDED SQL: AN OVERVIEW

We begin with an example (Fig. 11.1)—an ESQL version of the sample EQUEL program from Section 10.2.

```
DATA DIVISION .
WORKING-STORAGE SECTION .

EXEC SQL BEGIN DECLARE SECTION END-EXEC

        01   GIVENSNO   PIC X(5) .
        01   RANK       PIC S9(5) USAGE COMP .
        01   CITY       PIC X(15) .

EXEC SQL END DECLARE SECTION END-EXEC

EXEC SQL INCLUDE SQLCA END-EXEC

PROCEDURE DIVISION .

EXEC SQL WHENEVER SQLERROR STOP END-EXEC

EXEC SQL CONNECT "s_sp_p" END-EXEC

EXEC SQL BEGIN TRANSACTION END-EXEC

        MOVE "S4" TO GIVENSNO .

EXEC SQL SELECT S.STATUS, S.#CITY
        INTO    :RANK, :CITY
        FROM    S
        WHERE   S.SNO = :GIVENSNO  END-EXEC

        DISPLAY "Rank and city for supplier ", GIVENSNO,
                "are ", RANK, "and ", CITY .

        IF RANK < 25 THEN
           EXEC SQL DELETE FROM S
                   WHERE S.SNO = :GIVENSNO END-EXEC .

EXEC SQL END TRANSACTION END-EXEC

EXEC SQL DISCONNECT END-EXEC
```

Fig. 11.1 An ESQL/COBOL program (example—most COBOL details omitted)

Points arising:

1. Every ESQL database statement must begin with EXEC SQL and end with a language-specific terminator. (Note that, by contrast with EQUEL, it is *statements* that are specially flagged, not lines.) For COBOL, the terminator is END-EXEC. For other languages, see the RTI manuals.

2. Declarations of host variables that will be used within ESQL statements must appear in a special declaration section, bracketed by the special statements

```
EXEC SQL BEGIN DECLARE SECTION END-EXEC
```

and

```
EXEC SQL END DECLARE SECTION END-EXEC
```

3. After any ESQL statement has been executed, feedback information is returned to the program in an area called the SQL Communication Area (SQLCA). In particular, a numeric status value is returned in a field of the SQLCA called SQLCODE. A zero value means that the statement executed successfully; a positive value means that the statement did execute, but constitutes a warning that some exceptional condition occurred (e.g., a value of $+100$ indicates that no data was found to satisfy the request); and a negative value means that an error occurred and the statement did not execute successfully. Another field of the SQLCA, called SQLERRD(3), contains a count of the number of records accessed by the most recent ESQL statement.

The SQL Communication Area is included in the program by means of the special statement

```
EXEC SQL INCLUDE SQLCA END-EXEC
```

4. The WHENEVER statement is provided to simplify the process of testing for exceptional conditions after each ESQL statement. Its syntax is:

```
EXEC SQL WHENEVER condition action END-EXEC
```

where "condition" is one of the following—

```
NOT FOUND
SQLWARNING
SQLERROR
```

—and "action" is CONTINUE or STOP or a GO TO statement or a CALL statement. WHENEVER is not an executable statement; rather, it is a directive to the ESQL preprocessor. The STOP, GO TO, and CALL formats cause the preprocessor to insert statements after each ESQL statement to STOP or GO TO the specified label or CALL the specified procedure,* as appropriate, if the specified "condition" occurs; the CONTINUE format causes the preprocessor not to insert any such statements (the implication being that the programmer will insert appropriate statements by hand). The three "conditions" are defined as follows:

```
NOT FOUND      means      SQLCODE = 100

SQLWARNING     means      a warning condition exists (field
                          SQLWARN0 of the SQLCA is set to 'W')

SQLERROR       means      SQLCODE < 0
```

Each WHENEVER statement the preprocessor encounters on its sequential scan through the program text for a particular condition overrides the previous one it found for that condition. At the start of the program text there is an implicit WHENEVER for each of the three possible conditions, specifying CONTINUE in each case.

5. CONNECT and DISCONNECT are the ESQL analogs of the EQUEL statements INGRES and EXIT (see Chapter 10).

6. References to host variables in ESQL statements must be prefixed with a colon (:). As a consequence, EQUEL-style dereferencing is unnecessary (and in fact illegal); the ESQL preprocessor always knows whether a given symbol refers to a host variable or to a special ESQL object such as a database field.

7. ESQL does not support anything directly analogous to the RETRIEVE-loop of EQUEL. Instead, multiple-record retrieval is always performed by means of cursors (see later). On the other hand, ESQL does support what we will call a "singleton SELECT"—i.e., a SELECT statement for which the retrieved table contains at most one row. See Fig. 11.1 for an example. Note that a singleton SELECT (unlike a regular SELECT) requires an INTO clause to specify the variables into which values are to be retrieved.

8. ESQL data manipulation statements support a REPEATED option (analogous to the REPEAT option in EQUEL). The REPEATED keyword

---

*Or PERFORM the specified paragraph in COBOL.

appears immediately prior to the SQL verb (e.g., EXEC SQL REPEATED SELECT . . .).

9. Null values are handled by indicator variables, as in EQUEL. For example:

```
EXEC SQL SELECT P.WEIGHT
         INTO   :WT:WTIND
         FROM   P
         WHERE  P.PNO = :GIVENPNO END-EXEC

IF WTIND = -1 THEN ...
```

Indicator variables can be specified in the INTO clause (as shown) and in the SET clause on UPDATE and in the VALUES list on INSERT but should *not* be specified in a WHERE clause. To repeat from Chapter 10: We will generally ignore indicator variables in this book.

10. Finally, ESQL, like EQUEL, provides a complete set of facilities for accessing the INGRES Forms Management System. All of the statements available in EQUEL/FORMS—DISPLAY, INITIALIZE, ACTIVATE, etc., etc.—are also available in ESQL/FORMS. Syntactically the ESQL/FORMS statements are very similar to their EQUEL/FORMS counterparts. The major differences are merely that:

(a) Each ESQL/FORMS statement begins with EXEC FRS and ends with a language-specific terminator (END-EXEC in COBOL), instead of being set off by a double number sign (##) on each line as in EQUEL and EQUEL/FORMS;

(b) Blocks of code that are to be considered as a unit (e.g., following ACTIVATE) are bracketed by the special statements

```
EXEC FRS BEGIN END-EXEC
```

and

```
EXEC FRS END END-EXEC
```

instead of by opening and closing braces—"{" and "}"—as in EQUEL and EQUEL/FORMS.

11.6 EMBEDDED SQL: CURSORS

The cursors and cursor operations of ESQL are basically very similar to their analogs in EQUEL. Figure 11.2 shows a simple example (an ESQL version of the EQUEL example of Fig. 10.2). The example is intended to be self-explanatory.

```
EXEC SQL DECLARE X CURSOR FOR
          SELECT S.SNO, S.SNAME, S.STATUS
          FROM    S
          WHERE   S.CITY = :Y END-EXEC

EXEC SQL OPEN X END-EXEC
EXEC SQL WHENEVER NOT FOUND ... END-EXEC

          PERFORM BEGIN-RET-LOOP THROUGH END-RET-LOOP
                  UNTIL no more records to come .
BEGIN-RET-LOOP .
              EXEC SQL FETCH X
                    INTO :ALPHA, :BETA, :GAMMA END-EXEC
              process ALPHA, BETA, GAMMA
END-RET-LOOP .

EXEC SQL CLOSE X END-EXEC
```

Fig. 11.2 Example of the use of a cursor (ESQL)

The ESQL cursor operations can be regarded primarily as just syntactic variants on the corresponding EQUEL operations:

ESQL statements	*EQUEL equivalents*
DECLARE ... CURSOR	DECLARE CURSOR ...
OPEN	OPEN CURSOR
FETCH	RETRIEVE CURSOR
UPDATE ... CURRENT	REPLACE CURSOR
DELETE ... CURRENT	DELETE CURSOR
CLOSE	CLOSE CURSOR

The syntax of the SQL statements is as follows.

1. DECLARE CURSOR:

```
EXEC SQL DECLARE cursor CURSOR FOR [ REPEATED ]
               select-operation
             [ FOR [ DEFERRED | DIRECT ] UPDATE
                 [ OF ( field [, field ] ... ) ] ] END-EXEC
```

The "select-operation" can include DISTINCT and/or ORDER BY and/or UNION.

2. OPEN:

```
EXEC SQL OPEN cursor END-EXEC
```

3. FETCH:

```
EXEC SQL FETCH cursor
          INTO  variable [, variable ] ... END-EXEC
```

4. UPDATE CURRENT:

```
EXEC SQL UPDATE table
         SET    field = expression [, field = expression ] ...
         WHERE  CURRENT OF CURSOR END-EXEC
```

5. DELETE CURRENT:

```
EXEC SQL DELETE
         FROM   table
         WHERE  CURRENT OF CURSOR END-EXEC
```

6. CLOSE:

```
EXEC SQL CLOSE cursor END-EXEC
```

EXERCISES

11.1 Give SQL solutions to Exercises 4.1–4.32 from Chapter 4 (where possible or applicable).

11.2 Give SQL solutions to Exercises 5.1–5.12 from Chapter 5 (where possible or applicable).

11.3 Give ESQL solutions to Exercises 10.1–10.3 from Chapter 10 (where possible or applicable).

ANSWERS TO SELECTED EXERCISES

11.1 We have numbered the following solutions as 11.1.*n*, where 4.*n* is the number of the original exercise in Chapter 4.

11.1.1
```
SELECT J.*
FROM   J
```

11.1.2
```
CREATE LJ AS
       SELECT J.JNO, J.JNAME, J.CITY
       FROM   J
       WHERE  J.CITY = 'London'
```

11.1.3
```
SELECT SPJ.SNO
FROM   SPJ
WHERE  SPJ.JNO = 'J1'
ORDER  BY SPJ.SNO
```

11.1.4
```
SELECT SPJ.*
FROM   SPJ
WHERE  SPJ.QTY BETWEEN 300 AND 750
```

11.1.5
```
SELECT DISTINCT P.COLOR, P.CITY
FROM   P
```

11.1.6
```
SELECT  P.*
FROM    P
WHERE   ( P.WEIGHT * 454 ) < 7000
```

11.1.7
```
SELECT  J.JNO, J.CITY
FROM    J
WHERE   J.CITY LIKE '_o%'
```

11.1.8
```
SELECT  DISTINCT J.JNAME
FROM    J, SPJ
WHERE   J.JNO = SPJ.JNO
AND     SPJ.SNO = 'S5'
```

Or:
```
SELECT  J.JNAME
FROM    J
WHERE   J.JNO IN
        ( SELECT  SPJ.JNO
          FROM    SPJ
          WHERE   SPJ.SNO = 'S5' )
```

Or:
```
SELECT  J.JNAME
FROM    J
WHERE   EXISTS
        ( SELECT  SPJ.JNO
          FROM    SPJ
          WHERE   SPJ.SNO = 'S5'
          AND     SPJ.JNO = J.JNO )
```

From this point on we will not normally bother to show more than one possible solution.

11.1.9
```
SELECT  DISTINCT P.COLOR
FROM    P, SPJ
WHERE   P.PNO = SPJ.PNO
AND     SPJ.SNO = 'S1'
```

11.1.10
```
SELECT  DISTINCT SPJ.PNO
FROM    SPJ, J
WHERE   SPJ.JNO = J.JNO
AND     J.CITY = 'London'
```

11.1.11
```
SELECT  DISTINCT SPJ.JNO
FROM    SPJ, SPJ SPJX
WHERE   SPJ.PNO = SPJX.PNO
AND     SPJX.SNO = 'S1'
```

11.1.12
```
SELECT  DISTINCT SPJ.SNO
FROM    SPJ, SPJ SPJX, SPJ SPJY
WHERE   SPJ.PNO = SPJX.PNO
AND     SPJX.SNO = SPJY.SNO
AND     SPJY.PNO = P.PNO
AND     P.COLOR = 'Red'
```

11.1.13
```
SELECT  DISTINCT S.SNO
FROM    S, S SX
WHERE   S.STATUS < SX.STATUS
AND     SX.SNO = 'S1'
```

11.1.14
```
SELECT  S.SNO, P.PNO, J.JNO
FROM    S, P, J
WHERE   S.CITY = P.CITY
AND     P.CITY = J.CITY
```

```
11.1.15   SELECT S.SNO, P.PNO, J.JNO
          FROM   S, P, J
          WHERE  S.CITY <> P.CITY
          OR     P.CITY <> J.CITY
          OR     J.CITY <> S.CITY

11.1.16   SELECT S.SNO, P.PNO, J.JNO
          FROM   S, P, J
          WHERE  S.CITY <> P.CITY
          AND    P.CITY <> J.CITY
          AND    J.CITY <> S.CITY

11.1.17   SELECT DISTINCT SPJ.PNO
          FROM   S, SPJ, J
          WHERE  SPJ.SNO = S.SNO AND S.CITY = 'London'
          AND    SPJ.JNO = J.JNO AND J.CITY = 'London'

11.1.18   SELECT DISTINCT S.CITY, J.CITY
          FROM   S, SPJ, J
          WHERE  S.SNO = SPJ.SNO AND SPJ.JNO = J.JNO

11.1.19   SELECT DISTINCT SPJ.PNO
          FROM   S, SPJ, J
          WHERE  SPJ.SNO = S.SNO
          AND    SPJ.JNO = J.JNO
          AND    S.CITY = J.CITY

11.1.20   SELECT DISTINCT SPJ.JNO
          FROM   S, SPJ, J
          WHERE  SPJ.SNO = S.SNO
          AND    SPJ.JNO = J.JNO
          AND    S.CITY <> J.CITY

11.1.21   SELECT DISTINCT LEFT = SPJ.PNO, RIGHT = SPJX.PNO
          FROM   SPJ, SPJ SPJX
          WHERE  SPJ.SNO = SPJX.SNO
          AND    SPJ.PNO < SPJX.PNO

11.1.22   SELECT X = COUNT ( DISTINCT SPJ.JNO )
          FROM   SPJ
          WHERE  SPJ.SNO = 'S1'

11.1.23   SELECT Y = SUM ( SPJ.QTY )
          FROM   SPJ
          WHERE  SPJ.SNO = 'S1'
          AND    SPJ.PNO = 'P1'

11.1.24   SELECT J.JNO
          FROM   J
          WHERE  J.CITY =
               ( SELECT MIN ( J.CITY )
                 FROM   J )

11.1.25   SELECT SPJ.PNO, SPJ.JNO, Z = SUM ( SPJ.QTY )
          FROM   SPJ
          GROUP  BY SPJ.PNO, SPJ.JNO

11.1.26   SELECT DISTINCT SPJ.PNO
          FROM   SPJ
          GROUP  BY SPJ.PNO, SPJ.JNO
          HAVING AVG ( SPJ.QTY ) > 320
```

11.1.27 Cannot be done (set functions cannot be nested in SQL).

11.1.28
```
SELECT P.*, X = SUM ( SPJ.QTY )
FROM   P, SPJ
WHERE  SPJ.PNO = P.PNO
GROUP  BY P.PNO, P.PNAME, P.COLOR, P.WEIGHT, P.CITY
```

Unlike its QUEL counterpart, this SQL statement will not retrieve information for parts that are not currently supplied. A SQL version that will include such information is the following:

```
SELECT P.*, X = SUM ( SPJ.QTY )
FROM   P, SPJ
WHERE  SPJ.PNO = P.PNO
GROUP  BY P.PNO, P.PNAME, P.COLOR, P.WEIGHT, P.CITY

UNION

SELECT P.*, 0
FROM   P
WHERE  NOT EXISTS
       ( SELECT *
         FROM   SPJ
         WHERE  SPJ.PNO = P.PNO )
```

11.1.29
```
SELECT DISTINCT SPJ.JNO
FROM   SPJ
WHERE  SPJ.PNO = 'P1'
GROUP  BY SPJ.PNO, SPJ.JNO
HAVING AVG ( SPJ.QTY ) >
       ( SELECT MAX ( SPJ.QTY )
         FROM   SPJ
         WHERE  SPJ.JNO = 'J1' )
```

11.1.30
```
SELECT DISTINCT SPJ.SNO
FROM   SPJ
WHERE  SPJ.PNO = 'P1'
AND    SPJ.QTY >
       ( SELECT AVG ( SPJ.QTY )
         FROM   SPJ
         GROUP  BY SPJ.PNO, SPJ.JNO )
```

11.1.31
```
SELECT DISTINCT SPJ.PNO
FROM   SPJ
WHERE  EXISTS
       ( SELECT J.JNO
         FROM   J
         WHERE  SPJ.JNO = J.JNO
         AND    J.CITY = 'London' )
```

We have interpreted the question as referring to SQL EXISTS rather than QUEL ANY.

11.1.32
```
SELECT J.JNO
FROM   J
WHERE  NOT EXISTS
       ( SELECT SPJ.*
         FROM   SPJ
         WHERE  SPJ.SNO = S.SNO AND S.CITY = 'London'
         AND    SPJ.PNO = P.PNO AND P.COLOR = 'Red'
         AND    SPJ.JNO = J.JNO )
```

11.2 We have numbered the following solutions as 11.2.*n*, where 5.*n* is the number of the original exercise in Chapter 5.

11.2.1
```
UPDATE P
SET    COLOR = 'Orange'
WHERE  P.COLOR = 'Red'
```

11.2.2
```
DELETE
FROM   J
WHERE  J.JNO NOT IN
     ( SELECT SPJ.JNO
       FROM   SPJ )
```

11.2.3
```
UPDATE SPJ
SET    QTY = SPJ.QTY * 1.1
WHERE  SPJ.SNO IN
     ( SELECT SPJ.SNO
       FROM   SPJ
       WHERE  SPJ.PNO IN
            ( SELECT P.PNO
              FROM   P
              WHERE  P.COLOR = 'Red' ) )
```

11.2.4
```
DELETE
FROM   SPJ
WHERE  SPJ.JNO IN
     ( SELECT J.JNO
       FROM   J
       WHERE  J.CITY = 'Rome' )

DELETE
FROM   J
WHERE  J.CITY = 'Rome'
```

11.2.5
```
INSERT INTO S ( SNO, SNAME, CITY )
VALUES ( 'S10', 'White', 'New York' )
```

11.2.6
```
CREATE LP ( PNO ) AS
       SELECT SPJ.PNO
       FROM   SPJ
       WHERE  SPJ.SNO IN
            ( SELECT S.SNO
              FROM   S
              WHERE  S.CITY = 'London' )
       OR     SPJ.JNO IN
            ( SELECT J.JNO
              FROM   J
              WHERE  J.CITY = 'London' )
```

11.2.7
```
CREATE LJ ( JNO ) AS
       SELECT J.JNO
       FROM   J
       WHERE  J.CITY = 'London'

INSERT INTO LJ ( JNO )
       SELECT SPJ.JNO
       FROM   SPJ
       WHERE  SPJ.SNO IN
            ( SELECT S.SNO
              FROM   S
              WHERE  S.CITY = 'London' )
```

Actually this problem can also be solved by means of a single CREATE operation, provided we can rely on the fact that every value of SPJ.JNO should also appear as a value of J.JNO:

```
CREATE LJ ( JNO ) AS
       SELECT J.JNO
       FROM   J
       WHERE  J.CITY = 'London'
       OR     J.JNO IN
              ( SELECT SPJ.JNO
                FROM   SPJ
                WHERE  SPJ.SNO IN
                       ( SELECT S.SNO
                         FROM   S
                         WHERE  S.CITY = 'London' ) )
```

11.2.8
```
UPDATE S
SET    STATUS = S.STATUS + 10
WHERE  S.STATUS <
       ( SELECT S.STATUS
         FROM   S
         WHERE  S.SNO = 'S4' )
```

11.2.9
```
SELECT S.CITY
FROM   S
UNION
SELECT P.CITY
FROM   P
UNION
SELECT J.CITY
FROM   J
ORDER  BY 1
```

It is possible (and required, in the case of a query involving UNION) to refer to result columns in the ORDER BY clause by their ordinal position (1, 2, . . .) as well as by name.

11.2.10
```
SELECT J.*, SPJ.SNO, SPJ.PNO, SPJ.QTY
FROM   J, SPJ
WHERE  J.JNO = SPJ.JNO
UNION
SELECT J.*, 'bbbbb', 'bbbbbb', 0
FROM   J
WHERE  NOT EXISTS
       ( SELECT SPJ.JNO
         FROM   SPJ
         WHERE  SPJ.JNO = J.JNO )
```

11.2.11
```
SELECT P.*, J.JNO, J.JNAME
FROM   P, J
WHERE  P.CITY = J.CITY
UNION
SELECT P.*, 'bbb', 'bbb'
FROM   P
WHERE  NOT EXISTS
       ( SELECT J.JNO
         FROM   J
         WHERE  J.CITY = P.CITY )
UNION
SELECT 'bbb', 'bbb', 'bbb', 0, J.CITY, J.JNO, J.JNAME
FROM   J
WHERE  NOT EXISTS
       ( SELECT P.PNO
         FROM   P
         WHERE  P.CITY = J.CITY )
```

```
11.2.12   SELECT  S.SNO, S.SNAME, S.STATUS, SCITY = S.CITY,
                  P.PNO, P.PNAME, P.COLOR, P.WEIGHT, PCITY = P.CITY,
                  J.JNO, J.JNAME, JCITY = J.CITY,
                  SPJ.QTY
          FROM    S, P, J, SPJ
          WHERE   S.SNO = SPJ.SNO
          AND     P.PNO = SPJ.PNO
          AND     J.JNO = SPJ.JNO
          UNION
          SELECT  S.SNO, S.SNAME, S.STATUS, SCITY = S.CITY,
                  'bbb', 'bbb', 'bbb', 0, 'bbb',
                  'bbb', 'bbb', 'bbb',
                  0
          FROM    S
          WHERE   NOT EXISTS
                ( SELECT  SPJ.SNO
                  FROM    SPJ
                  WHERE   SPJ.SNO = S.SNO )
          UNION
          SELECT  'bbb', 'bbb', 0, 'bbb',
                  P.PNO, P.PNAME, P.COLOR, P.WEIGHT, PCITY = P.CITY,
                  'bbb', 'bbb', 'bbb',
                  0
          FROM    P
          WHERE   NOT EXISTS
                ( SELECT  SPJ.PNO
                  FROM    SPJ
                  WHERE   SPJ.PNO = P.PNO )
          UNION
          SELECT  'bbb', 'bbb', 0, 'bbb'
                  'bbb', 'bbb', 'bbb', 0, 'bbb',
                  J.JNO, J.JNAME, JCITY  = J.CITY,
                  0
          FROM    J
          WHERE   NOT EXISTS
                ( SELECT  SPJ.JNO
                  FROM    SPJ
                  WHERE   SPJ.JNO = J.JNO )
```

12

Storage Structure

12.1 INTRODUCTION

In this chapter we present a brief overview of the storage structure of an INGRES database. We also describe the INGRES statements that have a direct bearing on that structure. The statements in question are listed below:

QUEL statements	*SQL equivalents*
CREATE	CREATE TABLE
RETRIEVE INTO	CREATE TABLE AS
DESTROY (base table)	DROP [TABLE]
MODIFY	MODIFY
INDEX	CREATE INDEX
DESTROY (index)	DROP [INDEX]
RELOCATE	RELOCATE

Three other statements are also relevant—CREATEDB, DES-TROYDB, and SYSMOD. However, these three statements are not part of QUEL per se (nor of SQL); instead, they are categorized as *system-level* statements—i.e., they are "utility" commands to the machine's operating system, not to the INGRES DBMS. INGRES's system-level commands in general are the subject of Chapter 13, but the functions of the three just mentioned are described in the present chapter.

Each INGRES system supports one special database, the *database data-*

base or DBDB (already briefly discussed in Chapter 8), together with any number of *user databases*:

- The DBDB is used by the INGRES system manager and by INGRES itself for various control purposes. Among other things, it contains a list of the users and databases known to the system, and an indication as to which users are allowed to access which databases.

- Each user database, in turn, contains a set of system tables and a set of user tables (each possibly with a corresponding set of indexes). The system tables are discussed in Chapter 6. User tables—or rather, the *stored versions* of those tables, which henceforth we will refer to as *stored tables*—are discussed in the present chapter; so also are indexes on those stored tables.

At any given time, a given QUEL or SQL user is always operating within the context of a single INGRES database. The database in question is specified as a parameter to the command by which the user signs on to the system—for example, the interactive INGRES or RTINGRES command (see Chapter 13), or the embedded INGRES or CONNECT operation (see Chapters 10 and 11). We will refer to that database as "the current database" in this chapter. We now proceed to amplify the foregoing ideas.

12.2 DATABASES

An INGRES database can be regarded as a dynamically extendable collection of *pages*, where a page is a block of physical storage space (it is the unit of I/O, i.e., the unit transferred between primary and secondary storage in a single I/O operation). Each page is 2048 bytes in size. A database can contain any number of pages.

From the user's point of view, a database consists of a collection of logically related objects—that is, a collection of stored tables that belong together in some way, together with their associated indexes. A given stored table and all its associated indexes must be wholly contained within a single database. Thus, the database is the *logical unit of processing*; as explained in Section 12.1, QUEL or SQL statements are constrained to operate within the boundaries of a single database. For example, it is not possible to join two tables from two different databases.*

---

*We are ignoring here the possibility that the "single database" might in fact be virtual and might span multiple physical databases. See the description of INGRES/STAR in Chapter 2 or Chapter 21.

The command to create a new database is

```
CREATEDB database
```

where "database" is the name of the new database. The user issuing the command, who must have previously been given the authority to create new databases by the system manager, becomes the DBA for that new database. An entry identifying the database is made in the DBDB. *Note*: CREATEDB includes a number of additional parameters—one that specifies whether the new database is public or private (see Chapter 8), plus a number of others that are beyond the scope of this chapter. See the RTI manuals for more information.

To destroy an existing database, the command is

```
DESTROYDB database
```

The entry for the specified database is removed from the DBDB. A given database can be destroyed only by the DBA for that database (or by the system manager).

Each database occupies one or more "areas" or "locations," each of which consists of either a single storage volume (i.e., disk), or some subset of such a volume. A single database can thus span any number of storage volumes, and a single storage volume can contain portions of any number of databases. The locations available for use by a given database are defined by the system manager and are recorded in the DBDB. When a new table is created in a given database, the creator can specify that it be stored in a named location (see Section 12.4 for more information). The table can also be subsequently moved from one location to another within its containing database; again, see Section 12.4 for details.

12.3   STORED RECORDS

A stored record is the stored representation of a record of a base table (the "base record"). It consists of a stored record prefix (containing control information such as the stored record length), plus a set of stored fields—i.e., stored forms of the fields that make up that base record. Each stored record is wholly contained within a single page, with a maximum stored record length of 2008 bytes. One page can contain multiple stored records.

Each stored field, in turn, consists of:

- A two-byte length prefix (if the field is varying length—see Section 12.5), giving the length of the actual data (including the null indicator prefix, if there is one—see below);

- A one-byte null indicator prefix (if nulls are allowed), indicating whether the value, if any, in the data part of the field (a) is to be taken as a genuine data value or (b) is to be ignored (i.e., interpreted as null);

- The actual data value (if nonnull).

All stored fields are byte-aligned. There are no gaps between fields. *Note*: In a compressed structure (see Section 12.5), string fields occupy only as many bytes as are needed to store the actual value.

Internally, stored records are addressed by "tuple ID" or TID; for example, all pointers within indexes are TIDs. TIDs are implemented as shown in Fig. 12.1. The TID for a stored record R consists of two parts—the page number of the page P containing R, and an offset from the bottom of P (sometimes called a line number) identifying a slot that contains, in turn, the offset of R from the top of P. This scheme represents a good compromise between the speed of direct addressing and the flexibility of indirect addressing: Records can be rearranged within their page—e.g., to close up the gap when a record is deleted or to make room when a record is inserted—without having to change TIDs (only the local offsets at the foot

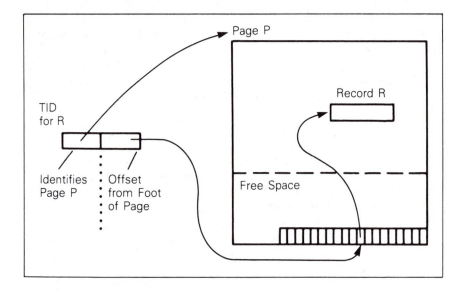

Fig. 12.1 Implementation of TIDs

of the page have to change); yet access to a record given the TID is fast, involving only a single page access.*

12.4 STORED TABLES

A stored table is the stored representation of a base table. It consists of a single operating system file, containing a set of stored records (one for each "base record" in the base table in question). Each stored table normally occupies multiple pages. A single page cannot contain stored records from multiple files.

- For the HEAP and CHEAP storage structures (see Section 12.5), records are stored wherever there happens to be room, on any available page. *Note*: The same is true for the HEAPSORT and CHEAPSORT structures, except at the time of the MODIFY that establishes the structure—see Section 12.5—when the records are initially stored in sorted order.

- For the other storage structures, records are stored on pages in accordance with the indexing or hashing scheme in effect (again, see Section 12.5). When the table is first loaded, all records are stored on *primary* pages (i.e., pages that are directly accessible via the index or hash). If a page subsequently becomes full, INGRES allocates another page—another primary page, if the structure is BTREE or CBTREE, an overflow page otherwise (see Fig. 12.2). The same thing happens if that new page becomes full in turn. All overflow pages for a given primary page are chained off that original primary page (does not apply to BTREE or CBTREE).

In QUEL, stored tables are created by means of the CREATE (or RETRIEVE INTO) statement and destroyed by means of the DESTROY statement, as we already know. The SQL equivalents are CREATE TABLE (or CREATE TABLE AS) and DROP. However, there is one aspect of table creation that we have not previously considered and needs to be discussed here—the ability to specify the *area* or location into which the new table is to go. For example (QUEL):

```
CREATE S_AREA : S
     ( SNO    = CHAR(5)   NOT NULL,
       SNAME  = CHAR(20)  NOT NULL WITH DEFAULT,
       STATUS = I2        NOT NULL WITH DEFAULT,
       CITY   = TEXT(15)  NOT NULL WITH DEFAULT )
```

---

*Unless it is necessary to go to an overflow page. See Section 12.4.

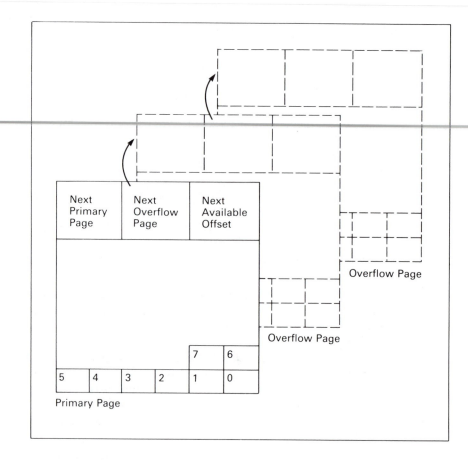

Fig. 12.2 Page layout for hash/isam structures

Here the new table (the suppliers table S) is to be stored in the location called S_AREA. That location must have been defined as a valid location for the current database by the INGRES system manager. If the optional "location:" prefix is omitted when a new table is created (as it has been in all examples in this book prior to this point), the new table is stored in the *default* location for the current database. The default location (usually "DB_INGRES") is also defined by the system manager.

It is also possible to move a given stored table from one location to another by means of the QUEL (or SQL) RELOCATE statement:

```
RELOCATE table TO location
```

For example:

```
RELOCATE S TO DIFF_AREA
```

Again, DIFF_AREA must have previously been defined as a legal location for the current database. Existing views and indexes on the table remain valid after any such relocation.

12.5 MODIFYING THE STRUCTURE OF A STORED TABLE

In INGRES (unlike most other relational systems at the time of writing), different stored tables can have significantly different storage structures. Each such table can thus be stored in the form most suitable for the ways in which it is to be used. Furthermore, the structure for a given stored table can be modified at any time, without in any way affecting the logic of existing applications; in other words, the storage structure is—of course— "transparent to the user."

The structures currently supported are as follows:

```
BTREE       CBTREE
HASH        CHASH
ISAM        CISAM
HEAP        CHEAP
HEAPSORT    CHEAPSORT
```

In brief:

- The optional "C" prefix—as in, e.g., CBTREE—specifies that the data is to be compressed on the disk. At the time of writing, compression consists merely of removing trailing blanks from CHAR and VCHAR (TEXT) and C string fields, thereby converting such fields to varying length. For simplicity, we ignore the possibility of compression in most of what follows.

- BTREE means that the stored table is represented as an indexed file, where the index is structured as a B-tree. A B-tree is a multi-level or tree-structured index that satisfies the property that the tree is always *balanced*; i.e., for all time, all leaf entries in the structure are at the same distance from the root of the tree, and this property continues to hold as new entries are inserted into the tree and existing entries are deleted. As a result, the index provides uniform and predictable performance for retrieval operations. Details of how this effect is achieved are beyond the scope of this book. The BTREE structure is good for data that is often accessed either directly or sequentially on the basis of values of the indexed field.

- HASH means that the stored table is represented as a hashed file, using a standard division/remainder algorithm supplied as part of the INGRES product. HASH is good for data that is frequently accessed directly on the basis of an equality condition on the hash field.

- ISAM ("indexed sequential access method") is somewhat similar to BTREE, but is a less dynamic structure; once created (via the MODIFY operation—see below), the index is never restructured. (As a result, it may sometimes be necessary to search an overflow chain to find some desired record.) In practice BTREE is usually—but not invariably—preferable to ISAM.

- HEAP means that the stored table is represented as a randomly ordered sequential file (new records are stored wherever there happens to be room). HEAP storage is primarily intended for small and/or shortlived tables.

- Finally, HEAPSORT means that the stored table is represented as a heap, but a heap that is sorted into a specified order. The sorting is done when the MODIFY operation is executed (see below); however, the sort order is not maintained in the face of subsequent updates (e.g., new records are still added wherever there happens to be room, as in HEAP).

Tables created via the QUEL CREATE or SQL CREATE TABLE operation are automatically created as HEAP. Tables created via the QUEL RETRIEVE INTO or SQL CREATE TABLE AS operation are automatically created as CHEAP.* However, the structure for any given stored table can be changed via the MODIFY operation to some other form, say to a BTREE structure, at any time after that table is created. Furthermore (as already indicated), the storage structure can be changed thereafter as often as desired.

The MODIFY Operation

We now proceed to discuss the MODIFY operation in some detail. First, a number of (important) generalities:

1. The overall purpose of MODIFY is to reorganize a stored table and (probably) to change the storage structure of that table—e.g., from BTREE to HASH—at the same time. It operates by constructing a new version of

---

*Actually the initial storage structure for such tables depends on the setting of the INGRES "ret_into" option. The explanation here assumes the default setting, which is CHEAP. See the RTI manuals for more information.

the table with the new structure, and then destroying the old version after the new version has been built.

2. The "table" operand to MODIFY must identify a stored (i.e., base) table, not a view.

3. MODIFY eliminates duplicate records from the new table *in all cases* (i.e., regardless of whether UNIQUE is specified—see below), except when the new storage structure is HEAP or CHEAP.

4. In fact, duplicate records can be introduced only into tables stored as HEAP or HEAPSORT (or CHEAP or CHEAPSORT). Any attempt to introduce a duplicate record into a table stored in any other structure will not succeed. Tables in INGRES thus *always* satisfy a "no duplicates" integrity constraint, except for the various flavors of "heap" (which are best regarded as anomalous anyway, since most tables will probably have one of the other structures in practice). The optional UNIQUE specification in MODIFY represents a *stronger* constraint; in effect, it says that records are to be unique, not just on the combination of all of their fields, but rather on the combination of some subset of their fields.*

5. If UNIQUE is specified but the existing table already violates the specified uniqueness constraint, the MODIFY will fail and no reorganization will occur.

6. MODIFY also includes certain additional parameters, not discussed here, that have to do with such things as the amount of free space to be left in each page on the disk. Of course, INGRES automatically supplies appropriate default values if such parameters are left unspecified.

7. If the table to be modified has been indexed via one or more INDEX operations (see Section 12.6), those indexes will automatically be destroyed by the MODIFY. Thus it may be necessary to follow the MODIFY by an appropriate set of INDEX operations to reconstruct such indexes.

Now for the details:

MODIFY: Format 1 (HEAP, CHEAP)

```
MODIFY table TO [C]HEAP
```

The specified table is modified to HEAP or CHEAP, as specified.

---

*In practice UNIQUE can and should be used to enforce primary key uniqueness.

MODIFY: Format 2 (HEAPSORT, CHEAPSORT)

```
MODIFY table TO [C]HEAPSORT
     [ ON field [ direction ] [, field [ direction ] ] ... ]
```

The specified table is modified to HEAPSORT or CHEAPSORT, as specified, in accordance with the specifications in the ON clause. Duplicate records are removed. If no "direction" (:ASCENDING or :DESCENDING, abbreviated :A or :D, in QUEL; ASC or DESC in SQL) is specified for a given field, ascending sequence is assumed. The left-to-right order of specifying fields corresponds to major-to-minor sorting in the usual way. *Note*: All fields of the table not explicitly specified in the ON clause are considered to be implicitly specified, in the left-to-right order in which they were originally defined, following those fields (if any) specified explicitly.

The sort order and the "no duplicates" property are not maintained as subsequent updates are made to the table.

MODIFY: Format 3 (ISAM, CISAM)

```
MODIFY table TO [C]ISAM
     [ UNIQUE ] [ ON field [, field ] ... ]
```

The specified table is modified to ISAM or CISAM, as specified. Duplicate records are removed. The index is on the combination of fields specified in the ON clause; omitting the ON clause is equivalent to specifying an ON clause naming just the first field of the table (as defined by the left-to-right order of naming columns when the table was originally created). The index sequence is defined by ascending values of the field combination identified by the (explicit or implicit) ON clause. If UNIQUE is not specified, remaining fields act as minor sort fields exactly as for HEAPSORT. If UNIQUE is specified, no two records in the table will be allowed to have the same value for the indexed field (combination) at the same time, so long as the table retains the ISAM/CISAM structure; INGRES will reject any attempt to violate this constraint. If UNIQUE is specified and the table already violates the constraint, the MODIFY fails and the storage structure of the table is not changed. Even if UNIQUE is not specified, any attempt to create a duplicate record or to update an existing record in such a way that it becomes a duplicate will fail, so long as the table retains the ISAM/CISAM structure.

MODIFY: Format 4 (HASH, CHASH)

```
MODIFY table TO [C]HASH
     [ UNIQUE ] [ ON field [, field ] ... ]
```

The specified table is modified to HASH or CHASH, as specified. Duplicate records are removed. The hash is on the combination of fields specified in the ON clause; omitting the ON clause is equivalent to specifying an ON clause naming just the first field of the table (as defined by the left-to-right order of naming columns when the table was created). If UNIQUE is specified, it means that no two records in the table will be allowed to have the same value for the hash field (combination) at the same time, so long as the table retains the HASH/CHASH structure; INGRES will reject any attempt to violate this constraint. If UNIQUE is specified and the table already violates the constraint, the MODIFY fails and the storage structure of the table is not changed. Even if UNIQUE is not specified, any attempt to create a duplicate record or to update an existing record in such a way that it becomes a duplicate will fail, so long as the table retains the HASH/CHASH structure.

MODIFY: Format 5 (BTREE, CBTREE)

```
MODIFY table TO [C]BTREE
     [ UNIQUE ] [ ON field [, field ] ... ]
```

The specified table is modified to BTREE or CBTREE, as specified. Duplicate records are removed. The index is on the combination of fields specified in the ON clause; omitting the ON clause is equivalent to specifying an ON clause naming just the first field of the table (as defined by the left-to-right order of naming columns when the table was originally created). The index sequence is defined by ascending values of the field combination identified by the (explicit or implicit) ON clause. If UNIQUE is not specified, remaining fields act as minor sort fields exactly as for HEAPSORT. If UNIQUE is specified, no two records in the table will be allowed to have the same value for the indexed field (combination) at the same time, so long as the table retains the BTREE/CBTREE structure; INGRES will reject any attempt to violate this constraint. If UNIQUE is specified and the table already violates the constraint, the MODIFY fails and the storage structure of the table is not changed. Even if UNIQUE is not specified, any attempt to create a duplicate record or to update an existing record in such a way that it becomes a duplicate will fail, so long as the table retains the BTREE/CBTREE structure.

Examples

1. MODIFY P TO CHEAP

2. MODIFY SP TO HEAPSORT ON SNO:A, PNO:D

The records of table SP are physically sorted into ascending QTY order (by default) within descending PNO order (as specified) within ascending SNO order (as specified). Although UNIQUE is not (and cannot be) specified, duplicate records are removed nonetheless. (Of course, if the SP table in fact satisfies a uniqueness constraint on the composite field (SNO,PNO), as it should do, then there will be no duplicate records, and furthermore the sorting of records into QTY order within (SNO,PNO) order will have no effect.)

3. MODIFY S TO BTREE UNIQUE ON SNO

Table S is sorted into SNO order and a B-tree is built on that field. No two records of S are allowed to have the same SNO value; the MODIFY will fail—i.e., the storage structure will remain unchanged—if that constraint is already violated by existing records. If the MODIFY succeeds, subsequent attempts to introduce a duplicate SNO value into the S table will fail.

4. MODIFY SP TO CHASH UNIQUE ON SNO, PNO

Table SP is reorganized into a hash-addressed structure, compressed, with hash access via values of the composite field (SNO,PNO). No two records of SP are allowed to have the same value for that composite field; the MODIFY will fail if that constraint is already violated by existing records. If the MODIFY succeeds, subsequent attempts to introduce a duplicate (SNO,PNO) value into the SP table will fail.

The SYSMOD Operation

We conclude this rather lengthy section with a brief mention of the INGRES system-level command SYSMOD. The purpose of SYSMOD is to modify the storage structure of some or all of the system tables for a specified database, in order to improve performance. In general, as more and more data definition operations are performed on a given database, so the system tables in that database will tend to become more and more disorganized, and overall performance will tend to deteriorate. The SYSMOD operation should be executed on each database at the time of creation, and periodically thereafter in order to avoid an unacceptable level of performance deterioration. The syntax of SYSMOD is:

```
SYSMOD database [ table(s) ]
```

where "table(s)" stands for a list of specific system tables (such as RELATION, ATTRIBUTE, INDEXES, etc.). Omitting the "table(s)" specification is equivalent to specifying a list of all the system tables in "database."

Note that the storage structures for the system tables are predetermined (in fact, they are nearly all HASH); there is no way to alter those structures. It is also not possible to create any additional indexes on those tables via an INDEX operation.

12.6 INDEXES

A given stored table can have any number of additional indexes (over and above the index that already exists as part of that table's principal storage structure for ISAM/CISAM/BTREE/CBTREE). Such additional indexes are useful if the table is frequently accessed on the basis of the indexed field(s). They are created by means of the INDEX statement in QUEL, or the CREATE INDEX statement in SQL. The format is:

QUEL:

```
INDEX ON table IS index ( field [, field ] ... )
```

SQL:

```
CREATE INDEX index ON table ( field [, field ] ... )
```

where "table" identifies a base table, not a view (for both QUEL and SQL). For example (QUEL):

```
INDEX ON S IS XSC ( CITY )
```

Once created, of course, the index is automatically maintained by INGRES.

Each additional index occupies its own separate operating system file. The index can be regarded as a special kind of stored table. For example, the index created by the INDEX operation shown above can be regarded as a table as follows:

```
xsc  |city |tid  |
     |-----------|
     | ... | ... |
     |     |     |
```

Here "city" represents the city value from some supplier record, and "tid" represents the tuple ID for that record.

Each additional index is initially stored as ISAM on the combination of all of its fields, TID included.* However, it can later be changed to some other structure via MODIFY, just as a stored table can.

Indexes created via the QUEL INDEX operation (or the SQL CREATE INDEX operation) can be destroyed via the QUEL DESTROY operation (or the SQL DROP [INDEX] operation). For example:

```
DESTROY XSC
```

It is not permitted to create an index on another index, nor on a system table.

EXERCISES

12.1 Write a suitable set of MODIFY operations to enforce primary key uniqueness for the suppliers-parts-projects database.

12.2 What are the main advantages of indexes? What are the main disadvantages?

12.3 "Uniqueness" of a field or field combination is a logical property, but it is enforced in INGRES by means of a particular storage structure, which is a physical construct. Discuss.

ANSWERS TO SELECTED EXERCISES

```
12.1   MODIFY S     TO BTREE UNIQUE ON SNO
       MODIFY P     TO BTREE UNIQUE ON PNO
       MODIFY J     TO BTREE UNIQUE ON JNO
       MODIFY SPJ   TO BTREE UNIQUE ON SNO, PNO, JNO
```

---

*Actually the initial storage structure for indexes depends on a parameter to the INGRES command; the explanation here assumes the default value for that parameter. See the RTI manuals for more information.

12.2 The advantages of indexes are as follows:

   (a) They speed up direct access based on a given value for the indexed field (combination). Without the index (or a hash), a sequential scan would be required.

   (b) They speed up sequential access based on the indexed field (combination). Without the index, a sort would be required.

   (c) In INGRES in particular, certain indexes serve to enforce certain uniqueness constraints.

The disadvantages are as follows:

   (a) They take up space in the database. The space taken up by indexes can easily exceed that taken up by the data itself in a heavily indexed database.

   (b) While an index may well speed up retrieval operations, it will at the same time slow down update operations. Any APPEND/INSERT or DELETE on the indexed table, or REPLACE/UPDATE on the indexed field (combination) will require an accompanying update on the index.

12.3 An unfortunate state of affairs. INGRES is not quite as data independent as it ought to be.

13

INGRES System Commands

13.1 INTRODUCTION

As mentioned in Section 12.1, INGRES provides a number of *system-level commands*—i.e., commands that operate at the level of the machine's operating system, instead of at the level of the INGRES DBMS per se. (Despite this fact, it is convenient to treat the commands in this, the "INGRES DBMS" part of the book.) Examples of such commands are CREATEDB, DESTROYDB, and SYSMOD. In this chapter we give a brief summary of the INGRES system commands, under the following headings:

1. Terminal Monitors

2. Preprocessors

3. Database utilities

4. Frontend subsystems

The categorization is a little arbitrary in places; some of the commands do not fit very neatly into any of the four groups identified above. Also, our descriptions of most of the commands are deliberately very sketchy; most optional parameters are simply ignored. However, we do describe a few of the commands at somewhat more length—particularly those in Category 3, the "database utilities" category, the discussion of which gives us an opportunity to complete our treatment of a few miscellaneous QUEL/

SQL features not previously dealt with in any detail (COPY, SAVE, WITH JOURNALING).

It is worth mentioning that the availability of the INGRES/MENU interface means that most of the Category 1 and 4 commands above do not usually need to be issued directly. See Chapter 15 or Section 2.3.

13.2 TERMINAL MONITORS

INGRES provides two Terminal Monitors, one for QUEL and one for SQL. Each supports interactive access to INGRES databases via its respective language. Each also provides certain additional facilities—e.g., a macro feature, the ability to edit query text, the ability to run "scripts" of multiple statements in batch mode, and so on (details beyond the scope of this book). The system-level command to invoke the Terminal Monitor is:

```
QUEL database
```

or

```
SQL database
```

(as applicable). *Note*: In earlier versions of INGRES, the QUEL command could alternatively be spelled "INGRES."

INGRES also provides two forms-based interfaces to the two Terminal Monitors, called IQUEL and ISQL, respectively. These interfaces can be invoked from INGRES/MENU (see Chapter 15).

13.3 PREPROCESSORS

INGRES provides QUEL and SQL preprocessors for the following host languages: Ada, BASIC, C, COBOL, FORTRAN, Pascal, and PL/I. They are invoked by the system-level command:

```
command  file
```

where "file" contains the program text to be preprocessed, and "command" is as indicated below:

host language	*EQUEL*	*Embedded SQL*
Ada	EQA	ESQLA
BASIC	EQB	ESQLB
C	EQC	ESQLC
COBOL	EQCBL	ESQLCBL
FORTRAN	EQF	ESQLF
Pascal	EQP	ESQLP
PL/I	EQPL	ESQLPL

For example, the command

```
EQCBL MYPGM
```

invokes the EQUEL/COBOL preprocessor on the program contained in the file MYPGM.

There is one additional command that should be mentioned in this section, the DCLGEN command. DCLGEN (usual pronunciation: "deckle gen") is intended for use in conjunction with ESQL programs (not EQUEL programs). Such programs may optionally contain special DECLARE TABLE statements for any INGRES table that they intend to process. For example, an ESQL program that operates on the suppliers table S might include the statement:

```
EXEC SQL DECLARE S TABLE
            ( SNO     CHAR(5)  NOT NULL,
              SNAME   CHAR(20) NOT NULL WITH DEFAULT,
              STATUS  SMALLINT NOT NULL WITH DEFAULT,
              CITY    CHAR(15) NOT NULL WITH DEFAULT )
END-EXEC
```

The purpose of the DECLARE TABLE statement is purely to make the program more self-documenting. It is obvious from the example that such statements are nothing more than a slight textual variation on the corresponding CREATE TABLE statements of SQL. The "declarations generator" DCLGEN will construct such DECLARE TABLE statements on the user's behalf. DCLGEN is invoked via the command

```
DCLGEN  language  database  table  file  structure
```

where "language" is the relevant host language, "database" and "table" between them identify the relevant INGRES table, "file" identifies a file to which the DCLGEN output is to be written, and "structure" is the name of a host-language structure that DCLGEN will also generate. For example, the command

```
DCLGEN COBOL S_SP_S S SFILE SREC
```

will cause DCLGEN to read the definition of the table S in the INGRES dictionary for database S_SP_P and generate both of the following:

- an ESQL DECLARE statement for that table;
- a corresponding COBOL declaration for a structure (the COBOL term is "record") the same shape as that table, to be used as a target for retrieval operations and/or a source for update operations against that table. The structure is called SREC.

These declarations are written into the file SFILE. They can be incorporated into an ESQL/COBOL program via the ESQL statement

```
EXEC SQL INCLUDE SFILE END-EXEC
```

13.4   DATABASE UTILITIES

DBDB Commands

The following commands operate on the database database (DBDB).

```
* ACCESSDB
```

ACCESSDB provides a forms-based interface by which the INGRES system manager can update information in the DBDB—for example, to specify that some user is allowed to create new databases, or to specify the valid locations for a given database (see Chapters 8 and 12).

```
* CATALOGDB
```

CATALOGDB provides a read-only forms-based interface to the DBDB. It allows the user to see a list of databases he or she owns (i.e., has created) or has access to, or to see the locations that are valid for a specified database.

```
* FINDDBS
```

FINDDBS can be used only by the INGRES system manager. Its purpose is to help in the process of reconstructing the DBDB after some disastrous error has occurred. For more information, see the RTI manuals.

Performance Commands

The following commands have to do with various aspects of database performance.

* OPTIMIZEDB

As explained in Chapter 2, the INGRES optimizer makes its optimization decisions on the basis of certain statistics that are kept in the INGRES dictionary. Some of those statistics (e.g., the number of tuples in each relation) are maintained continuously and are always up to date; others are updated only on request, because the overhead of maintaining them continuously would be too great. Those latter statistics are updated by OPTIMIZEDB. For each specified attribute of each specified relation, OPTIMIZEDB (a) counts the number of distinct values of that attribute, (b) determines the corresponding maximum and minimum values, and (c) constructs a histogram showing the number of times each distinct value appears. Such statistics are used by the optimizer for attributes that are referenced within a WHERE clause (only; they are not used for attributes that are referenced only within a target list and/or a SORT BY clause).

Every time a significant amount of update activity occurs on a given database, it is a good idea to follow that activity with an OPTIMIZEDB operation. It is also good practice to follow each OPTIMIZEDB by a SYSMOD operation (see Chapter 12).

* STATDUMP

The STATDUMP command produces a report showing the current values of the OPTIMIZEDB statistics in the dictionary.

* SYSMOD

See Chapter 12.

Recovery Commands

The following commands have to do with various aspects of database recovery.

* CKPDB

The CKPDB ("checkpoint database") command performs the necessary preparation for the recovery process that will be required if the database is subsequently destroyed (e.g., if a disk crash occurs). In other words, CKPDB "takes a checkpoint" of the current state of the specified database—i.e., it dumps the current contents of that database to a checkpoint file. It also invalidates all previous checkpoints for the database.*

CKPDB also turns journaling on or off (as specified by a command parameter) for the specified database. "Journaling on" means that update operations on tables created WITH JOURNALING (see Chapters 3 and 11) are automatically logged in a journal file; "journaling off" means that such updates are not logged (and hence that updates applied since the last checkpoint will not be recoverable in the event of a disk crash). The normal situation would be to have journaling turned on, but to specify WITH JOURNALING only for reasonably permanent (long-lived) tables.

```
* ROLLFORWARDDB
```

ROLLFORWARDDB should be invoked after a disk (hardware) crash has occurred. Its purpose is to reconstruct the database (a) by reloading it from the last checkpoint or (b) by redoing the updates from the journal since the last checkpoint or (c) by a combination of first (a) and then (b). Which of (a), (b), (c) applies depends on parameters to the ROLLFORWARDDB command.

```
* AUDITDB
```

AUDITDB reads the database journal (see the description of CKPDB above) and creates an audit trail in another file, in a form suitable for COPYing into an INGRES table. (That INGRES table can then be processed via normal INGRES facilities—e.g., via SQL SELECT statements. Note that COPY is the normal QUEL and SQL load/unload utility function.) The audit trail contains information regarding updates (additions, deletions, replacements) made since the last checkpoint; parameters specify the precise updates to be audited—e.g., updates before or after a specified time, on a specified table or on all tables, by a specified user or by all users, etc.

```
* PURGEDB
```

---

*The reader is cautioned that the term "checkpoint" is used in different systems with very different meanings.

PURGEDB is used to clean up a database by destroying obsolete tables. Obsolete tables are (a) temporary tables created by INGRES itself while processing certain other INGRES operations (e.g., certain aggregate operations)*, and (b) user-created tables whose expiration date has passed. When a user creates a new table, the expiration date for that table is set (by default) to "never." However, the QUEL/SQL SAVE operation—syntax:

```
SAVE table UNTIL month day year
```

—allows the user to establish an earlier expiration date for specific tables, if desired.

PURGEDB is invoked automatically during system restart after a system crash has occurred.

Miscellaneous Commands

```
* CREATEDB
```

See Chapter 12.

```
* DESTROYDB
```

See Chapter 12.

```
* COPYDB
```

QUEL and SQL provide a COPY statement whose purpose (as mentioned under AUDITDB above) is basically to serve as the INGRES load/unload utility. In other words, COPY allows the user to copy an operating system file into an INGRES table (load), or vice versa (unload). For full details of the COPY statement, the reader is referred to the RTI manuals.

The primary purpose of the COPYDB system-level command is to facilitate the copying of *entire databases* (though it can be used on individual tables also). It does this by creating two files—one (COPY.OUT) containing COPY statements to unload all tables (and indexes) out of the specified database, and another (COPY.IN) containing COPY statements to load

---

*INGRES normally purges such tables automatically. In the event of a system crash, however, it is possible that one or more such tables may be left in the database.

them all back in again. These two files can then be used in conjunction with the QUEL or SQL command to take one database and use it to construct another, possibly on a different system. For example, to copy the database OLD to another one NEW:

```
/* first create the necessary COPY statements    */
  COPYDB OLD
/* now execute the COPY statements in COPY.OUT    */
  QUEL OLD <COPY.OUT
/* finally execute the COPY statements in COPY.IN */
  QUEL NEW <COPY.IN


 * UNLOADDB
```

UNLOADDB is like COPYDB but supports the copying of views, security constraints, integrity constraints, and report definitions as well as base tables and indexes.

13.5 FRONTEND SUBSYSTEMS

The INGRES frontend subsystems are as follows (see Chapter 2):

- INGRES/MENU
- INGRES/QUERY: Query-By-Forms (QBF)
- INGRES/FORMS: Visual-Forms-Editor (VIFRED)
- INGRES/REPORTS: Report-Writer and Report-By-Forms (RBF)
- INGRES/GRAPHICS: Visual-Graphics-Editor (VIGRAPH)
- INGRES/APPLICATIONS: Applications-By-Forms (ABF)

They can be invoked by means of a variety of system-level commands, as follows.

- INGRES/MENU is invoked via the INGRES command (see Chapter 2 or Chapter 15). *Note*: In some versions of INGRES, the INGRES command is spelled RTINGRES.

- INGRES/QUERY is invoked by means of either the QBF command or the QUERY command. The QBF command supports both query definition and query execution (see Chapter 16); the QUERY command supports query execution only.

- INGRES/FORMS is invoked via the VIFRED command (see Chapter 17).

- INGRES/REPORTS is invoked via one of the commands REPORT, RBF, or SREPORT. Reports are written under the control of "report specifications," which are kept in the INGRES dictionary. Report specifications can be created either by means of the Report-Writer report specification language or by means of the forms-based interface invoked by the RBF command (see Chapter 18). The SREPORT command saves a report specification in the dictionary, and the REPORT command produces a report in accordance with such a saved specification; again, see Chapter 18.

- INGRES/GRAPHICS is invoked by means of either the VIGRAPH command or the RUNGRAPH command. The VIGRAPH command supports both graph specification and graph generation (see Chapter 19); the RUNGRAPH command supports graph generation only.

- INGRES/APPLICATIONS is invoked via the ABF command.

Finally, there are four further commands that must be mentioned: COPYFORM, COPYREP, COPYGRAPH, and COPYAPP. Briefly, these commands allow a given INGRES form, report specification, graph specification, or application (according to the command in question) to be copied from one database to another. Thus, for example, an application can be developed, tested, and debugged using Applications-By-Forms (ABF) on a test database, and then copied over to the production database via COPYAPP when it has reached operational status.

PART **III**

THE INGRES APPLICATION DEVELOPMENT SYSTEM

14

Visual Programming

14.1 INTRODUCTION

As explained in Chapter 2, the overall INGRES system can be regarded as consisting of several more or less distinct subsystems—a single "backend" subsystem, which is the INGRES DBMS per se, and an integrated set of "frontend" subsystems, which together constitute the INGRES *Application Development System*. See Fig. 14.1 (an expanded version of Fig. 2.1 from Chapter 2).

As the figure indicates, the INGRES Application Development System contains the following forms-based subsystems:*

- INGRES/MENU   — a forms-based frontend to the entire INGRES system

- INGRES/QUERY   — for data retrieval and update and data entry via forms

- INGRES/FORMS   — for form definition and editing via forms

---

*From the point of view of the backend, of course, the frontend subsystems are nothing more than built-in (i.e., RTI-provided) applications, as explained in Chapter 2. User-developed applications can also be regarded as INGRES frontends; see Chapter 20.

243

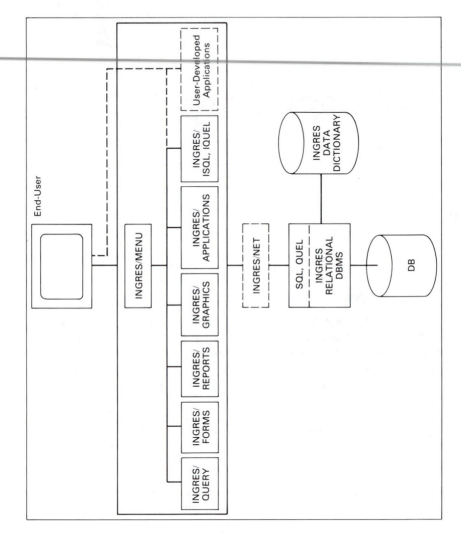

Fig. 14.1 Overall structure of INGRES

- INGRES/REPORTS   —   for forms-based report definition and report generation
- INGRES/GRAPHICS   —   for forms-based business graphics definition and graph generation
- INGRES/APPLICATIONS   —   for forms-based definition and testing of forms-based applications

This part of the book discusses the INGRES forms-based frontends in some detail. The present chapter provides some general background information concerning the overall process of interacting with forms-based applications—the process of "Visual Programming," as it is known in INGRES. Chapters 15–20 then go on to discuss the individual subsystems in depth.

One final preliminary remark: For obvious reasons, it is not really possible to include any Exercises or Answers sections in this part of the book. However, if the reader has access to an INGRES system, then we strongly recommend at least trying out some of the examples discussed in the text. There is no substitute for genuine hands-on experience.

14.2 FORMS AND FRAMES

Forms

As already explained, the INGRES frontend subsystems use *forms* to communicate with the user.* An INGRES form can be regarded as a display-screen version of an ordinary paper form. One advantage of such forms is that they can be used both for input and for output—i.e., both for entering data into the system and for displaying information to the user. A simple example of the use of a form is shown in Figs. 14.2–14.4 below. Figure 14.2 represents a possible "default form" (see Chapter 16) for the parts table P; Fig. 14.3 shows an INGRES/QUERY retrieval request expressed by means of that form; and Fig. 14.4 shows one of the retrieved records, displayed by means of that same form once again.

Now a little terminology. An INGRES form is made up of two kinds of component, "fields" and "trim." *Fields* are the portions of the form that are used for data entry and data display; *trim* is everything else. In the

---

*In this part of the book we will normally take the term "user" to refer to an *end-user* specifically.

```
|--------------------------------------------------------|
| TABLE IS p                                             |
|                                                        |
| pno:           pname:                    color:        |
|                                                        |
| weight:        city:                                   |
|                                                        |
|                                                        |
|--------------------------------------------------------|
```

Fig. 14.2 Default form for table P

```
|--------------------------------------------------------|
| TABLE IS p                                             |
|                                                        |
| pno:           pname:                    color: Red    |
|                                                        |
| weight: < 25    city:                                  |
|                                                        |
|                                                        |
|--------------------------------------------------------|
```

Fig. 14.3 Example of an INGRES/QUERY retrieval request:
            "Find all red parts weighing less than 25 pounds"

```
|--------------------------------------------------------|
| TABLE IS p                                             |
|                                                        |
| pno: P1      pname: Nut                  color: Red    |
|                                                        |
| weight: 12     city: London                            |
|                                                        |
|                                                        |
|--------------------------------------------------------|
```

Fig. 14.4 One of the records in response to the INGRES/QUERY
            request of Fig. 14.3

example of Figs. 14.2–14.4, there are five fields and a single piece of trim ("TABLE IS p"). In general:

- Each field, in turn, has three components—a *title*, a *data window*, and a set of *attributes*:

  - The *title* is the name of the field as it is displayed on the form. The titles in the example are "pno:", "pname:", "color:", "weight:", and "city:". Note that the title of a field in a form is not necessarily the same as the name of the corresponding field in the database; in fact, a corresponding field in the database might not even exist, as we will see in Chapter 17.

  - The *data window* is the space in which data values are actually displayed and/or entered.

  - The *attributes* represent internal control information. They govern such matters as the display format of data values as they appear in the data window, whether the user is allowed to change those values by overtyping, whether values are displayed in color or underlined or in reverse video, and so on. Attributes are "hidden from the user"—i.e., they do not appear as part of the field as displayed on the screen.

- Trim is used to make the displayed form more understandable and more usable. Such items as headings, comments, other explanatory text, displayed instructions to the user, etc., are all examples of trim.

Both fields and trim are discussed in more detail in Chapter 17.

Table Fields

INGRES forms frequently include *table fields*. A table field can be regarded as the display-screen analog of a *repeating group* (see Section 1.2 in Chapter 1); in other words, it consists of a single displayed field containing multiple displayed values (different numbers of values on different screens, in general). Table fields allow multiple rows and columns of data to be displayed and/or manipulated within the confines of a single form. An example of a form containing a table field (with some sample data values) is shown in Fig. 14.5. Table fields are discussed in detail in Chapter 17.

Frames

A *frame* is the combination of a form and a *menu*. The menu is a list of operations that may be executed using the form. An example is shown in Fig. 14.6. Note that the menu appears at the bottom of the frame (the standard position in INGRES).

```
|-----------------------------------------------------------------|
|                                                                 |
|  Supplier and parts supplied:                                   |
|                                                                 |
|  Supplier information:                                          |
|                                                                 |
|     supplier : S1                                               |
|     name     : Smith                                            |
|     status   : 20                                               |
|     city     : London                                           |
|                                                                 |
|  Shipments for supplier S1:                                     |
|                                                                 |
|              |part  |quantity|                                  |
|              |---------------|                                  |
|              |P1    |     300|                                  |
|              |P2    |     200|                                  |
|              |P3    |     400|                                  |
|              |P4    |     200|                                  |
|              |P5    |     100|                                  |
|              |P6    |     100|                                  |
|              |---------------|                                  |
|                                                                 |
|-----------------------------------------------------------------|
```

Fig. 14.5 Example of a form with a table field (with some sample values)

To select an operation from a menu, the user presses the terminal *menu key*,* then types the name of the required operation and presses the carriage return key. (Alternatively, the menu operations can be mapped to terminal PF keys, in which case they can be selected via a single keystroke.) After

```
|-----------------------------------------------------------------|
|                                                                 |
|  TABLE IS p                                                     |
|                                                                 |
|  pno: P1        pname: Nut                   color: Red         |
|                                                                 |
|                                                                 |
|  weight: 12        city: London                                |
|                                                                 |
|                                                                 |
|                                                                 |
|                                                                 |
|  Next    Append    Replace    Delete    Help    End :           |
|                                                                 |
|-----------------------------------------------------------------|
```

Fig. 14.6 Example of a frame (form plus menu)

---

*Which key serves as the menu key depends upon the specific terminal being used. It is the PF1 key on DEC VT100 terminals, the ESC (escape) key on most others.

executing the indicated operation, INGRES either displays the same frame again or moves on to another one, depending on the application. Numerous examples of this process appear throughout the next few chapters. *Note*: When selecting a menu option in practice, it is usually convenient not to type the entire operation name but merely enough leading characters of that name to be unambiguous (e.g., "H" for "Help").

By convention, every menu in INGRES includes a "Help" menu item, and usually an "End" menu item also (for returning to the previous frame). Selecting "Help" causes another frame to appear, with the following menu:

```
WhatToDo   Keys   Field   Help   End   :
```

Each of these options in turn causes a screen of help text to be displayed. "WhatToDo" produces text describing how to use the form; "Keys" produces text showing which keys on the keyboard (in particular, which PF keys) perform which functions; "Field" produces text tailored to the specific fields on the form; "Help" produces text describing the general help facilities; and "End" (as always) returns the user to the previous frame. Within any of these text screens, it is possible to scroll through the text, also to use the "Find" operation to search for occurrences of some specified string of characters. "Find" can be useful if the set of help text is very extensive and the user wishes to go straight to the portion dealing with some specific facility.

14.3 SCREEN CONTROL COMMANDS

INGRES provides a number of special control commands for moving the screen cursor around within a displayed form and performing other related functions. We summarize the most important ones below, just to give some idea of the range of commands available. *Note*: Details of these commands vary from terminal to terminal and from installation to installation; the ones shown below are the system defaults for the DEC VT100 terminal. The symbol ^ represents the terminal CTRL (control) key.

^H — Move cursor one space left

^L — Move cursor one space right

^J — Move cursor down one line
or scroll table field up one row

^K — Move cursor up one line
or scroll table field down one row

TAB — Move cursor to next field
        or to next column within a table field

^P — Move cursor to previous field
        or to previous column within a table field

^F — Scroll table field up one page*

^G — Scroll table field down one page

^N — Insert new empty row into a table field

^A — Repeat value in this field from previous screen

^E — Toggle between insert mode and overtype mode

^D — Delete character

^X — Clear field

RET — Clear rest of field to right of cursor

The functions of ^H, ^L, ^J, ^K can alternatively be performed by means of the cursor arrow keys on most terminals. In addition, it is possible to assign the functions of specific control commands (also of specific menu items, incidentally) to specific PF keys, and thereby make life a little easier for the user, but the details are beyond the scope of this text.

---

*A "page" here refers to the capacity of the table field (in terms of rows) as it is displayed on the screen.

15

INGRES/MENU

15.1 INTRODUCTION

As explained in Chapter 2, the entire INGRES system is presented to the user as a single integrated forms-based application, by virtue of the INGRES component called INGRES/MENU. INGRES/MENU is invoked by the command:

```
INGRES database
```

where "database" is the name of the required INGRES database. (As mentioned earlier, the INGRES command is spelled RTINGRES in some versions of the system.) INGRES responds by displaying the main INGRES/MENU frame, as shown in Fig. 15.1 (a repeat of Fig. 2.4; note that the major part of the form in that frame consists of a single large table field). The user can then perform any of the following operations:

1. Execute predefined queries (where "query" includes retrieval, update, and data entry operations)

2. Run predefined reports or graphs (i.e., generate reports or graphs in accordance with predefined report or graph specifications)

3. Define new reports via the Report-Writer

```
!--------------------------------------------------------------!
!                                                              !
! INGRES/MENU                              Database: s_sp_p    !
!                                                              !
! To run a highlighted command, place the cursor over it and   !
! select the "Go" menu item.                                   !
!                                                              !
! +---------+------------------------------------------------+ !
! |Commands |Description                                     ! !
! +=========+================================================+ !
! |QUERY    |RUN QUERY to retrieve, modify, or append data   ! !
! |REPORT   |RUN default or saved REPORT                     ! !
! |RUNGRAPH |RUN saved GRAPH defined by VIGRAPH              ! !
! |         |                                                ! !
! |QBF      |Use QUERY-BY-FORMS to develop/test query defns  ! !
! |RBF      |Use REPORT-BY-FORMS to design/modify reports    ! !
! |VIGRAPH  |Use VIGRAPH to design/modify/test graphs        ! !
! |ABF      |Use APPLICATIONS-BY-FORMS to design/test applicns! !
! |         |                                                ! !
! |TABLES   |CREATE, MANIPULATE, or LOOKUP tables in database ! !
! |VIFRED   |EDIT forms by using the VISUAL-FORMS-EDITOR     ! !
! |QUEL     |ENTER interactive QUEL statements               ! !
! |SQL      |ENTER interactive SQL statements                ! !
! |SREPORT  |SAVE REPORT-WRITER reports in the database      ! !
! +---------+------------------------------------------------+ !
!                                                              !
! Go  History  CommandMode  DBswitch  Shell  Help  Quit :      !
!                                                              !
!--------------------------------------------------------------!
```

Fig. 15.1 Main INGRES/MENU frame (slightly simplified)

4. Invoke any of the forms-based frontends INGRES/QUERY, INGRES/ FORMS, INGRES/REPORTS, INGRES/GRAPHICS, or INGRES/ APPLICATIONS

5. Invoke INGRES/ISQL or INGRES/IQUEL, the forms-based front-ends to the SQL and QUEL Terminal Monitors

6. Perform forms-based data definition operations

Items 1–4 in this list are the subject of the next few chapters (Chapters 16–20); items 5 and 6 are described in the remaining sections of the present chapter. The INGRES/MENU main frame menu—

```
Go  History  CommandMode  DBswitch  Shell  Help  Quit :
```

—is described below.

- *Go*: Invoke an INGRES/MENU function from the list in the body of the form (as indicated by the instructions at the top of the form; refer to Fig. 15.1).

- *History*: Obtain a list of the INGRES/MENU functions invoked since the start of the current INGRES session.

- *CommandMode*: Switch INGRES/MENU into "command mode," in which INGRES/MENU functions can be invoked by system-level commands as described in Chapter 13 instead of by using the INGRES/MENU main frame. Using the main frame is the normal mode of operation; command mode is primarily intended for more experienced users.

- *DBswitch*: Close the current database and open another (for further processing via INGRES/MENU).

- *Shell*: Escape to the operating system level, thus allowing the user to execute operating system commands. Logging out from the operating system will then return the user to INGRES/MENU. A good example of the use of this facility occurs in conjunction with the Report-Writer (see Chapter 18): The user might escape to the operating system level in order to create a report specification via the system text editor, then return to INGRES/MENU to compile that specification (via the SREPORT function) and produce the actual report (via the REPORT function).

- *Help*: See Section 14.2.

- *Quit*: Terminate INGRES/MENU and return control to the operating system.

15.2 TABLE UTILITIES

The INGRES/MENU table utilities are invoked by selecting "TABLES" from the list of functions on the INGRES/MENU main frame. The table utilities provide a forms-based interface for performing certain data definition (and related) operations—in QUEL terms, basically the operations of CREATE, DESTROY, and HELP, for base tables (only).

Selecting TABLES from the INGRES/MENU main frame leads to a frame such as that shown in Fig. 15.2. The table field in that frame contains a list of user tables in the database, together with the names of their owners. The cursor can be moved around within that table field via control commands as explained in Chapter 14; in addition, the menu items "Top," "Bottom," and "Find" allow quick movement to, respectively, the top or bottom of the table field or the position of a specified string of characters (e.g., the string "cjdate") within the table field. The "Help" and "End" options have their usual meanings; the "Create," "Destroy," and "Examine" options correspond respectively to the QUEL operations CREATE, DESTROY, and HELP (for base tables). "Destroy" and "Examine" are

```
!------------------------------------------------------------------!
!                                                                  !
! INGRES TABLE UTILITY                        Database: s_sp_p     !
!                                                                  !
!             +------------+------------+                          !
!             |Table Name  |Owner       |                          !
!             +------------+------------+                          !
!             |s           |cjdate      |                          !
!             |p           |cjdate      |                          !
!             |sp          |cjdate      |                          !
!             |            |            |                          !
!             |            |            |                          !
!             +------------+------------+                          !
!                                                                  !
! Create   Destroy   Examine   Find   Top   Bottom  Help   End :   !
!                                                                  !
!------------------------------------------------------------------!
```

Fig. 15.2 Table utility frame (example)

straightforward: In each case, the user simply positions the cursor on the row of the table field representing the desired table, then selects the required option from the menu, and the operation is then executed (in the case of "Examine," the output is displayed via another form). "Create" needs a little additional explanation, however. Selecting the "Create" option leads to the frame shown in Fig. 15.3.

This frame is largely self-explanatory; the user defines the new table by entering rows into the table field, giving the column names for the new table

```
!------------------------------------------------------------------!
!                                                                  !
! INGRES TABLE UTILITY                        Database: s_sp_p     !
!                      Creating a New Table                        !
!                                                                  !
! Enter the name of the new table:                                !
!                                                                  !
! Enter the column   +------------+------------+                  !
! specifications      |Column Name |Data Format |                 !
! of the new table:  +============+============+                  !
!                     |            |            |                  !
!                     |            |            |                  !
!                     |            |            |                  !
!                     |            |            |                  !
!                     |            |            |                  !
!                     +------------+------------+                  !
!                                                                  !
! InsertLine Delete Blank Move GetTableDef Save Find Top ...       !
!                                                                  !
!------------------------------------------------------------------!
```

Fig. 15.3 Frame for creating a new table

and their corresponding "data formats" (data types). The data types are specified in either QUEL or SQL, depending on whether QUEL or SQL is the default language for the installation (see the RTI manuals for details). The menu items have the following meanings:

- *InsertLine*: Add a new blank row to the table field in a specified position (to allow for the definition of another column).
- *Delete*: Delete a row from the table field.
- *Blank*: Clear the entire form.
- *Move*: Move a row of the table field to a different position.
- *GetTableDef*: Fetch the definition of an existing base table from the INGRES dictionary into the table field. This option makes it easy to create a new table whose definition is similar to that of some existing table (or some combination of existing tables).
- *Save*: Create the table in the database.

The remaining menu items—"Find," "Top," "Bottom," "Help," and "End" (the last two not shown for reasons of space)—have their standard meanings.

15.3 IQUEL AND ISQL

Interactive QUEL (IQUEL) and Interactive SQL (ISQL) are forms-based interfaces to the QUEL and SQL Terminal Monitors. They are invoked by selecting the QUEL or SQL option (as appropriate) from the INGRES/ MENU main frame. In this section we restrict our attention to ISQL only, for reasons of simplicity; of course, all of our discussions apply with only minor changes to IQUEL also.

Selecting SQL from the INGRES/MENU main frame leads to a frame such as that shown (with a sample query entered) in Fig. 15.4. The major part of that frame consists of a large single-column table field, which is used both for entry of the SQL statement(s) to be executed (*input mode*) and for display of any messages or results arising from execution of those statements (*output mode*). Since it is a table field, INGRES's usual control commands can be used to move around within it and to edit the text it contains. Figures 15.4 and 15.5 show, respectively, an example of the ISQL frame being used in each of the two modes (i.e., input mode and output mode). The menu items in each case are broadly self-explanatory, except as noted below.

```
|--------------------------------------------------------------|
|                                                              |
| Enter SQL Statements                      Database: s_sp_p   |
| +----------------------------------------------------------+ |
| | select s.sno, s.sname, s.status                          | |
| | from    s                                                | |
| | where   s.city = 'London'                                | |
| |                                                          | |
| |                                                          | |
| |                                                          | |
| |                                                          | |
| |                                                          | |
| +----------------------------------------------------------+ |
| Go  Resume  Complete  Blank  Edit  File  Help  Quit :        |
|                                                              |
|--------------------------------------------------------------|
```

Fig. 15.4 ISQL main frame (input mode)

```
|--------------------------------------------------------------|
|                                                              |
| End of Output                                 Line 1/13      |
| +----------------------------------------------------------+ |
| | >select s.sno, s.sname, s.status                         | |
| | >from    s                                               | |
| | >where   s.city = 'London'                               | |
| |                                                          | |
| |  |sno |sname |status|                                    | |
| |  |------------------|                                    | |
| |  |S1  |Smith |   20 |                                    | |
| |  |S4  |Clark |   20 |                                    | |
| |  |------------------|                                    | |
| |  End of Request -- 2 Rows                                | |
| |                                                          | |
| |                                                          | |
| +----------------------------------------------------------+ |
| Top  Bottom  File  Help  End :                               |
|                                                              |
|--------------------------------------------------------------|
```

Fig. 15.5 ISQL main frame (output mode)

The following menu items (all of them from input mode) require a little additional explanation:

- *Go*: Execute SQL statement(s) and display results immediately (contrast "Complete" below).

- *Resume*: Switch back to output mode and resume inspecting the current output (used after "End" has been selected in output mode to switch back to input mode).

- *Complete*: Execute SQL statement(s) but do not display results until processing is complete (contrast "Go" above).

- *Blank*: Clear the table field. *Note*: The "Blank" option appears as a standard item in numerous menus (an example has already been given in Fig. 15.3). Its purpose is always to erase all user-specified entries from the form, so that a new set of entries can then be made. We will not bother to repeat this explanation every time we encounter the "Blank" option in a menu.
- *Edit*: Invoke the system text editor to edit the statement(s) in the table field.
- *File*: Read statements from a specified file into the table field *or* write the contents of the table field into a specified file.

16

INGRES/QUERY

16.1 INTRODUCTION

INGRES/QUERY is a forms-based subsystem that permits users with no knowledge of QUEL or SQL to perform simple data manipulation operations (both retrievals and updates) on data stored in INGRES databases. A simple example of an INGRES/QUERY retrieval operation was shown in Section 14.2; refer back to that section if you need to refresh your memory on the basic idea. In this chapter we examine the facilities of INGRES/QUERY in somewhat more detail.

INGRES/QUERY consists of a single component, *Query-By-Forms* or QBF. QBF supports two basic functions: *join definition** and *query execution*, invoked from INGRES/MENU (somewhat confusingly) by the QBF option and the QUERY option, respectively. The query execution function was what was illustrated in Section 14.2 — i.e., it is the function that allows queries to be formulated and executed (and the results returned) by means of a predefined form. (*Note*: We follow standard QBF usage in referring to the operation as a query, though as already indicated QBF is not limited to read-only processing.) That predefined form, in turn, can be either of the following:

---

*Sometimes referred to—more accurately—as *query* definition.

1. a default form, built automatically by QBF;

2. a customized form, defined via the Visual-Forms-Editor VIFRED and identified to QBF by a "QBFName."

Which of the two cases applies in any given situation depends on a parameter specified by the user when query execution is invoked. The process of customizing forms via VIFRED is described in Chapter 17; default forms are described in the next section of the present chapter.

There are also two kinds of *query target*—that is, two kinds of object on which query execution can be performed in QBF:

1. *named tables* (base tables or views);

2. *join definitions* (abbreviated JoinDefs), created via the join definition function of QBF. A JoinDef can be regarded as an extended kind of *view** (in the usual relational sense of that term).

Which of the two cases applies in any given situation depends (again) on a parameter specified when query execution is invoked. JoinDefs are described in detail in Section 16.3. Note carefully that both named tables and JoinDefs can be accessed either by default forms or by customized VIFRED forms.

16.2 DEFAULT FORMS

If the user invokes the query execution phase of QBF and does not specify a customized form (via a "QBFName"), QBF automatically builds a *default* form for the query target. As explained in Section 16.1, that query target can be either a named table or a JoinDef. We consider the named table case first. The default form in this case can be either of two types, "single-row format" or "table-field format." An example of the first type is shown in Fig. 16.1 (which is basically a repeat of Fig. 14.2). As you can see, the form consists of a set of displayed fields, one for each field in the specified table, arranged on the screen top to bottom and left to right in accordance with the declared widths of those fields and named in accordance with their declared names. The declared widths and names are taken from the definition of the specified table in the dictionary, of course.

The second type of default form for a named table consists of a single

---

*The INGRES terminology is not very good here. It would be more accurate to say that a JoinDef corresponds to an extended kind of view *definition*—and hence that the query target (i.e., the object that can be queried) is the object *defined* by the JoinDef, not the JoinDef itself. But we will stay with the "official" terminology, in order to be consistent with the RTI manuals.

```
!-------------------------------------------------------------------!
!                                                                   !
!                   Query Target Name is p                          !
!                                                                   !
!  TABLE IS p                                                       !
!                                                                   !
!                                                                   !
!  pno:          pname:                      color:                 !
!                                                                   !
!                                                                   !
!  weight:       city:                                              !
!                                                                   !
!                                                                   !
!-------------------------------------------------------------------!
```

Fig. 16.1 Default form for table P (single-row format)

table field; for an example, see Fig. 16.2. Which of the two types is used
in a given situation depends once again on a parameter specified when query
execution is invoked.

  We turn now to the case in which the query target is a JoinDef. The
layout of the default form for a JoinDef depends in part on parameters
specified at the time the JoinDef is created (see Section 16.3). We give a
typical example here. Recall from the previous section that a JoinDef is
basically an extended kind of view (more properly, view *definition*). Suppose, therefore, that a JoinDef S_SP is created in which suppliers and shipments are joined over supplier numbers. Then the default form for this
JoinDef might look as shown in Fig. 16.3. As you can see, the form essen-

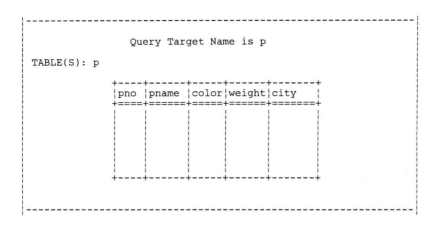

Fig. 16.2 Default form for table P (table-field format)

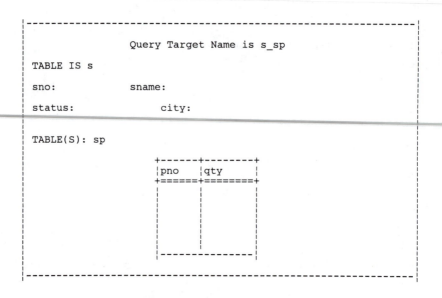

```
!---------------------------------------------------------------!
!                     Query Target Name is s_sp                 !
! TABLE IS s                                                    !
! sno:              sname:                                      !
! status:              city:                                    !
```

```
! TABLE(S): sp                                                  !
!                  +------+--------+                            !
!                  !pno   !qty     !                            !
!                  +======+========+                            !
!                  !      !        !                            !
!                  !      !        !                            !
!                  !      !        !                            !
!                  !      !        !                            !
!                  !      !        !                            !
!                  !--------------!                             !
!---------------------------------------------------------------!
```

Fig. 16.3 Default form for a JoinDef (example)

tially consists of a combination of a single-row-format default form for S (the suppliers table) and a table-field-format default form for SP (the shipments table)—except that the SNO (supplier number) field has been omitted from the display for SP.

16.3 JOIN DEFINITION

First it is necessary to explain exactly what is meant by the term "join" in the context of a QBF join definition (JoinDef). JoinDefs in QBF support two types of join, referred to as a Master/Master (or Detail/Detail) join and a Master/Detail join, respectively. For simplicity, we restrict our attention to the case of joins involving only two tables, though QBF actually permits any number of tables up to 10.*

- A Master/Master (or Detail/Detail) join is basically just an ordinary natural join (refer back to Chapter 4, Section 4.3, if you need an explanation of this term). As such, it does not include any rows from

---

*To be precise, a single group of Masters joined via Master/Master joins, together with—optionally—a single group of Details joined via Detail/Detail joins, the two groups then being joined via a single Master/Detail join.

either table that have no matching rows in the other. For example, if we created a Master/Master JoinDef between suppliers (the S table) and shipments (the SP table) over supplier numbers, and then used the QBF query execution function to examine that join, no row would appear for supplier S5, because supplier S5 does not currently supply any parts.

- A Master/Detail join, by contrast, is basically a *left outer* natural join* between the Master table and the Detail table (in that order). As such, it *does* include rows from the Master table that have no matching rows in the Detail table (but not the other way around). For example, if we created a Master/Detail JoinDef between the S table (Master) and the SP table (Detail) over supplier numbers, and then used the QBF query execution function to examine that join, a row would appear for supplier S5 even though supplier S5 does not currently supply any parts.

In general, a JoinDef (either type) has four principal components:

- a set of table specifications
- a set of join specifications
- a set of update/delete rules
- a set of display specifications

Aside: It is also possible to create a "join" definition involving just one table. In this way it is possible (a) to associate a permanent table-field-format default form with a named table, and/or (b) to eliminate unneeded fields of the named table from that form. See the subsections on join specification and display specification later in this section.

We now proceed to illustrate the process of join definition, using the case of a JoinDef between suppliers and shipments as the basis for our examples.

Table Specification

The tables to be joined are specified via a Table Entry form. An example is shown in Fig. 16.4. The example includes some sample entries—a JoinDef name, one Master table name, one Detail table name, and a request for table field format. This last item means that a single Master row will be displayed with all its corresponding Detail rows (in a table field) when the JoinDef is used with its default form. The optional range variable speci-

---

*See "The Outer Join," in *Relational Database: Selected Writings*, by C. J. Date (Addison-Wesley, 1986) for a formal definition of this term and many related terms.

```
|--------------------------------------------------------------|
| QBF - JoinDef Definition - Table Entry Form                  |
|                                                              |
| JoinDef Name: s_sp                                           |
|                                                              |
| Enter the table names and corresponding optional range       |
| variables in the tables below.                               |
|                                                              |
| Master Tables:                     Detail Tables:            |
| +------------+--------------+       +------------+--------------+ |
| |Table Name  |Range Variable|       |Table Name  |Range Variable| |
| +============+==============+       +============+==============+ |
| | s          |              |       | sp         |              | |
| |            |              |       |            |              | |
| |            |              |       |            |              | |
| |            |              |       |            |              | |
| +------------+--------------+       +------------+--------------+ |
|                   Table Field Format? (y/n): y               |
|                                                              |
| Select the "Go" menu item to run the Join Definition.        |
|                                                              |
| Go Blank ChangeDisplay Joins Rules Save Help End Quit :      |
|                                                              |
|--------------------------------------------------------------|
```

Fig. 16.4 The Table Entry form (example)

fications allow the user to introduce range variables to be used in place of the table names in the QUEL or SQL statements generated by QBF for operating on this JoinDef (necessary if the JoinDef involves a join of a table with itself, and possibly useful as a shorthand in other situations also).

The "ChangeDisplay," "Joins," and "Rules" menu options invoke the display, join, and rule specification phases, respectively, of the join definition process—see the next three subsections. "Save" creates the JoinDef and saves it in the dictionary. "Go" also creates the JoinDef but then invokes the QBF query execution function, so that the JoinDef can be immediately used or tested. The other menu items have the obvious meanings.

Join Specification

The join specifications are defined via a Join Specification form. An example is shown in Fig. 16.5 (a continuation of the example begun in Fig. 16.4). QBF automatically makes entries in this form to specify (a) the type of join—MD ("Master/Detail") in the example—and (b) a join condition involving equality matching over like-named columns—"S.SNO = SP.SNO" in the example. If QBF's default entries are exactly the ones required, which in practice they frequently will be, there is of course no need

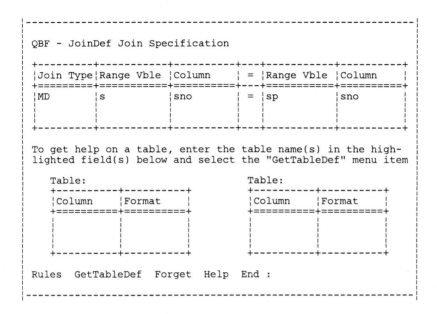

```
|-----------------------------------------------------------------|
| QBF - JoinDef Join Specification                                |
|                                                                 |
| +---------+-----------+-----------+---+-----------+-----------+  |
| |Join Type|Range Vble |Column     | = |Range Vble |Column     |  |
| +=========+===========+===========+===+===========+===========+  |
| |MD       |s          |sno        | = |sp         |sno        |  |
| |         |           |           |   |           |           |  |
| |         |           |           |   |           |           |  |
| +---------+-----------+-----------+---+-----------+-----------+  |
|                                                                 |
| To get help on a table, enter the table name(s) in the high-    |
| lighted field(s) below and select the "GetTableDef" menu item   |
|                                                                 |
|    Table:                            Table:                     |
|    +----------+----------+           +----------+----------+     |
|    |Column    |Format    |           |Column    |Format    |     |
|    +==========+==========+           +==========+==========+     |
|    |          |          |           |          |          |     |
|    |          |          |           |          |          |     |
|    |          |          |           |          |          |     |
|    +----------+----------+           +----------+----------+     |
|                                                                 |
| Rules   GetTableDef   Forget   Help   End :                     |
|-----------------------------------------------------------------|
```

Fig. 16.5 The Join Specification form (example)

to modify them. If they do need to be modified, however, then the two table fields in the lower half of the form can be used (in conjunction with the "GetTableDef" menu option) to display information regarding the columns of the tables to be joined, in order to assist in the process of deciding exactly what the join specifications should be. The other menu items (other than the obvious ones) have the following meanings:

- *Rules*: Invoke the rule specification phase.
- *Forget*: Cancel any changes made to the form, then same as "End."
- *End:* Save the join specifications and return to the previous frame.

Rule Specification

The rule specifications are defined via an Update/Delete Rules form. An example is shown in Fig. 16.6 (again a continuation of the S_SP example). The purpose of this form is to allow the JoinDef creator to specify the effect of QBF Update Mode operations—REPLACE and DELETE in QUEL terms, UPDATE and DELETE in SQL terms—on the JoinDef. (QBF Up-

```
|-----------------------------------------------------------------|
|                                                                 |
| QBF - JoinDef Update & Delete Rules                             |
|                                                                 |
| Update Information:                                             |
| +------------+------------+-------+                             |
| |Table Name  |Column Name |Update?|    To enable modification   |
| +============+============+=======+    of join field values in  |
| |s           |sno         |no     |    UPDATE Mode, enter "Yes" |
| |sp          |sno         |no     |    under Update? column.    |
| |            |            |       |                             |
| +------------+------------+-------+                             |
|                                                                 |
| Delete Information:                                             |
| +------+----------+----------+-------+                          |
| |Type  |Table Name|Range Vble|Delete?|  To disable deletion of  |
| +======+==========+==========+=======+  rows in a table during  |
| |Master|s         |s         |no     |  UPDATE Mode, enter "No" |
| |Detail|sp        |sp        |yes    |  under Delete? column.   |
| |      |          |          |       |                          |
| +------+----------+----------+-------+                          |
|                                                                 |
| Joins  Forget  Help  End :                                      |
|                                                                 |
|-----------------------------------------------------------------|
```

Fig. 16.6 The Update/Delete Rules form (example)

date Mode is discussed in Section 16.4.) For our example, the possibilities are as follows:

- REPLACE/UPDATE on field SNO: Can be allowed or disallowed; if allowed, the REPLACE/UPDATE can be applied to either or both of tables S and SP. Note that only one "SNO" field, not two, will be displayed when the JoinDef is used.

- REPLACE/DELETE on any other field: Always allowed.

- DELETE: Can be allowed or disallowed; if allowed, the DELETE can be applied to either or both of tables S and SP.

Note that adding new records, to either Master or Detail (APPEND in QUEL, INSERT in SQL), is always allowed. The effect of such additions is explained in Section 16.4.

Aside: Of course, all updates in INGRES, via QBF or otherwise, are always subject to the INGRES authorization rules. The user is never allowed to perform any operation that would violate such a rule.

Again QBF automatically makes entries in the form corresponding to certain frequent requirements—namely, "REPLACE (or UPDATE) not allowed" ("no" against both join fields in the Update Information table field), and "DELETE allowed, and applied to both tables" ("yes" against both tables in the Delete Information table field). If these entries are exactly the ones required, which they may or may not be in practice, there is of course no need to modify them. In the example, however, we have made one change to QBF's default specifications: DELETEs are to be applied to the Detail table (table SP) only. The menu options should be self-explanatory.

Display Specification

The default display specifications for the JoinDef—which control the layout of the default form for the JoinDef—are basically as defined by the "Table Field Format?" entry on the Table Entry form. However, the Change Display form allows the JoinDef creator to make a slight change to those specifications, namely by eliminating any unwanted fields from the display. (Note that join fields cannot be eliminated.) For details, see the RTI manuals.

16.4 QUERY EXECUTION

The query execution function of QBF has three modes: Append Mode, Retrieve Mode, and Update Mode.* The mode can be specified in a variety of ways—for example, by selecting an appropriate menu option from the query execution main frame. We discuss each mode in turn. Again we use the S_SP JoinDef as the basis for our examples. If the query target is in fact not a JoinDef but instead a single named table, and/or the display does not include a table field, some of the options to be discussed will not apply (and in some cases the menus will therefore be slightly different), but the overall principles illustrated are generally valid.

Append Mode

Append Mode is used to add new rows to existing tables. Invoking Append Mode for the S_SP JoinDef will lead to the frame shown in Fig. 16.7. (Of course, we are ignoring the possibility that a customized VIFRED form might be used in place of the default form.) The user can now enter field values for one new row in the suppliers table and any number of corre-

---

*Append and Update Modes cannot be used for views—though they *can* be used for JoinDefs.

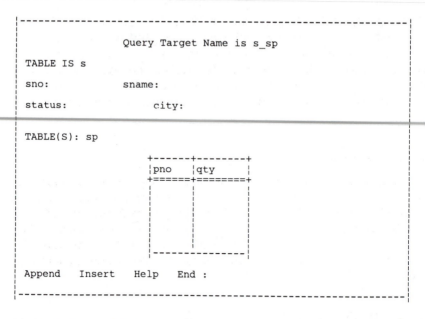

```
 ------------------------------------------------------------------
|                    Query Target Name is s_sp                      |
| TABLE IS s                                                        |
| sno:              sname:                                          |
| status:              city:                                       |
|                                                                  |
| TABLE(S): sp                                                     |
|               +------+---------+                                 |
|               |pno   |qty      |                                 |
|               +======+=========+                                 |
|               |      |         |                                 |
|               |      |         |                                 |
|               |      |         |                                 |
|               |      |         |                                 |
|               |      |         |                                 |
|               +---------------+                                  |
| Append   Insert   Help   End :                                   |
 ------------------------------------------------------------------
```

Fig. 16.7 Append Mode (example)

sponding new rows in the shipments table. The "Append" menu item will then cause the new rows to be added to the database. The "Insert" menu item is for creating a new empty row in the table field, to make room for a new Detail table row. *Note*: Adding a new Detail row for an *existing* Master record is done via Update Mode (see later).

After the "Append" has been successfully executed, QBF blanks out all fields on the form in preparation for a new set of values to be entered by the user.

We remark that QBF Append Mode provides the usual (and certainly the most convenient) method of performing data entry in INGRES. As soon as a new INGRES table has been created—probably via the table utilities of INGRES/MENU—QBF Append Mode can be used with the QBF default form for the table (either single-row format or table-field format) to load records into that table. We remind the reader also of the "control A" command (^A—see Section 14.3), which can be used to repeat the value of a given field from one screen to the next during this process—particularly useful for data entry, since it is frequently the case that each new record to be entered during data entry is rather similar to its predecessor.

Retrieve Mode

Retrieve Mode has two states, the Query state and the Go state. The Query state is used to formulate the desired query; the Go state is used to retrieve and browse through the result of executing that query. In the Query state, the user specifies the desired query by making entries in fields of the form in accordance with the following rules:

- The entry against a given field can be any combination of simple comparisons involving that field (and no other fields), constants, AND and OR operators, and parentheses—except that actual references to the field are elided, and the "=" comparison operator can optionally be elided also. String constants do not need to be enclosed in quotes. Here are some valid entries:

Field:	*Expression*:
city	Paris or London
city	<> Paris and <> London
city	*vill*
status	< 10 or (> 25 and < 55)

- Entries against distinct fields—all nontable fields and table fields also, if there are any—are assumed to be ANDed together.
- Entries in distinct rows of a table field are assumed to be ORed together.

Figure 16.8 is a QBF representation of the query "Find supplier and shipment information for suppliers with status greater than 15, located in London or Paris, who supply either part P1 or part P2 in a quantity greater than 150." For interest, an equivalent SQL formulation would be:

```
SELECT   S.SNO, S.SNAME, S.STATUS, S.CITY, SP.PNO, SP.QTY
FROM     S, SP
WHERE  ( S.STATUS > 15
AND      ( S.CITY = 'London' OR S.CITY = 'Paris' ) )
AND        S.SNO = SP.SNO
AND      ( ( SP.PNO = 'P1' AND SP.QTY > 150 ) OR
           ( SP.PNO = 'P2' AND SP.QTY > 150 ) )
```

The menu items have the obvious meanings, except as follows:

- *LastQuery*: Redisplay the previous query for further editing (useful if a query is very similar to the one before).
- *Order*: Specify an ordering for the result of the query (both for Master rows and for Detail rows within each Master row). The options available correspond basically to the options supported by the QUEL SORT

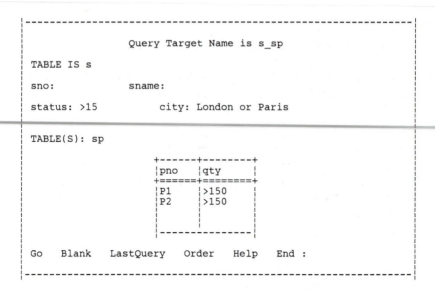

```
-----------------------------------------------------------------
|                Query Target Name is s_sp                      |
|  TABLE IS s                                                   |
|  sno:              sname:                                     |
|  status: >15           city: London or Paris                 |
-----------------------------------------------------------------
|  TABLE(S): sp                                                |
|                  +------+---------+                          |
|                  |pno   |qty      |                          |
|                  +======+=========+                          |
|                  |P1    |>150     |                          |
|                  |P2    |>150     |                          |
|                  |      |         |                          |
|                  |      |         |                          |
|                  |----------------|                          |
|  Go    Blank   LastQuery   Order   Help   End :              |
-----------------------------------------------------------------
```

Fig. 16.8 Retrieve Mode—Query state (example)

BY clause or the SQL ORDER BY clause; thus they allow ordering to be requested on the basis of any combination of fields, in any major-to-minor sequence (except that Master fields must precede Detail fields with respect to that sequence), with either ascending or descending ordering specified for each field. See the RTI manuals for details.

Selecting the "Go" option from the Query state menu causes the query to be executed and the Go state to be entered. Assuming that the user has specified ascending part number order within ascending supplier number order for the result, the first screen to be displayed will look like Fig. 16.9.

The "NextMaster" menu item will cause the next Master row and its corresponding Detail rows to be displayed. The "Query" option returns QBF to the Query state; the "End" option terminates QBF Retrieve Mode entirely. We remind the reader that if the set of shipments for a given supplier is too large to fit on the screen, then it is possible to scroll through the shipments table field while keeping the supplier information at the top of the screen unchanged (see Section 14.3).

Update Mode

Like Retrieve Mode, Update Mode has two states, the Query state and the Go state. The Query state is identical to the Query state of Retrieve Mode.

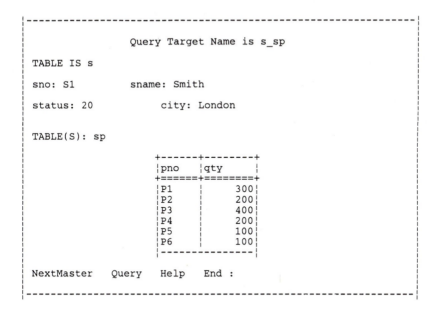

```
| -------------------------------------------------------------- |
|                                                                |
|                   Query Target Name is s_sp                    |
|                                                                |
| TABLE IS s                                                     |
|                                                                |
| sno: S1          sname: Smith                                  |
|                                                                |
| status: 20             city: London                           |
|                                                                |
|                                                                |
| TABLE(S): sp                                                   |
|                    +------+--------+                           |
|                    |pno   |qty     |                           |
|                    +======+========+                           |
|                    |P1    |    300 |                           |
|                    |P2    |    200 |                           |
|                    |P3    |    400 |                           |
|                    |P4    |    200 |                           |
|                    |P5    |    100 |                           |
|                    |P6    |    100 |                           |
|                    |--------------|                           |
|                                                                |
| NextMaster   Query   Help   End :                              |
|                                                                |
| -------------------------------------------------------------- |
```

Fig. 16.9 Retrieve Mode—Go state (example)

The Go state is used to display the result of executing queries specified in the Query state, and also (of course) to make changes—i.e., replacements and deletions—to that data. By way of example, consider Fig. 16.10, which is an example of a Go state display for QBF Update Mode (actually it is identical to Fig. 16.9, except for the menu).

Replacing existing data is done by simply typing new values over the old ones on the screen. New Detail records can be created in the same way, by simply typing in values in a new row in the table field after all existing rows. *Deleting* existing data is a little more complicated, however. Selecting the "Delete" option from the menu leads to another menu, as follows:

```
Master   AllRows   Row   Help   End :
```

The "Master" option causes the current Master record and all its corresponding Detail rows to be deleted. The "AllRows" option causes all current Detail rows to be deleted. The "Row" option causes just the Detail row on which the cursor is currently positioned to be deleted.

Note carefully, however, that the replacements and deletions are not

```
:-----------------------------------------------------------------:
:               Query Target Name is s_sp                         :
:  TABLE IS s                                                     :
:  sno: S1          sname: Smith                                  :
:  status: 20          city: London                              :
:                                                                 :
:  TABLE(S): sp                                                   :
:                +------+---------+                               :
:                :pno   :qty      :                               :
:                +======+=========+                               :
:                :P1    :     300 :                               :
:                :P2    :     200 :                               :
:                :P3    :     400 :                               :
:                :P4    :     200 :                               :
:                :P5    :     100 :                               :
:                :P6    :     100 :                               :
:                :----------------:                               :
:                                                                 :
:  NextMaster   Query   Delete   Save   Help   End :              :
:-----------------------------------------------------------------:
```

Fig. 16.10 Update Mode—Go state (example)

actually applied to the database until the user selects the "Save" menu item on the Go state display. The most efficient method of using QBF for updating is to perform all required changes on the data currently displayed, then move on to the next record, make all required changes to it, and so on, and finally issue "Save" to apply all requested changes to the actual data.

Note: If the query target is a JoinDef, it is possible that a requested change will have no effect because of the update/delete rules specified when that JoinDef was defined. It is the user's responsibility to be aware of the changes that QBF will honor.

16.5 CONCLUSION

It should be apparent from everything that has been said in this chapter so far that QBF allows simple forms-based applications to be created very simply. Indeed, through its JoinDef facility, QBF allows the simple forms-based *creation* of reasonably powerful applications that are themselves forms-based in turn. It can fairly be claimed, in fact, that most data entry requirements, most ad hoc retrieval requirements, and many update requirements, can all be handled by the "basic" QBF facilities described in this chapter. But of course some applications do require more sophisticated facilities. For example, some applications require more complex screen layouts; some require certain validation or integrity checks to be applied to data entered by the application user; and so on. However, it may still be possible to build those applications without having to resort to application programming in the conventional sense (COBOL, EQUEL, EQUEL/ FORMS, and the like). The facilities of the Visual-Forms-Editor (VIFRED), discussed in the next chapter, make it possible to build QBF applications that are much more sophisticated than those supported by the "basic" QBF facilities described in this chapter. Thus, the topic of Chapter 17 can be seen as a natural follow-on to the material we have been discussing in the present chapter.

17

INGRES/FORMS

17.1 INTRODUCTION

INGRES/FORMS is a forms-based subsystem that supports the creation of forms for use with the query execution function of QBF or with user-developed applications (i.e., applications built by means of EQUEL/ FORMS or ESQL/FORMS or INGRES/APPLICATIONS—see Chapters 10, 11, and 20, respectively). In the case of QBF, INGRES's default forms will often be adequate for the task at hand; however, as indicated at the end of Chapter 16, there are bound to be some situations in which it is necessary to use some kind of specially customized form instead of the QBF default. In the case of user-written applications, of course, the question of defaults does not arise; customized forms are obviously mandatory for such applications. In this chapter we examine the process of building customized forms in some detail.

INGRES/FORMS consists of a single component, the *Visual-Forms-Editor* or VIFRED. The major purpose of VIFRED is to support the creation of new forms, either from scratch or by editing some existing form. (*Note*: In the latter case, the existing form may be—and very often will be—one of the default forms created by QBF.) Once created, the new form can be used with any number of applications (in general) and with any number of tables (again in general); indeed, it is very desirable that related applications and/or tables use the same form, for reasons of consistency and usability.

Consider the sample forms shown in Chapter 16 in conjunction with the query execution function of QBF (Section 16.4). In all of those examples, there was an obvious correspondence between fields on the form and fields in the database. *It is important to understand, however, that such a correspondence is not an essential aspect of forms in general.* Basically, a form is just an interface to some application program. To that program, the fields in the form are basically just named positions on the screen; the program may display output values at those positions and/or retrieve input values from those positions, but whether those values are derived from the database in the case of output, or stored in the database in the case of input, is completely up to the application program in question. In other words, any correspondence between fields on the form and fields in the database must be established by application program logic. In the case of the forms mentioned above, there is such a correspondence, because the application program in question—namely, the query execution portion of QBF—establishes it. As a counterexample, consider the case of the forms used for QBF join definition (see, e.g., Fig. 16.4), where no such correspondence exists.*

It follows from the foregoing that it is not the connexion (if any) between the form and the database that is significant in a forms-based application, but rather the connexion between the form and the application program. How is that connexion established? The answer is as follows:

- First, each form has a name (specified when the form is "saved" via VIFRED—see Section 17.2). When the application program executes, it invokes the form by that name (e.g., via the FORMINIT operation; see Section 10.6).

- Second, each field on the form has an associated *internal field name* (specified as part of the field definition—see Section 17.4), by which the field can be referenced by the application program. The internal field name may or may not be the same as the name, or rather *title*, by which the field is known to the application user. (A field's title can be regarded as the field's *external* name.)

It should also be clear from the foregoing that there need not be any obvious correspondence between the name of the form and the name of a

---

*On the other hand, of course, there *is* a correspondence between the fields of those join definition forms and fields of the *dictionary*.

table in the database, nor between the title of a field on the form and the name of a field in the database (see Fig. 17.1). Indeed, it would be perfectly possible, though perhaps unusual, to develop a forms-based application that did not access the database at all.

17.2 THE CURSOR MENU

VIFRED is invoked from INGRES/MENU via the VIFRED option. This option leads directly to the VIFRED top frame, which displays a list (actually a table field) of existing forms and a menu that includes options to destroy, edit, or rename any of those existing forms or to create a new form. Choosing the "Create" option leads to the following menu:

```
BlankForm    TableDefault    JoinDefDefault    Help    End :
```

Each of "BlankForm," "TableDefault," and "JoinDefDefault" creates a new form that can subsequently be customized via the VIFRED editing process: "BlankForm" creates a completely empty form, "TableDefault" creates a default form for a specified table (or for several specified tables in combination), and "JoinDefDefault" creates a default form for a specified JoinDef. In all three cases VIFRED then displays the created

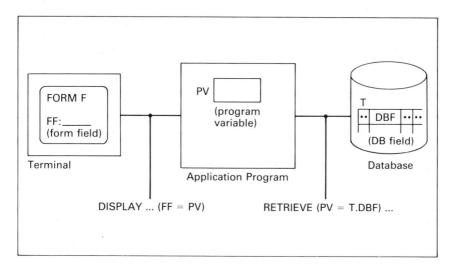

Fig. 17.1 Form vs. application program vs. database

form with the *cursor menu*.* This menu, which is really VIFRED's main menu, is also displayed (with the form to be edited) if the user selects the "Edit" option from the VIFRED top frame.

By way of example, suppose we specify the "Create" option, followed by the "TableForm" option and (in response to a VIFRED prompt) "table P." VIFRED responds with the frame shown in Fig. 17.2. The form in that frame is basically the QBF default form for table P, except that (a) each field includes a "picture" of its data window, consisting of a data format code ("C" or "I" in the example) and a string of underscore characters of an appropriate length, and (b) the form terminates in a special "End-of-Form" line, which will move up or down the screen as the form contracts or expands during the editing process.

As Fig. 17.2 illustrates, the cursor menu offers the following options:

```
Create  Delete  Edit  Move  Undo  Order  Save  ... :
```

A brief description of these options will serve to indicate the range of facilities provided by VIFRED.

```
|--------------------------------------------------------------|
| TABLE IS p                                                   |
|                                                              |
| pno: c_____   pname: c_____   color: c_____|
|                                                              |
| weight: i_____    city: c_____                   |
|                                                              |
| ---------End-of-Form--------------------End-of-Form--------- |
|                                                              |
| Create Delete Edit Move Undo Order Save Help End Quit :      |
|--------------------------------------------------------------|
```

Fig. 17.2 Default form for table P, with the cursor menu

---

*So called because its functions are very much bound up with the positioning of the cursor on the screen. Editing forms in VIFRED is a highly visual process, in keeping with the general idea of Visual Programming. For example, to move a form component from one location to another, the user uses the cursor to identify the component to be moved, selects the "Move" menu item, then uses the cursor again to identify the target location. VIFRED is a "what you see is what you get" editor (WYSIWYG, pronounced "whizzy wig").

- *Create*: Create a new form component—trim, a blank line, a field, or a table field. (Recall from Chapter 14 that forms are made up of fields and "trim." Trim consists of character strings—instructions, legends, explanatory text, etc.— that are used to make the form more readable. The string "TABLE IS p" in Fig. 17.2 is a simple example of trim.)

- *Delete*: Delete an existing form component.

- *Edit*: Edit an existing form component (see Sections 17.3 and 17.4).

- *Move*: Move an existing form component from one location to another (again, see Sections 17.3 and 17.4).

- *Undo*: Undo the previous operation on the form.

- *Order*: Specify a "tabbing order" for fields on the form (i.e., the sequence in which fields will be accessed via repeated use of the TAB key when the form is used). The default sequence is top to bottom, left to right. Note that display-only fields (see Section 17.4) do not participate in the tabbing order at all.

- *Save*: Save the form definition in the dictionary under a specified form name. *Note*: If the form is to be used with QBF, the "Save" menu option permits the specification of a "QBFName" by which the form may be invoked from QBF. Each QBFName corresponds to the use of a particular form with a particular table or JoinDef; since the same form can be used with several distinct tables (or JoinDefs), the same form may be invoked via several distinct QBFNames.

One final point: All form components in INGRES are *rectangular*. Furthermore, distinct components (i.e., distinct rectangles) are not allowed to overlap. If the user attempts to move a component to a position where it would overlap with one or more existing components, VIFRED will make the requested move, but will also automatically reposition those existing components as necessary in order to avoid the overlap. If this automatic rearranging is not to the user's taste, it is always possible either to "Undo" the move or to perform further moves to compensate.

17.3 EDITING TRIM

In this section and the next we use the term "editing" to include all of the operations of creation, deletion, moving, and modification of form components (trim and fields). We deal with trim first because it is simpler. A trim component can be any string of characters that is wholly contained within a single line on the form; thus, for example, a two-line title actually consists of two separate form components—i.e., two separate pieces of trim.

Creating Trim

The "Create" option in the cursor menu leads to the following submenu:

```
Trim    Field    TableField    Line    Help    End :
```

The "Line" option creates a new blank line immediately above the line the cursor is currently positioned on. The "Trim" option causes VIFRED to prompt for text for the desired trim, and inserts that text starting at the point the cursor is currently positioned on. The "Field" and "TableField" options are discussed in Section 17.4.

Moving Trim

To move a trim component, the user positions the cursor on that component and selects the "Move" option from the cursor menu. A submenu is then displayed, with options to move the trim left or right or to center it on the line or to move it to another place on the form entirely.

Modifying Trim

To modify a trim component, the user positions the cursor on that component and selects the "Edit" option from the cursor menu. The trim can then be modified simply by overtyping.

Deleting Trim

To delete a blank line or trim component, the user positions the cursor on that line or component and selects the "Delete" option from the cursor menu.

17.4 EDITING FIELDS

Recall from Chapter 14 that a field on a form has three components: a title, a data window, and a set of attributes. As explained in Section 17.1, the title is the name of the field as it is displayed on the form (*not* the field's internal name); the data window is the space in which data values are actually displayed and/or entered; and the *attributes* represent internal control information, governing such matters as the display format of data values as they appear in the data window, whether the user is allowed to change those values by overtyping, whether values are displayed in color or in reverse video, and so on. Attributes are "hidden from the application user"—i.e., they are not explicitly displayed on the screen. We are now in a position to amplify these ideas.

Title

Most fields have a title or external name (though untitled fields are possible). The internal name defaults to the external name if no new internal name is specified (see the subsection "Attributes" below).

Data Window

The data window for each field includes a *format specification*, indicating how values will be displayed in the field. The permitted format specifications and their meanings are as follows:

Format:	*Data displayed as*:
Cn[.w]	string of not more than n characters, not more than w characters per line
Iw	integer of not more than w digits
Fw[.d]	fixed point number of not more than w digits, with decimal point d digits from the right
Ew[.d]	floating point number of w digits precision, with decimal point d digits from the right
Gw[.d]	same as Fw[.d] if room, else same as Ew[.d]

Format C is used for string and date data types, the other formats are used for numeric and money data types. In all cases, the format specification can optionally be preceded by a plus or minus sign (meaning that values are to be displayed right- or left-justified, respectively, within the field); minus (left) is the default.

Attributes

The attributes of a field consist of the field's internal name, an optional validation check and associated message, and a set of display attributes. Of these, the internal field name has already been discussed. The *validation check* is a predicate to be applied to values entered into the field by the application user; the *message* is a message to be displayed if the validation check fails. The validation predicate can involve the field under consideration, other fields from the same form, constants (including the special partial-match comparison characters), the usual scalar comparison operators, the Boolean operators AND, OR, and NOT, and parentheses. It can also include the special comparisons

```
field  IN  list
```

(where "list" is a comma-separated list of constants enclosed in square brackets), and

```
field  IN  table.column
```

(where "table" is a table in the database and "column" is a column of that table). Examples:

```
/* in a form for table P : */
CITY  IN  ["London", "Rome", "Paris", "New York", "Athens" ]

/* in a form for table SP : */
SNO   IN  S.SNO
```

The first of these examples means that the only valid part cities are the ones listed; the second means that any value entered for the supplier number field in the SP table must already exist as a value for the supplier number field in the S table. Note, therefore, that the second of these formats effectively provides a limited amount of referential integrity support (see Appendix B). A limitation is that the check is applied only against the set of values in "table.column" *at the time the form is initialized* (i.e., at FORMINIT time; see Section 10.6). Thus, e.g., if the application inserts supplier S6 into the S table and then tries to insert a shipment for supplier S6 into the SP table, that second insert will fail.

Display Attributes

The possible display attributes are as follows. They are mostly self-explanatory, except as noted.

- Box Field (draw a box around the field)
- Keep Previous Value (display the value entered into the field on the previous form)
- Mandatory Field (user must enter a value)
- Reverse Video
- Blinking
- Underline

- Brightness Change
- Query Only (user can type a value into the field only in Query state)
- Force Lower Case (upper case automatically converted)
- Force Upper Case (lower case automatically converted)
- No Auto Tab (reaching the end of the field on data entry does not cause an automatic tab to the next field)
- No Echo (data entered in the field is not displayed)
- Display Only (user cannot type a value into the field at all)
- Color

Creating Fields

As explained under "Creating Trim" in the previous section, the "Create" option in the cursor menu leads to the following submenu:

```
Trim   Field   TableField   Line   Help   End :
```

The "Field" option creates a new field at the point the cursor is currently positioned on. A new menu is displayed:

```
Title   Data   Attributes   Forget   Help   End :
```

The "Title" option causes VIFRED to prompt for the title of the new field—for example, "Part Quantity:". The "Data" option allows the specification of the format for the new field—for example, "I4". The "Attributes" option leads to the Attribute form (see Fig. 17.3); entries in that form are straightforward.

Moving Fields

Moving a field is very similar to moving a trim component (as with a trim component, it involves the "Move" menu item), except that options are provided to move the title and the data window separately. For example, the title could be moved to a position above the data window on the form. Otherwise, the process is basically as described in Section 17.3.

Modifying Fields

To modify a field, the user positions the cursor on that field and selects the "Edit" option on the cursor menu. VIFRED then displays the "Field Edit" menu, which provides separate options for modifying the field title and/or

```
|-------------------------------------------------------------------|
|                                                                   |
| VIFRED - Attributes for Field                                     |
| +--------------------+---+                                        |
| |Attribute           |Set|   Default Value for Field:             |
| +====================+===+                                        |
| |Box Field           |n  |                                       |
| |Keep Previous Value |n  |   Internal Name for Field              |
| |Mandatory Field     |n  |   (12 characters only):                |
| |Reverse Video       |n  |                                       |
| |Blinking            |n  |                                       |
| |Underline           |n  |   Validation Check on Field:           |
| |Brightness Change   |n  |                                       |
| |Query Only          |n  |                                       |
| |Force Lower Case    |n  |                                       |
| |Force Upper Case    |n  |                                       |
| |No Auto Tab         |n  |                                       |
| |No Echo             |n  |                                       |
| |Display Only        |n  |   Validation Error Message:            |
| |END OF ATTRIBUTES   |   |                                       |
| +--------------------+---+                                        |
|                                                                   |
|                              Color: 0                             |
|                                                                   |
|                                                                   |
| Next    Previous    Help    End :                                 |
|                                                                   |
|-------------------------------------------------------------------|
```

Fig. 17.3 The Attribute form

format specification and/or display attributes. The actual modification is done (as usual) by simple overtyping.

Deleting Fields

To delete a field, the user positions the cursor on that field and selects the "Delete" option from the cursor menu (the process is identical to that for deleting any other kind of component—see Section 17.3).

Table Fields

VIFRED provides facilities analogous to those already discussed for the creation, movement, modification, and deletion of table fields. The details are beyond the scope of this text.

17.5 UTILITY FUNCTIONS

The VIFRED top frame includes one menu item not so far discussed, the "Utilities" option. Selecting the "Utilities" option leads to the following menu:

```
Compile   Print   QBFNames   Help   End :
```

The "QBFNames" option has already been discussed (tacitly) under "Save" in Section 17.2. The "Compile" and "Print" options are described briefly below.

- *Compile*: Generate a file containing a set of operating system macro statements representing the definition of the specified form. Those statements can subsequently be compiled (via an appropriate operating system command), and the resulting code linked into the EQUEL or ESQL program that needs to use the form. That program can then use ADDFORM instead of FORMINIT to initialize the form at run time. ADDFORM is much faster than FORMINIT.

- *Print*: Generate a file containing a "picture" of the specified form that is suitable for printing on a line printer (useful for application documentation purposes).

18

INGRES/REPORTS

18.1 INTRODUCTION

The term "report" is used to mean a set of formatted output from the database, displayed on the terminal screen or printed via the line printer ("hard copy"). Several examples of reports are shown later in this chapter. INGRES/REPORTS is the INGRES subsystem that supports the production of such reports; it consists of two components, the *Report-Writer* and *Report-By-Forms* (RBF), invoked from INGRES/MENU by the REPORT option and the RBF option, respectively. Briefly:

- The Report-Writer is the component that actually creates the displayed or printed report. The detailed content and layout of the report are controlled by means of a *report specification*.

- Report-By-Forms is used to create report specifications. "Report-By-Forms" is thus something of a misnomer, since the component does not actually produce any reports per se; instead, it produces report *definitions* (i.e., report specifications). RBF is really a (forms-based) forms *editor*, much like VIFRED—except that the forms that RBF is designed to edit are, specifically, the forms that make up a report specification, as will shortly be made clear.

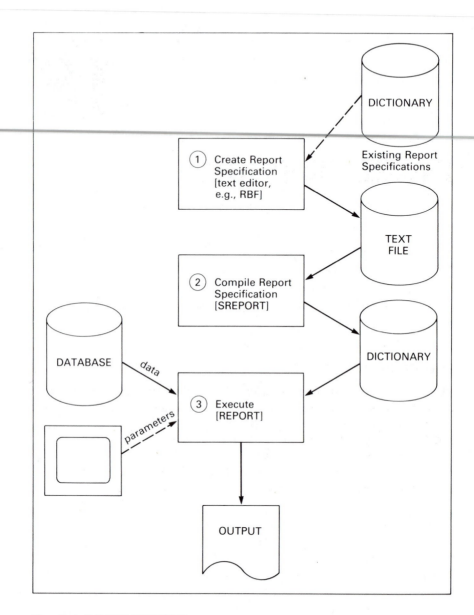

Fig. 18.1 INGRES/REPORTS

Figure 18.1 shows in outline the steps involved in producing an INGRES report.

Explanation:

1. Report specifications are created by means of an appropriate editor— either a conventional text editor or (perhaps more simply) RBF. In either case the new report specification can be generated by modifying one that already exists.

2. Once created, the report specification is compiled and saved in the INGRES dictionary. This function is performed via the SREPORT option of INGRES/MENU. SREPORT can also be invoked directly from RBF.

3. The Report-Writer (invoked via the INGRES/MENU REPORT option) reads the compiled report specification from the dictionary, the data from the database, and (optionally) parameters from the terminal, and generates the required report.

Note: It is possible to bypass Steps 1 and 2 and invoke the Report-Writer directly, specifying just the name of the table (possibly a view) from which the report is to be produced. In this case, INGRES automatically generates a *default* report specification for the specified table, so in fact there is always a report specification (default or user-generated) to control the details of how the finished report will look. The report produced by means of a default report specification is called a *default report*. We shall have more to say on default reports in Section 18.2.

18.2 DEFAULT REPORTS

Suppose it is desired to produce a report showing supplier cities, suppliers in those cities, the parts they supply, and the corresponding quantities. Suppose too that an appropriate table (actually a view) exists containing precisely the required information:

```
DEFINE VIEW CITYSHIPS
     ( CITY      = S.CITY,
       SUPPLIER  = S.SNO,
       PART      = SP.PNO,
       QUANTITY  = SP.QTY )
     WHERE S.SNO = SP.SNO
```

Invoking the Report-Writer on view CITYSHIPS, using the INGRES default report specification facility, will produce a report looking something like that shown in Fig. 18.2.

```
!-----------------------------------------------------------------!
| 18-JAN-87                                            11:41:19   |
|                 Report on Table: Cityships                     |
|                                                                |
|   City            Supplier          Part           Quantity    |
|                                                                |
|   London          S1                P1                 300     |
|                   S1                P2                 200     |
|                   S1                P3                 400     |
|                   S1                P4                 200     |
|                   S1                P5                 100     |
|                   S1                P6                 100     |
|                   S4                P2                 200     |
|                   S4                P4                 300     |
|                   S4                P5                 400     |
|   Paris           S2                P1                 300     |
|                   S2                P2                 400     |
|                   S3                P2                 200     |
|                                                                |
|                            - 1 -                               |
!-----------------------------------------------------------------!
```

Fig. 18.2 A default report

Explanation: The report consists of a single page. That page in turn consists of:

- a page heading line, containing the date and time;
- a title ("Report on Table: Cityships," underlined);
- a set of column headings, underlined (see below);
- a set of data lines;
- a page footing line, containing the page number.

The column headings (which are the same as the names of the columns as given in the INGRES dictionary) appear left to right across the page in the order in which the columns appear in their containing table. That latter order is significant, because by default it determines the sort order for the data lines in the body of the report—in the case at hand, supplier sequence within city sequence. In general, the sort order for a default report is defined to be ascending values of the second column within ascending values of the first column. Also, values are displayed for the first column only when a value change occurs in that position (i.e., when a "control break" occurs in that position).

Control Breaks

As just indicated, a value change in a column that is being used to control the sequence of data lines in the report is known as a control break. The concept of control breaks is an extremely important one in report writing, because (as we shall see later) it is possible to specify a variety of special actions to be performed when such a break occurs. In addition to the "value change" kind of control break just mentioned, control breaks are also considered to occur:

- at the beginning of the report;
- at the end of each page of the report (a "page break");
- at the end of the report.

18.3 REPORT-BY-FORMS

Default reports are adequate in many cases, but sometimes it is desirable to produce a report that is more carefully tailored to some specific requirement. Tailored reports require a user-generated report specification. User-generated report specifications can be created in two ways:

(a) They can be created interactively through RBF. This is probably the simpler method, though not necessarily the more efficient.

(b) They can be created using the Report-Writer's "report specification language," which does provide certain additional facilities not supported under method (a) but which also requires some degree of conventional programming expertise.

Of course, the basic advantage of using RBF is precisely that (like VIFRED) it is a *visual* editor. That is, the process of defining the report specification consists of screen-based interaction with an RBF picture of the current layout of the report; components of that picture can be created, moved, deleted (etc.) by means of menu options and appropriate cursor operations, very much as in VIFRED. By contrast, using the Report-Writer's report specification language is more akin to writing a program in a conventional programming language such as COBOL or PL/I. In this section we take a look at what is involved in constructing report specifications via RBF; the Report-Writer's report specification language is discussed in Section 18.4.

RBF is invoked from INGRES/MENU via the RBF option. This option leads directly to the RBF top frame, which displays a list of existing report specifications and a menu that includes options to destroy, edit, or rename any of those existing specifications or to create a new one. Choosing the "Create" option causes RBF to prompt for the name of an existing table (possibly a view) and then creates a default report specification for that table; the layout for that default specification is then displayed via the RBF Report Layout frame. Likewise, choosing the "Edit" option for an existing report specification causes RBF to display the Report Layout frame for that existing specification. Figure 18.3 shows a possible Report Layout frame for the default specification for table CITYSHIPS (see Section 18.2).

The Report Layout frame is the major frame in RBF. It is used throughout the RBF report specification process to show the layout of the report in its current stage of definition. The body of the frame (i.e., the report layout *form*) is broadly self-explanatory; note the similarity to the VIFRED default form for a table (compare Fig. 17.2 in Chapter 17). The menu is also very similar to the corresponding VIFRED menu (again, compare Fig. 17.2):

- *Create*: Create a new report specification component—trim, a blank line, a new column (heading and detail line entry), or a new column heading line.

- *Delete*: Delete an existing component.

- *Edit*: Edit an existing component (much as in VIFRED; see Sections 17.3 and 17.4). In particular, "Edit" allows data display format specifications to be edited, again much as in VIFRED (see the "Data Window" subsection in Section 17.4).

- *Move*: Move an existing component from one location to another (once again much as in VIFRED).

- *Undo*: Undo the previous operation.

- *Order*: Define the report sort order, control breaks, and aggregation operations (see below).

```
|--------------------------------------------------------------|
| -----------Title-------------------------Title----------     |
|              Report on Table: Cityships                      |
| -------Column-Headings----------------Column-Headings------- |
|   City            Supplier           Part          Quantity  |
| ---------Detail-Lines-------------------Detail-Lines-------   |
|   c_____  c____              c_____      i_____  |
| ---------End-of-Detail-----------------End-of-Detail-------   |
|                                                              |
|                                                              |
| Create Delete Edit Move Undo Order ReportOptions Save ... :  |
|--------------------------------------------------------------|
```

Fig. 18.3 Report Layout frame for the CITYSHIPS default report

- *ReportOptions*: Define page length, underlining behavior, and similar cosmetic details.

- *Save*: Compile the report specification (via SREPORT) and save it in the dictionary under a specified name.

Note: The RBF top frame also permits an RBF-created report specification to be *archived*—i.e., it allows such a specification to be written out to an operating system file in the form of Report-Writer specification language statements. That file can then be edited further by means of a standard text editor to produce a report specification that is more sophisticated than the facilities of RBF alone can support. This feature provides a quick means of "getting started" if it is necessary to produce a specification that is beyond the capabilities of RBF per se.

Sort Order, Control Breaks, and Aggregation

The "Order" option on the Report Layout menu leads to the Order Columns frame, which is used to specify sort control and control break columns. For instance, in the CITYSHIPS example, we might designate CITY, SUPPLIER, and PART (in that major-to-minor order) as sort columns, with CITY as a control break column; see Fig. 18.4. *Note*: Duplicate rows are always eliminated during the sorting process.

Next, we can call up the Column Options frame for each column in turn. The Column Options frame is used to specify the actions to be taken

```
!--------------------------------------------------------------!
!                                                              !
! RBF - Order Columns                                          !
!                                                              !
! Scroll through the column names. Select the sorting sequence !
! (0-127), sorting direction ("a" or "d"), and whether to break!
! ("y" or "n") for each column.                                !
!                                                              !
!       +------------------------------------------------+     !
!       |Column Name |Sequence |Direction |Break? |       !
!       |============|=========|==========|=======|       !
!       |city        |1        |a         |y      |       !
!       |supplier    |2        |a         |n      |       !
!       |part        |3        |a         |n      |       !
!       |quantity    |0        |          |       |       !
!       |            |         |          |       |       !
!       |            |         |          |       |       !
!       +------------------------------------------------+     !
!                                                              !
! ColumnOptions    Top    Bottom    End   :                    !
!                                                              !
!--------------------------------------------------------------!
```

Fig. 18.4 Order Columns frame for CITYSHIPS

```
|-------------------------------------------------------------------|
| RBF - Column Options                                              |
|                                                                   |
| Column name: City                    Break Column: y             |
|                                                                   |
| When to print values: b              (b=break, p=pages, t=both,  |
|                                       a=always)                   |
| Lines to skip on break: 1            (-1 to skip to new page)     |
| Selection criteria at run time: n    (n=none, v=value, r=range)  |
|                                                                   |
| Enter "x" to select Aggregation/Break combinations for column.   |
|                                                                   |
| +-----------------------------------------------------------+     |
| |Aggregate         | Over Report | Over Breaks | Over Pages |     |
| |==================+=============+=============+============|     |
| |Count             |             |             |            |     |
| |Count (unique)    |             |             |            |     |
| +------------------+-------------+-------------+------------+     |
|                                                                   |
| Help    End   :                                                  |
|                                                                   |
|-------------------------------------------------------------------|
```

Fig. 18.5 Column Options frame for column CITY

on the column when a control break occurs, plus certain other information.
To call up the Column Options frame for column CITY, for example, we
position the cursor on the row for CITY in the Order Columns frame, then
choose the "ColumnOptions" menu item. For simplicity, we show the Col-

```
|-------------------------------------------------------------------|
| RBF - Column Options                                             |
|                                                                  |
| Column name: Quantity                Break Column: n            |
|                                                                  |
| Selection criteria at run time: n   (n=none, v=value, r=range)  |
|                                                                  |
| Enter "x" to select Aggregation/Break combinations for column.  |
|                                                                  |
| +----------------------------------------------------------+     |
| |Aggregate         | Over Report | Over Breaks | Over Pages|     |
| |==================+=============+=============+===========|     |
| |Count             |             |             |           |     |
| |Sum               |     x       |     x       |           |     |
| |Average           |             |             |           |     |
| |Minimum           |             |             |           |     |
| |Maximum           |             |             |           |     |
| +------------------+-------------+-------------+-----------+     |
|                                                                  |
| Help    End   :                                                 |
|                                                                  |
|-------------------------------------------------------------------|
```

Fig. 18.6 Column Options frame for column QUANTITY

umn Options frames for CITY and QUANTITY only (Figs. 18.5 and 18.6, respectively).

Explanation: The entries "When to print values" and "Lines to skip on break" are included only for control break columns (i.e., CITY but not QUANTITY, in our example). The "b" ("When to print values") means "Print on control breaks." The "n" ("Selection criteria at run time") means "None." If instead we had specified "v" (value) or "r" (range), the Report-Writer would prompt for a (range of) value(s) for the column each time a report is produced using this specification; in this way, tailored reports for specific cities and/or quantities could be produced. Notice that the only aggregate options offered for CITY are "Count" and "Count (unique)," because CITY is a string column and counting is the only aggregation that makes sense (in fact we have chosen not to specify any aggregation for CITY at all). By contrast, the aggregate options offered for QUANTITY include the full set of possibilities; we have requested totaling

```
:-------------------------------------------------------------:
: 18-JAN-87                                          11:46:07 :
:                   Report on Table: Cityships                :
:                                                             :
:  City               Supplier          Part       Quantity  :
:                                                             :
:  London             S1                P1              300   :
:                     S1                P2              200   :
:                     S1                P3              400   :
:                     S1                P4              200   :
:                     S1                P5              100   :
:                     S1                P6              100   :
:                     S4                P2              200   :
:                     S4                P4              300   :
:                     S4                P5              400   :
:  -----------------------------------------------------------:
:  Totals: London                                            :
:  Sum:                                               2200    :
:  -----------------------------------------------------------:
:                                                             :
:  Paris              S2                P1              300   :
:                     S2                P2              400   :
:                     S3                P2              200   :
:  -----------------------------------------------------------:
:  Totals: Paris                                             :
:  Sum:                                                900    :
:  -----------------------------------------------------------:
:                                                             :
:  ===========================================================:
:  Grand Totals: REPORT                                       :
:  Sum:                                               3100    :
:  ===========================================================:
:                             - 1 -                           :
:-------------------------------------------------------------:
```

Fig. 18.7 A tailored report for CITYSHIPS

("Sum") to be performed for each value of the control break column (i.e., for each CITY value) and also for the report as a whole.

The resulting report is shown in Fig. 18.7.

18.4 THE INGRES REPORT-WRITER

As explained in Section 18.1, an INGRES report specification consists (in its source or uncompiled form) of a set of statements in the Report-Writer's *report specification language.* That language can be regarded as a special-purpose *programming* language—a programming language, however, that is specifically oriented toward the construction of programs whose purpose is to produce customized formatted reports. Such programs can be created either *directly* by means of a standard operating system text editor, or *indirectly* (and "visually") by means of RBF. The first method requires more specialized skills on the part of the person creating the specification, but does provide certain features and functions (such as run-time conditional branching) not available via the simpler RBF method. In this section we take a very brief look at what is involved in creating a report specification directly, using the Report-Writer's report specification language.

By way of example, we show in Fig. 18.8 a possible report specification, slightly simplified, for a revised version of the customized CITYSHIPS report of Fig. 18.7 in Section 18.3.

Explanation:

1. All report specification language statements start with an initial dot or period (.). The .NAME statement merely assigns a name (CS_REP_SPEC—"CITYSHIPS report specification") to the report. The .QUERY statement defines the (derived) table from which the report is to be produced; to make the example a little more general, we no longer assume that view CITYSHIPS already exists. Also we use SQL instead of QUEL as the basis for our example, for no particular reason. The .QUERY statement can include parameters, in which case the Report-Writer will prompt for corresponding arguments when the report specification is processed. The .SORT statement specifies sort control columns (and therefore potential break columns also).

Note: Most Report-Writer statements can be abbreviated. For example, the statement .UNDERLINE can be abbreviated to just .UL (or even to just .U). For readability, we have not used any abbreviations in our example.

2. The next few statements specify the report heading and footing. The heading consists of:

(a) a line containing the current date (left-justified), the current time (right-justified), and the title "Shipments by City," centered and underlined;

(b) a single blank line;

(c) a line containing the column headings "City," "Supplier," "Part," and "Quantity," underlined, and printed at specified tab (column) positions;

(d) another blank line.

The footing consists of a blank line, followed by a line of equals signs, followed by a line "Grand Totals: REPORT," followed by a line including the total of all QUANTITY values (taken over the entire report), followed by another line of equals signs and a line containing a centered page number.

```
/* first a block of report setup statements: */

.NAME   CS_REP_SPEC
.QUERY SELECT CITY      = S.CITY,
              SUPPLIER = S.SNO,
              PART     = SP.PNO,
              QUANTITY = SP.QTY
       FROM   S, SP
       WHERE  S.SNO = SP.SNO
.SORT   CITY, SUPPLIER, PART

/* report layout: report header and footer specifications */

.HEADER REPORT
   .LEFT    .PRINT CURRENT_DATE
   .CENTER
      .UNDERLINE   .PRINT "Shipments by City"   .NOUNDERLINE
   .RIGHT   .PRINT CURRENT_TIME
   .NEWLINE 2
   .UNDERLINE
      .TAB 2    .PRINT "City"
      .TAB 19   .PRINT "Supplier"
      .TAB 38   .PRINT "Part"
      .TAB 52   .PRINT "Quantity"
   .NOUNDERLINE
   .NEWLINE 2

.FOOTER REPORT
   .NEWLINE 2
   .PRINT "==================================================="
   .NEWLINE   .TAB 2    .PRINT "Grand Totals: REPORT"
   .NEWLINE   .TAB 2    .PRINT "Sum:"
              .TAB 52   .PRINT SUM (QUANTITY) (F8)
   .NEWLINE
   .PRINT "==================================================="
   .NEWLINE
   .CENTER   .PRINT "- ", PAGE_NUMBER, " -"
```

Fig. 18.8 Example of a report specification (part 1 of 2)

```
/* report layout: CITY control break specifications */

.HEADER CITY
   .TFORMAT CITY (C15)

.FOOTER CITY
   .NEWLINE
   .PRINT "--------------------------------------------------"
   .NEWLINE   .TAB 2    .PRINT "Totals: ", CITY
   .NEWLINE   .TAB 2    .PRINT "Sum:"
                        .TAB 52   .PRINT CUM (CITY) SUM (QUANTITY) (F8)
   .NEWLINE
   .PRINT "--------------------------------------------------"
   .NEWLINE 2

/* report layout: data line specifications */

.DETAIL
   .TAB 2    .PRINT CITY (B15)
   .TAB 19   .PRINT SUPPLIER (C5)
   .TAB 38   .PRINT PART (C6)
   .TAB 52   .PRINT QUANTITY (F8)
   .NEWLINE
```

Fig. 18.8 Example of a report specification (part 2 of 2)

Note: In practice, we would probably want to specify page headings and footings as well as a heading and footing for the overall report, but we have omitted all such page specifications from our example for reasons of simplicity.

3. Next we indicate what is to be done when a CITY control break occurs:

- The specification .TFORMAT CITY (C15) in the header information defines a "temporary display format" for CITY of C15, meaning that when a control break occurs the new value of CITY is to be printed as a string of 15 characters. (The "normal" display format for CITY— see paragraph 4 below— is defined as B15, meaning that CITY values are "normally" printed as a string of 15 blanks.)

- The statements following the .FOOTER CITY statement define what is to be displayed before we move on to the next CITY value, namely a line of hyphens, followed by a line stating "Totals:" and giving the current CITY value, followed by a line including the total QUANTITY value accumulated (thanks to the CUM(CITY) specification) since the last CITY value change occurred, followed by another line of hyphens and a blank line.

4. Finally, we indicate what is to be displayed in a "normal" data (or detail) line—namely, the current SUPPLIER, PART, and QUANTITY val-

ues, printed at specified tab positions. (As already explained, CITY values
are "normally" blanked out in such detail lines.)

This concludes the explanation of our simple example. We stress the
point that the example is extremely simple and does little more than scratch
the surface of the Report-Writer's full range of capabilities. We conclude
this section (and this chapter) with a list of the major Report-Writer statements, in the hope that such a list will give a slightly better idea as to the
full extent of those capabilities.

Report Setup:

```
.NAME
.OUTPUT
.DATA
.QUERY
.SORT
```

Report Structuring:

```
.HEADER
.FOOTER
.DETAIL
```

Printing:

```
.PRINT
  - column values
  - constants
  - system variables
  - parameters
  - aggregates
  - expressions
.PRINTLN
```

Text Positioning:

```
.TAB
.NEWLINE
.CENTER
.LEFT
.RIGHT
.LINESTART
.LINEEND
```

Page Layout:

```
.PAGELENGTH
.FORMFEEDS
.LEFTMARGIN
.RIGHTMARGIN
.NEWPAGE
.NEED
```

Column Control:

```
.FORMAT
.POSITION
.WIDTH
.BLOCK
.ENDBLOCK
.TOP
.BOTTOM
.WITHIN
.ENDWITHIN
```

Miscellaneous:

```
.IF
.UNDERLINE
.NOUNDERLINE
.ULCHARACTER
.TFORMAT
```

19

INGRES/GRAPHICS

19.1 INTRODUCTION

The INGRES business graphics subsystem INGRES/GRAPHICS is somewhat analogous to the reports subsystem discussed in Chapter 18, except that the final "report" consists of a picture instead of rows and columns of text. For many kinds of data, a graph is a much more effective means of communication than a conventional report. As a trivial illustration, compare the graphical (bar chart) version of CITYSHIPS shown in Fig. 19.1 with the same data in conventional report form (see Fig. 18.7 in the previous chapter).

INGRES/GRAPHICS consists of a single component, the Visual-Graphics-Editor or VIGRAPH,* invoked from INGRES/MENU via the options VIGRAPH and RUNGRAPH. Graphs in INGRES are produced under the control of an appropriate *graph specification*, just as reports are produced under the control of an appropriate report specification. The INGRES/MENU option "VIGRAPH" supports the creation of both the original graph specification and the corresponding graph itself; the option

---

*VIGRAPH replaces an earlier INGRES subsystem called Graph-By-Forms (GBF). Facilities are available to convert GBF-style graph specifications into their VIGRAPH equivalents.

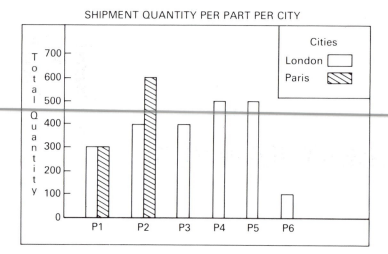

Fig. 19.1 A bar chart version of CITYSHIPS

"RUNGRAPH" supports the latter function only. Like report specifications, graph specifications are kept in the INGRES dictionary.

Although we began this section by likening VIGRAPH to INGRES/ REPORTS, the fact is that the various pieces of VIGRAPH are rather more tightly integrated than are the corresponding pieces of INGRES/ REPORTS. As a result, VIGRAPH is somewhat easier to use. For example, it is very easy at any stage during the graph specification creation process to display a rough "sketch" of the corresponding graph, or even the current version of the graph itself, and hence to see what further refinements are needed to the specification. (By contrast, it is not possible to write a report in the middle of creating a report specification, e.g., via RBF, without leaving the RBF environment and invoking the INGRES Report-Writer as a separate operation.) Also, VIGRAPH comes equipped with a set of predefined sample graph specifications (with a set of corresponding sample data values); and it is a trivial matter to modify one of those sample specifications so that it can be used to produce genuinely useful output from the real database. We will illustrate this process in Section 19.3.

One final preliminary remark: As indicated at the end of Section 14.1, it is a little difficult in a conventional textbook such as this one to describe the highly visually-oriented INGRES frontend subsystems in a fully satisfactory manner. For obvious reasons, this remark applies to the graphics subsystem with even more force than it does to most of the other frontends.

Once again, if the reader has access to an INGRES system, he or she is strongly recommended to try out some of the examples on the system while reading the book. To quote Section 14.1 again, there is no substitute for genuine hands-on experience.

19.2 GRAPH TYPES

VIGRAPH supports four basic graph types: bar charts, pie charts, scatter charts, and line charts (see examples in Figs. 19.2-19.5). In the case of bar charts, two further variations are available: clustered bar charts and stacked bar charts. The example of Fig. 19.1 was actually a clustered bar chart (multiple bars appeared clustered together for each part). A stacked bar chart version of the same data is given in Fig. 19.6.

In all cases, no matter what kind of graph is to be produced, the data to be graphed (sometimes called the graph *data set*) consists of a table, derived in some way from the tables of the underlying database. The table in question might be an existing base table or view, or it might be defined by means of a QUEL or SQL query whose result is the desired table. That table must have either two or three columns (referred to generically as the X, Y, and Z columns, respectively). For example, here is a QUEL view

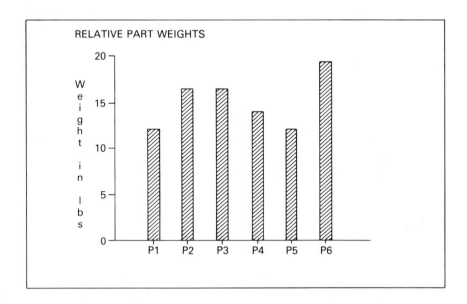

Fig. 19.2 A bar chart (example)

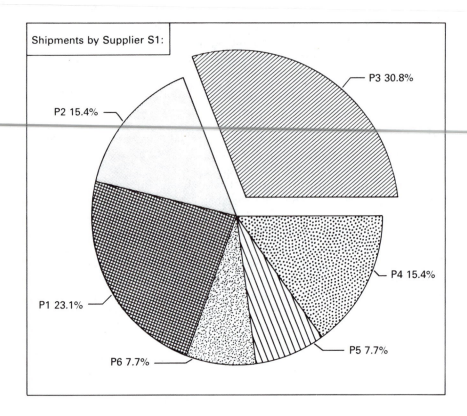

Fig. 19.3 A pie chart (example)

definition defining the data set for the bar chart shown in Fig. 19.1 of the previous section:

```
RANGE OF CS IS CITYSHIPS
DEFINE VIEW PQC
     ( X = CS.PART,
       Y = SUM ( CS.QUANTITY BY CS.CITY, CS.PART ),
       Z = CS.CITY )
```

The meanings of the three columns X, Y, and Z depend on the type of graph, as follows.

- *Bar chart*: X represents the independent variable (the labels on the bars); Z (if present) represents labels of "sub-bars" within each bar (i.e., for a clustered or stacked bar chart—see, e.g., "City" in Figs. 19.1 and

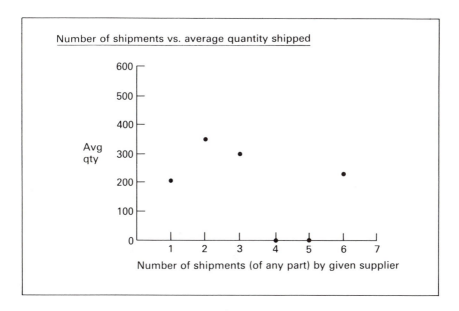

Fig. 19.4 A scatter chart (example)

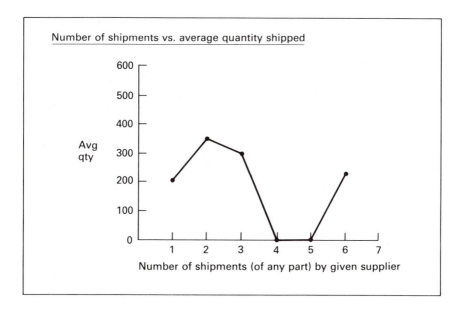

Fig. 19.5 A line chart (example)

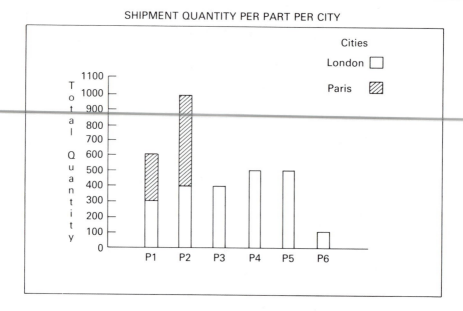

Fig. 19.6 A stacked bar chart (example)

19.6); Y represents the dependent variable (the bar or "sub-bar" heights).

- *Pie chart*: X represents the independent variable (the labels on the slices), Y represents the dependent variable (the slice areas, given as a percentage of the total). Z should not be present for this type of graph.

- *Scatter chart*: X and Y represent (X,Y)-coordinates, where (as usual) X represents the independent variable and Y the dependent variable. Different sets of points are plotted for each distinct value of Z. A different "mark" character can be used to represent the points in each such set.

- *Line chart*: A line chart is the same as a scatter chart, except that each individual set of plotted points is assumed to represent a continuous function. To display that function, VIGRAPH will connect adjacent points together by straight line segments, step curves, or continuous curved arcs. Alternatively, it will approximate the function by drawing a single straight line that is derived from the plotted points by least-squares regression analysis.

19.3 SPECIFYING THE GRAPH DATA SET

The VIGRAPH option of INGRES/MENU leads directly to the VIGRAPH top frame, which displays a list of existing graph specifications and a menu that includes options to destroy, edit, or rename any of those existing specifications or to create a new one. As explained in Section 19.1, VIGRAPH comes ready equipped with a set of sample graph specifications, so that the list of existing specifications will be nonempty (in general), even when VIGRAPH is invoked for the very first time. See Fig. 19.7.

The "CreateBlank," "Destroy," "Edit," and "Rename" menu options have the obvious meanings. (We remark in passing that creating a new specification by editing an existing one—the "Edit" option—is usually much faster than creating a brand new one from scratch—the "Create-Blank" option.) The "Plot," "Sketch," and "Profile" options have the following meanings:

- *Plot*: Draw the graph for the selected specification.

- *Sketch*: Draw a small sketch of the graph at bottom right on the screen.

- *Profile*: Display the VIGRAPH profile. The VIGRAPH profile contains a number of parameters that control VIGRAPH's operation—for

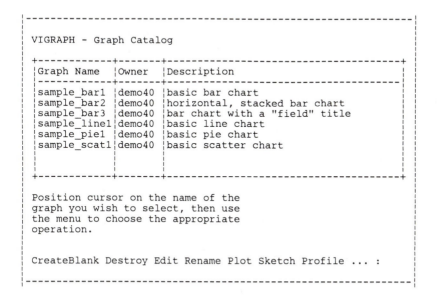

Fig. 19.7 The VIGRAPH top frame

example, the "presentation level" (level of resolution to be used when displaying graphs), device type for the plotting device, etc. Displaying the profile allows the user to review and/or change such parameters.

Suppose now that we wish to produce a simple bar chart report showing the relative status of suppliers in the suppliers table (table S). Selecting "Edit" on the sample graph specification "sample_bar1" will cause VIGRAPH to display a frame containing (a) the corresponding sample_bar1 graph itself, showing the predefined sample data values, (b) a "status line" displaying the text

```
Editing entire graph ...
```

in reverse video,* and (c) a menu that looks like this:

```
Create Delete Edit Move Size Undo MapData Layer Profile
Save Plot Help End Quit :
```

The important option at this point is "MapData," which allows us to define the graph data set. Selecting "MapData" leads to the frame shown in Fig. 19.8. At this point, we could if we wished invoke IQUEL or ISQL

```
:------------------------------------------------------------:
:                                                            :
: VIGRAPH - Data Mapping Specification                       :
:                                      Available columns      :
:                              +----------------------+       :
:                              |Column Name |Format   |       :
:                              |------------+---------|       :
: Table or view to graph:      |            |         |       :
:                              |            |         |       :
:                              |            |         |       :
:          Horizontal axis (X):|            |         |       :
:                              |            |         |       :
:            Vertical axis (Y):|            |         |       :
:                              |            |         |       :
:   Optional series column (Z):|            |         |       :
:                              |            |         |       :
:                  Sort: yes   +------------+---------+       :
:                                                            :
: ListTables  IQUEL  ISQL  ...  :                            :
:                                                            :
:------------------------------------------------------------:
```

Fig. 19.8 The Data Mapping Specification frame (initial)

---

*An appropriate status line appears at each distinct stage of graph specification creation or editing.

to specify a query whose result is the desired data set. In the particular case at hand, however, the desired data set already exists as a table in the database, namely table S. We can specify this table by choosing the "List-Tables" option and selecting table S from the list of tables in the frame that results, then returning to the Data Mapping Specification frame. Now table S will be identified as the "Table or view to graph" and the columns of that table (SNO, SNAME, STATUS, and CITY) will be listed in the "Available columns" table field, as shown in Fig. 19.9. We can now fill out the rest of the form to specify which column corresponds to the X-axis and which to the Y-axis; again, see Fig. 19.9.

Selecting "End" from the Data Mapping Specification frame menu will now cause VIGRAPH to display the bar chart graph again, but this time with "genuine" data instead of the dummy data provided with the product (see Fig. 19.10).

Of course, there is much more that could be done to this example in the way of improvement and refinement, but it does illustrate the point that VIGRAPH permits the production of (admittedly simple, but genuinely useful) graphs in a truly simple manner. In particular, it shows how the sample graph specifications provided with the product can serve as *templates* from which simple customized specifications can be produced with very little effort.

Note: Even though (as we have seen from the example) each graph specification does include a specification of the corresponding graph data

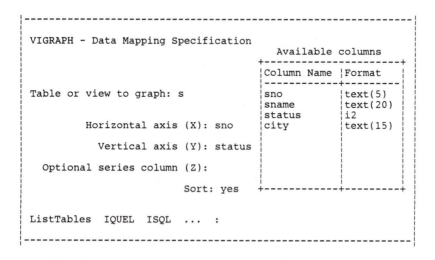

Fig. 19.9 The Data Mapping Specification frame (final)

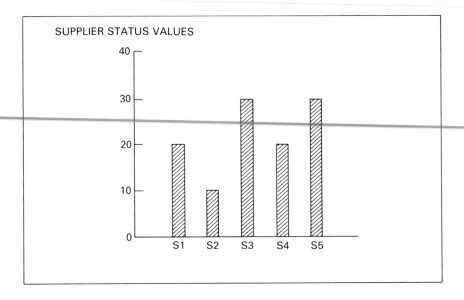

Fig. 19.10 A bar chart showing supplier status values

set, it is possible when invoking RUNGRAPH to designate a different table or view to be graphed instead. For details, see the RTI manuals.

19.4 EDITING GRAPH SPECIFICATIONS

The ''CreateBlank'' option in the VIGRAPH top frame menu leads to a blank editing frame. Choosing the ''Create'' option from that frame's menu leads to the following menu:

```
Trim Field BarChart LineChart ScatterChart PieChart Legend ... :
```

Each of these options causes an object of the indicated type to be created. *Note*: All objects in VIGRAPH are rectangular, as in VIFRED.* Therefore, the position and size for a new object can be specified (and indeed are specified) as follows:

---

*A difference is that in VIGRAPH objects can be *transparent*, meaning that distinct objects can overlap on the screen.

(a) The object's top left corner is identified by moving the cursor to the desired position and then executing the desired menu option ("Trim" or "Field" or . . .).

(b) The object's bottom right corner is identified by moving the cursor to the desired position immediately after executing the menu option and then pressing the menu key.

Once created, objects can be moved and/or resized and/or deleted and/ or subjected to a variety of further, more detailed editing operations. The nature of those more detailed operations depends to some extent on the nature of the object being edited. It is not our purpose in this book to go into complete detail on such topics; instead, we content ourselves with giving a basic indication of the kinds of editing that are possible in various cases. The following is *not* intended to be an exhaustive enumeration of the possibilities.

Trim and Fields

Trim and fields are very much as in VIFRED, except that the type font can also be varied.

Legend

For a given graph, the legend defines the graph's title (text, font, color), the font and color associated with each "Z"-variable value (see Section 19.2), the background color, and other items. Any of these specifications can be changed.

Bar Charts

- Different colors or hatch patterns can be specified for the background and for the bars. If a "Z" variable is specified, then different colors or hatch patterns can be specified for each distinct value of that variable—i.e., for each distinct "sub-bar."

- The bar chart can be switched from vertical to horizontal orientation and vice versa. If a "Z" variable is specified, the chart can be switched from clustered to stacked format and vice versa.

Pie Charts

- Different colors or hatch patterns can be specified for the background and for each of the pie slices.

- Any of the pie slices can be "exploded"—i.e., displaced outward along a radius from the pie center, with its edges no longer in contact with the rest of the pie. Different slices can be so displaced by differing amounts.
- The labels on the slices can be deleted or can have their text, font, or color changed.
- The pie can be rotated.

Line Charts

- Different colors can be specified for different curves on the graph (corresponding to different "Z" values), and different colors or hatch patterns can be specified for the areas under each of the curves.
- Different mark characters (dot, star, circle, etc.) can be specified for the data points on different curves. Different types of curve (solid, dotted, etc.) can be specified.
- Different connexion types (straight, curved, etc.) can be specified for each curve.

Scatter Charts

A scatter chart can be regarded as a degenerate case of a line chart. Thus, many (not all) of the same possibilities apply.

All Except Pie Charts

- Extra axes can be created (in addition to the left axis and bottom axis, which are supplied by default)—a right axis and/or a top axis. Axis headers (text describing the axes and running parallel to them) can be specified. A variety of styles (e.g., font, color) can be specified for axis labels (the values appearing at data points along the axes). Axis tick marks can appear inside, outside, or crossing the axis itself. Logarithmic scale can be specified.
- A grid can be superimposed on the graph.
- The chart type can be changed (e.g., from bar chart to line chart).

Text Charts

A text chart is a simple form of "graph" that does not include a pictorial chart at all, but only text (trim, fields, etc.). Such charts can still be useful as the basis for presenting purely textual information in a visually pleasing manner. VIGRAPH provides two features that are especially useful in the creation of such charts, namely bullet points and multiple-line trim (recall from Chapter 17 that trim is normally considered to be single-line). The ability to draw boxes around items is also particularly useful in the production of text charts. See the RTI manuals for details.

20

INGRES/APPLICATIONS

20.1 INTRODUCTION

The availability of the various INGRES subsystems described in Chapters 16–19 certainly reduces the need for conventional user-written application programs. Indeed, it may even be possible to avoid having to write any such programs at all in some installations. Usually, however, it will still be necessary to develop at least a few applications that are specialized to the installation's own particular needs. Even so, it may still be possible to avoid programming in the traditional sense (i.e., programming in a conventional language such as COBOL or PL/I), thanks to the subsystem called INGRES/APPLICATIONS.

INGRES/APPLICATIONS is an *application generator*—i.e., it is a tool for the rapid development of installation-specific applications. Application generators can be regarded as an advance over conventional high-level languages (COBOL, PL/I, etc.), just as those languages are an advance over assembler language and assembler language in turn was an advance over machine code. For this reason, application generators are sometimes referred to as *fourth generation* tools—machine code, assembler language, and high-level languages representing the first three generations—and the user interface to an application generator is accordingly sometimes called a "fourth generation language" (4GL). However, we choose not to adopt the 4GL terminology in this book, since it does not seem to have any very precise definition.

The user of an application generator such as INGRES/APPLICA-TIONS—i.e., the application designer—is typically not an ordinary end-user, but rather someone with a certain amount of DP expertise (though of course it is possible for end-users to use the system to develop their own applications if they want to). A typical application generator (and INGRES/APPLICATIONS is certainly typical in this regard) will present the designer with a very high-level application development interface, one whose functions include not only the usual arithmetic and control flow facilities of conventional languages, but also facilities for database access, terminal screen layout definition, screen input/output, screen data manipulation, and so on. Furthermore, the process of actually developing an application will typically be done, at least in part, not by writing code in any conventional manner, but rather by conducting some kind of interactive dialog with the system—in INGRES terms, by Visual Programming.

To concentrate now on INGRES specifically: The INGRES application generator INGRES/APPLICATIONS consists of a single component, Applications-By-Forms (ABF), invoked from INGRES/MENU by means of the "ABF" option. ABF is specifically designed to support the development of *forms-based* applications—i.e. (to repeat from earlier chapters), applications that communicate with the end-user by means of forms displayed on the screen. QBF, VIFRED, RBF, and VIGRAPH are all special cases of forms-based applications. So is ABF itself, for that matter; in other words, application development in ABF is itself very much a forms-based process, as we will see in Sections 20.3.

Application source code built by ABF during the application development process is kept in the INGRES dictionary (together with certain associated control information). The corresponding object code is kept in a set of files in what is called an *application directory*, which is also automatically maintained by ABF. When the application is fully debugged and ready to go into production, the designer can *install* it on the host system. Installation involves creating an "executable image" of the application (which is done via an appropriate ABF frame) and defining an operating system command by which that "image" can be invoked. Thereafter the application can be invoked directly from the operating system level, instead of having to access it through ABF. In effect, the application is now a new (installation-specific) INGRES frontend subsystem.

20.2 STRUCTURE OF AN ABF APPLICATION

Any forms-based application can be regarded as consisting of a hierarchical arrangement of frames (where as usual a frame consists of a form and an associated menu). See Fig. 20.1.

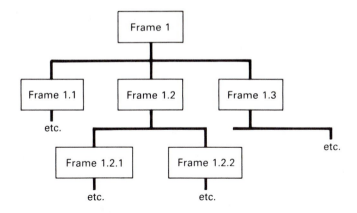

Fig. 20.1 Structure of a forms-based application

The hierarchy of Fig. 20.1 is interpreted as follows. Frame 1 represents the entry point to the application—i.e., it is the frame displayed when the user first invokes the application (the application top frame). Frames 1.1–1.3 represent three possible successor frames (corresponding to, e.g., three possible menu choices on frame 1—for example, "Produce sales report," "Enter new order," or "Update customer information," in a SALES application). Likewise, frames 1.2.1–1.2.2 represent two possible successor frames to frame 1.2, and so on. Note, incidentally, that several frames can share the same form, thus presenting a consistent set of interfaces to the application user at run time.

In order to create a forms-based application, therefore, the application designer needs to be able to specify:

1. The frames involved in the application;

2. For each frame, the form and menu items to be displayed;

3. For each frame, the sequence of operations to be performed if the application user performs some specific action on the frame, such as selecting a specific menu option. A typical sequence of operations will include operations to read values from the current form, and/or operations to perform database retrievals and/or updates (expressed in either SQL or QUEL), and/or an operation to invoke the frame to be displayed next.

There are four possible types of frame: user-specified frames, query frames, report frames, and graphics frames. The purposes of the four types are as follows:

- *User-specified* frames* are frames that are completely specific to the application in question (such as Frame 1, the top frame, in the SALES application sketched above). For each such frame, the designer specifies the name of the frame, the name of the associated form, the menu, and the set of operations associated with the frame (operations are discussed at the end of this section). If the associated form does not yet exist, the designer can create it using VIFRED, without leaving the ABF environment. The designer can also use QBF, again without leaving the ABF environment, if it becomes necessary to interrogate the database while building the application. In fact, it is possible to invoke the whole of INGRES/MENU, and therefore any of the INGRES subsystems (except for ABF itself), from within ABF. Thus, for example, it is possible to call up the QUEL or SQL Terminal Monitor at any time during the application development process.

- *Query* (or *QBF*) frames allow the application to make use of the built-in INGRES/QUERY code. Suppose, for example, that one of the menu choices the application is to offer to its end-user is "ad hoc query." Then, instead of writing explicit code to perform that function, the designer can simply incorporate the QBF code into the application directly (as a subroutine, in effect). For a QBF frame, the designer specifies the name of the frame, the corresponding form (which can be created via VIFRED, again without leaving ABF), and the name of the table or JoinDef on which QBF is to operate.

- Similarly, *report* frames allow the application to make use of the INGRES Report-Writer (again as a subroutine, in effect). The designer specifies the name of the frame, a form for the acquisition of run-time parameters for the report (if any), and the corresponding report specification (which can be built via RBF, once again without leaving ABF).

- Finally, *graphics* frames allow the application to make use of the built-in INGRES/GRAPHICS code. These frames are analogous to the report frames just discussed.

In the case of a user-specified frame, the application designer must also (as already stated) define the *operations* corresponding to the frame. This function is performed by means of the ABF *Operation Specification Language* (OSL), which can be regarded as a very high-level programming and database accessing language. OSL comes in two versions, OSL/SQL and OSL/QUEL. As the names suggest, the two versions differ merely in that

---

*"User" here refers to the application designer, not to the application end-user.

OSL/SQL supports the SQL statements SELECT, INSERT, UPDATE, and DELETE, whereas OSL/QUEL supports the QUEL analogs RETRIEVE, APPEND, REPLACE, and DELETE. *Note*: OSL can also invoke procedures written in one of the standard programming languages, such as C or COBOL (possibly with embedded QUEL or SQL statements). Such procedures should not be needed very often in practice, however, because most of the relevant functions are directly available from within OSL itself. The only major INGRES function not currently available in OSL but included in EQUEL and ESQL is the REPEAT option (see Section 10.2).

The application designer creates OSL text by means of a standard operating system text editor, which can be invoked directly from ABF. Section 20.4 discusses OSL in some detail.

20.3 BUILDING AN ABF APPLICATION

ABF is invoked from INGRES/MENU via the ABF option, which leads directly to the ABF top frame (the Application Definition frame), with menu as follows:

```
Help Create Define Destroy Image Options Rtingres Run Exit :
```

"Create" is used to initiate the construction of a new application; "Define" is used to create or modify objects (such as frames) within a previously created application. The other options (apart from "Help" and "Exit," whose purpose is obvious) have the following meanings:

- *Destroy*: Delete the application.
- *Image*: Create an executable image of the application (see Section 20.1).
- *Options*: Specify certain system options, such as the text editor to be used in creating OSL code.
- *Rtingres*: Invoke INGRES/MENU (see Section 20.2).
- *Run*: At any point during construction of the application, the designer can ask ABF to execute the current version, even though it may still be incomplete. ABF will invoke all the necessary compilers,* etc. to convert the application to (temporarily) executable form, and will then try to execute it. Syntax errors will be diagnosed. If a call is encountered to a frame or procedure that does not yet exist, ABF will display a

---

*Note, incidentally, that ABF applications *are* compiled—a significant performance advantage (most application generators are interpretive at the time of writing).

message, together with a trace of the control flow to that point. The application designer can then request execution to continue from a different point or can stop the run. When errors are discovered, the designer can use ABF to make corrections to frames and procedures, and can then try to execute the application again.

Selecting the "Define" option leads to another menu, which includes the following options:

- *Frame*: Create or edit or destroy (or . . .) frames and their associated form and OSL code.

- *Procedure*: Create or edit or destroy (or . . .) procedures written in a conventional programming language such as COBOL (possibly including statements of ESQL or ESQL/FORMS or EQUEL or EQUEL/ FORMS).

- *Table*: Create, examine, or destroy database tables (much as in the Table Utilities portion of INGRES/MENU—see Section 15.2).

The only one of these options we discuss any further here is "Frame." Suppose for the sake of the example that, in the application we are building, we wish to make use of a frame called SHIPMENT, which is to appear as shown in Fig. 20.2. Selecting the "Frame" option after "Define" causes ABF to prompt for a frame name. If a new name is specified (i.e., the frame does not yet exist), ABF then displays the New Frame Definition frame; by means of that frame, the designer indicates the kind of frame to be created (user-specified, QBF, etc.—see Section 20.2), and then chooses the "Create" menu option, which leads to the User Frame Definition frame. See

```
|----------------------------------------------------------------|
|                    Shipment Information                        |
| Supplier: _____          Supplier City: _____        |
|                                                                |
| Part:     _____            Part City: _____         |
|                                                                |
| Quantity: ____                                                 |
|                                                                |
|                                                                |
| Retrieve   Update   Append   Help   End   :                    |
|----------------------------------------------------------------|
```

Fig. 20.2 The user-specified frame SHIPMENT

```
 --------------------------------------------------------------
|                                                              |
|               User-Specified Frame Definition                |
|                                                              |
| Frame Name : shipment        Creation Date : 18-jan-87:11:47 |
|                                                              |
| Usage : USER                 Modification Date :          :  |
|                                                              |
| Form : shipment                                              |
|                                                              |
|                                                              |
|                                                              |
|                                                              |
| Help  Compile  Define  Destroy  Edit  Print  Vifred  End  :  |
|                                                              |
 --------------------------------------------------------------
```

Fig. 20.3 The User Frame Definition frame for SHIPMENT

Fig. 20.3, which represents a possible User Frame Definition frame for the user-specified frame SHIPMENT.

The user-specified SHIPMENT frame has an associated form (assumed by ABF by default to have the same name, SHIPMENT, but the designer can override this default) and an associated set of OSL code:

- The *form* can be created by selecting the "Vifred" menu option. See Chapter 17.

- The *OSL code* can be created by selecting the "Edit" menu option. See Section 20.4.

The only other User Frame Definition menu option we mention here is "Compile," which can be used to compile and syntax-check the OSL code created via the "Edit" menu option. *Note*: It is not absolutely necessary to invoke the "Compile" option, because ABF will automatically compile any uncompiled code when the application is executed.

As for the other types of frame (QBF or report or graphics frames): Creating such frames is essentially straightforward. In the case of a QBF frame, for example, a QBF Frame Definition frame allows the designer to specify the table or JoinDef (see Chapter 16) to be accessed and the corresponding form to be used (which can be a default form or can be created via VIFRED). For more details, see the RTI manuals.

20.4 OPERATION SPECIFICATION LANGUAGE (OSL)

The "Edit" option on the User Frame Definition frame for SHIPMENT causes ABF to create a file called SHIPMENT.OSQ and to invoke the operating system text editor on that file. The application designer can then

```
INITIALIZE =
    {
        sno   = "_____" ;
        scity = "_____" ;
        pno   = "_____" ;
        pcity = "_____" ;
        qty   = "____"
    }

"Retrieve" =
    {
        ...
        CALLFRAME GetShip ;
        ...
    }

"Update" =
    {
        ...
        CALLFRAME UpdShip ;
        ...
    }

"Append" =
    {
        ...
        CALLFRAME AppShip ;
        ...
    }

"Help" =
    {
        HELPFILE "Shipment Frame" ... ;
    }

"End" =
    {
        RETURN ;
    }
```

Fig. 20.4 OSL code for SHIPMENT (outline)

use the editor to create an appropriate set of OSL statements in that file. The OSL code for SHIPMENT is shown in outline in Fig. 20.4. *Note*: Exiting from the editor will return control to the User Frame Definition frame.

The OSL code for a given frame has the general form shown by the simplified BNF grammar of Fig. 20.5.

Explanation:

1. The OSL code for a given frame consists of an optional "initialization," followed by one or more "operations."

2. An "initialization" consists of a single INITIALIZE statement, which is executed each time the frame is started up (i.e., invoked from some point

```
1. frame-code
     ::=  [ initialization ] operation [ operation ] ...

2. initialization
     ::=  INITIALIZE
          [ ( field-allocation [, field-allocation ] ... ) ]
              = { statement [; statement ] ... }

3. field-allocation
     ::=  field  =  data-type

4. operation
     ::=  activator  =  { statement [; statement ] ... }

5. activator
     ::=  menu-item ¦ FIELD field ¦ KEY key

6. statement
     ::=  ... see text
```

Fig. 20.5 A BNF grammar for OSL

higher up in the application hierarchy; note that the initialization is *not* performed if, e.g., control is returned to the frame from some lower point in the hierarchy). The INITIALIZE statement performs some optional allocation of "hidden fields," followed by the execution of one or more other statements. Hidden fields are effectively temporary local variables; they can be used to hold intermediate results and the like, but they are not made visible to the application user as part of the displayed frame.

The other statements can be used (e.g.) to establish initial values for hidden fields and/or for fields displayed in the frame. We repeat the example from Fig. 20.4:

```
INITIALIZE =
   {
        sno   = "_____" ;
        scity = "_____" ;
        pno   = "_____" ;
        pcity = "_____" ;
        qty   = "_____"
   }
```

The purpose of this initialization code is merely to cause rows of underscore characters to be displayed in the specified fields. We have assumed that the internal names for the fields whose titles on the form are "Supplier:", "Part:", "Supplier City:", "Part City:", and "Quantity:" are "sno", "pno", "scity", "pcity", and "qty", respectively.

3. To allocate a hidden field, the designer simply specifies a name and a data type for that field at the appropriate point within the INITIALIZE statement.

4. The main body of the OSL code for a given frame consists of a sequence of "operations," one for each distinct "activator" available to the frame user. For each such activator, the application designer specifies a set of OSL statements to be executed if the corresponding "activation" occurs. That set of statements will frequently include a CALLFRAME statement to invoke this frame's successor down the hierarchy. CALLFRAME can also pass parameters to the frame it calls.

5. There are three ways in which the frame user can activate a frame operation:

- by selecting one of the menu items on the frame;
- by moving the screen cursor away from a particular field via an operation such as TAB;
- by pressing a specific terminal PF key.

The sample OSL code in Fig. 20.4 includes operations corresponding to the first of these possibilities only. For instance:

```
"Retrieve" =
    {
        ...
        CALLFRAME GetShip ;
        ...
    }
```

Here, if the frame user selects the "Retrieve" menu option, the set of code including the statement "CALLFRAME GetShip;" will be executed.

Here is an example of a field activation operation:

```
FIELD "pno" =
    {
        IF sno = "_____" OR pno = "_____"
            MESSAGE "Please specify both supplier and part" ;
            SLEEP 3 ;
        ELSE
            SELECT scity = S.CITY, pcity = P.CITY, qty = SP.QTY
            FROM   S, SP, P
            WHERE  SP.SNO = :sno
            AND    SP.PNO = :pno
            AND    S.SNO = SP.SNO
            AND    P.PNO = SP.PNO ;
            REDISPLAY ;
        ENDIF ;
    }
```

This code will be invoked when the frame user moves the screen cursor out of the field with title "Part:". At this point, if the user has specified both a supplier number and a part number, those values will be used as a basis for retrieving data from the database and the frame will be redisplayed with that new data; otherwise a message will be displayed and the application will wait for three seconds. *Note*: The REDISPLAY operation is actually unnecessary in this example; the form will automatically be redisplayed when all statements have been executed for the current operation.

After a field activation operation has been executed, the screen cursor will return to the field in question unless the OSL code includes a RESUME statement specifying some different position.

6. It is not our purpose here to give an exhaustive description of every OSL statement. Instead, we content ourselves with a short discussion of the four basic statement categories, followed in each case by a list of the statements available in that category. As with our discussions of EQUEL/ FORMS in Chapter 10 and the Report-Writer in Chapter 18, we hope that the lists will suffice to give some idea as to the range of facilities provided.

- Database statements:

  OSL includes almost all of the data manipulation function of SQL (or QUEL). In particular, it allows values to be retrieved from the database for display via a frame. It also allows values entered into a frame by the application user to be used to update the database or to condition further database retrievals. A special QUALIFICATION function is provided to simplify the process of creating WHERE clauses to reflect queries specified by the user in QBF style (see Section 16.4).

  Note: OSL does not currently include ESQL- or EQUEL-style cursors for dealing with multiple-record retrievals; instead, it uses a generalized form of the RETRIEVE-loop mechanism described in Chapter 10. It also does not support the EQUEL (or ESQL) REPEAT option (see Chapter 10).

```
SELECT [SQL]      (or RETRIEVE [QUEL])
INSERT [SQL]      (or APPEND   [QUEL])
UPDATE [SQL]      (or REPLACE  [QUEL])
DELETE [SQL]      (or DELETE   [QUEL])
```

- Form control statements:

  Form control statements control what appears on the screen. For example, the CLEAR statement clears one or more fields on the screen, the MESSAGE statement displays a single-line message at the foot of the screen, the assignment statement assigns the value of some expression to a field on the screen, and so on. Mention should also be made of the VALIDATE statement, which is used to cause the validation checks specified for the form (via VIFRED—see Chapter 17) to be applied. Special statements are also provided for dealing with table fields—namely, DELETEROW, INITTABLE, UNLOADTABLE, and VALIDROW.

```
assignment        NEXT
CLEAR             PROMPT
DELETEROW         REDISPLAY
HELPFILE          RESUME
INITIALIZE        SLEEP
INITTABLE         UNLOADTABLE
MESSAGE           VALIDATE
MODE              VALIDROW
```

- Control flow statements:

  Examples of control flow statements include various forms of IF statement, statements to call another (user-specified) frame, statements to call one of the INGRES-supplied frames (such as a QBF frame), statements to return to the previous frame, and statements to call a user-specified procedure.

```
CALLFRAME         EXIT
CALLPROC          ENDLOOP
CALL subsystem    IF - THEN - ELSE - ELSEIF - ENDIF
CALL SYSTEM       WHILE - DO - ENDWHILE
INITIALIZE        SLEEP
INITTABLE         UNLOADTABLE
MESSAGE           VALIDATE
MODE              VALIDROW
RETURN
```

- Miscellaneous statements:

  The statements INQUIRE_FORMS and INQUIRE_INGRES can be used to retrieve a variety of information concerning the run-time environment, such as error flags, terminal type, name or type or length of current field, count of number of rows processed, and so on.

```
INQUIRE_FORMS
INQUIRE_INGRES
```

20.5 OSL VS. EQUEL

At this point the reader may be wondering about the differences between OSL and EQUEL.* After all, both are application development languages. Both include database access functions, forms management functions, conditional logic, etc. When would one language be chosen in preference to the other?

The short answer is that OSL would probably always be the first choice. OSL is a much more succinct language than EQUEL. By way of illustration, consider Figs. 20.6 and 20.7, which show, respectively, an EQUEL version (actually an EQUEL/C version) and an OSL version of a trivial application—"Display the status of a specified supplier" (where the supplier number of the required supplier is provided as a parameter by the end-user).

The example of Figs. 20.6 and 20.7 does illustrate one important difference between EQUEL and OSL right away—namely, that in EQUEL program variables are used as intermediaries between the database and the

```
main( )
{
##   char   csno[5] ;
##   int    cstat ;
##   INGRES s_sp_p
##   FORMS
##   FORMINIT statform
##   DISPLAY statform QUERY
##   INITIALIZE
##   ACTIVATE MENUITEM "go"
##   {
##      GETFORM ( csno = sno )
##      RETRIEVE ( cstat = s.status )
##      WHERE    s.sno = csno
##      PUTFORM ( sno = csno, status = cstat )
##   }
##   ACTIVATE MENUITEM "return"
##   {
##      BREAKDISPLAY
##   }
##   ENDFORMS
##   EXIT
}
```

Fig. 20.6 A simple application (EQUEL/C)

---

*Throughout this section we take the term "EQUEL" to include EQUEL/FORMS. Also, of course, all of our discussions apply equally well to ESQL, mutatis mutandis.

```
"go" =
    {
         statform := RETRIEVE ( s.sno, s.status )
                      WHERE     s.sno = sno
    }
"return" =
    {
         RETURN
    }
```

Fig. 20.7 A simple application (OSL)

form, whereas in OSL the fields of the form *are* the program variables. Another obvious difference is that OSL automatically takes care of numerous housekeeping details that are the concern of the user (i.e., the application programmer) in EQUEL.

However, EQUEL does provide certain features that are not yet supported in OSL. Perhaps the most important is the REPEAT option (already mentioned in Section 20.2). A few additional such features (comparatively minor) are described in the RTI manuals. Given that the syntax of OSL is very close to that of EQUEL in many ways, the recommended method of proceeding is to define the application code by means of OSL initially, then modify that code subsequently if it proves desirable to incorporate EQUEL features that are not directly supported in OSL. Also, of course, an OSL program can always invoke an EQUEL procedure by means of the OSL statement CALLPROC.

DISTRIBUTED DATABASE SUPPORT

21

INGRES/STAR

21.1 INTRODUCTION

In this, the final chapter of the book, we take a look at one of the most
significant software product developments of recent years—INGRES/
STAR. As explained in Chapter 2, INGRES/STAR is a full distributed
database management system: It allows a single (distributed) database to
span any number of distinct sites, where those sites may involve a variety
of different CPUs and different operating systems and may be connected
together via a variety of different communication networks. An INGRES/
STAR database can consist of any arbitrary collection of relations from
any arbitrary collection of local ("component") databases at any arbitrary
set of such sites. Furthermore, any number of such distributed databases
can be defined, and distinct distributed databases can overlap. From the
user's point of view, however, each such distributed database then behaves
for data manipulation purposes as if it were *not* distributed, i.e., as if it
were a local database stored in its entirety at the user's own local site. See
Fig. 21.1 (a repeat of Fig. 2.7 from Chapter 2).

The advantages of such a system include the following, among many
others:

- *System transparency*: As already indicated, users and user programs
  are independent of the underlying machines, operating systems, and

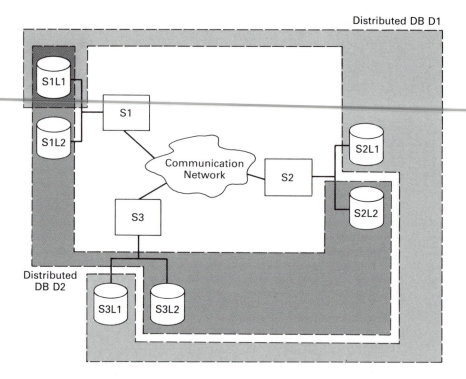

Fig. 21.1 INGRES/STAR

network protocols. Future releases of INGRES/STAR will allow them to be independent of the underlying DBMS also: It is planned to allow nonINGRES sites to participate in an INGRES/STAR network, and thereby to share data with INGRES sites or with other nonINGRES sites, by means of a mechanism known as a "gateway" (see Section 21.4).

- *Location transparency*: Users and user programs do not have to know where data is stored. As a result, data can be moved from one site to another in response to changing patterns of usage, without necessitating any rewriting of application programs.

- *Improved productivity*: As a consequence of the previous points, users have universal and uniform access to data throughout the network. Data manipulation operations (SQL or QUEL) work against the distributed database exactly as if it were an ordinary local database. Application programs (both user-provided applications and the built-in subsystems

QBF, RBF, etc.) therefore also operate exactly as if the database were purely local.

■ *Site autonomy*: Despite the fact that data is universally accessible, as explained in the previous paragraph, local sites can still maintain control (for security and integrity and performance purposes) of data that logically belongs to them—they do not have to relinquish such control to some remote "master" site. Also, local applications (i.e., applications that do not need access to remote data) remain truly local; they are not penalized in any way by the fact that their local data is now accessible to remote sites.

■ *Application portability*: Applications can be developed on a micro and can then run unchanged on a large mainframe (or vice versa). Applications can easily be moved from one site to another around the network.

■ *Capacity and performance*: Transaction volumes and database size are essentially unlimited because the network can grow to any size, again without necessitating the rewriting of application programs. Throughput is increased because of the parallelism inherent in the system structure. Response times can be reduced by placing data at the site at which it is most frequently used.

■ *Incremental growth*: Individual sites can be added, upgraded, and replaced in a transparent and nondisruptive fashion. Existing applications will continue to work after a nondistributed system has evolved into a distributed one; they will also continue to work as the distributed system itself evolves and new sites are added and/or data is redistributed across existing sites.

21.2 DATA DEFINITION

We begin by considering what is involved in defining an INGRES/STAR distributed database. First, it is important to understand that all data in a distributed database "really" exists in, and belongs to, some underlying local or "component" database. Thus, tables (that is, base tables) are created in their local database in the usual way. Likewise, storage structures (in QUEL terms, the MODIFY and INDEX operations), security constraints (DEFINE PERMIT in QUEL), and integrity constraints (DEFINE INTEGRITY in QUEL) are also all defined at the component site in the usual way. For the sake of the example, therefore, let us suppose that relations S, P, and SP already exist; further, let us suppose they are stored in three distinct local databases LS, LP, and LSP, at three distinct sites or *nodes* NS, NP, and NSP, respectively. Suppose now that we wish to define a single distributed database S_SP_P containing all three relations. We go through the following steps.

1. Suppose we are signed on to the INGRES site X, which for generality we assume is not one of the sites NS, NP, NSP. We issue the regular INGRES system command CREATEDB at site X (with a parameter, not shown below, to specify that this is a distributed database we are creating, instead of an ordinary local database):

```
CREATEDB   S_SP_P
```

The name of the new database is "S_SP_P"; it can be referenced at site X by that name (e.g., in the command that invokes INGRES/MENU at site X). An entry describing S_SP_P is made in the database database (DBDB) at site X. The user issuing the CREATEDB becomes the database administrator for the new database. Site X is said to be the "coordinator site" or "coordinator node" for database S_SP_P.

2. So far we have only specified that the distributed database exists; we have not indicated what tables it logically contains. The (SQL or QUEL) DEFINE LINK operation is used for this purpose:

```
DEFINE LINK S
       WITH NODE     = NS,
            DATABASE  = LS,
            TABLE     = S
```

(certain optional parameters not shown). We assume that this operation is executed in the context of distributed database S_SP_P (that is, database S_SP_P is the "current database"—e.g., it was the database nominated in the INGRES command when the user signed on to the system). A dictionary entry for link S is made at the coordinator site for database S_SP_P (i.e., site X). Now the name "S" can be used in the context of distributed database S_SP_P to refer to base table S in (component) database LS at node NS. For example, we can now execute SQL SELECT operations (etc.) in the context of database S_SP_P against that base table.

We define links to tables P and SP similarly:

```
DEFINE LINK P
       WITH NODE     = NP,
            DATABASE  = LP,
            TABLE     = P

DEFINE LINK SP
       WITH NODE     = NSP,
            DATABASE  = LSP,
            TABLE     = SP
```

Of course, it is not necessary that table "link names" in the distributed database be the same as the table names in the underlying component database (though for simplicity they all are in our example).

3. An existing link can be destroyed at any time by means of the (SQL or QUEL) DESTROY LINK operation—for example:

```
DESTROY LINK S
```

The effect of **DESTROY LINK** is to remove the indicated link from the current distributed database—i.e., it causes the underlying table to cease to be accessible from that database. It has no effect on the underlying table itself, of course.

4. To destroy an existing distributed database, the normal DESTROYDB system command is used:

```
DESTROYDB database
```

If "database" is a distributed database, the effect of DESTROYDB is simply to remove it from the INGRES/STAR system. The underlying local databases are not affected.

5. So far the new distributed database S_SP_P is directly accessible by name from site X only. (It can be accessed indirectly from other sites via the normal facilities of INGRES/NET, of course.) However, we can also make it directly accessible from additional sites Y, Z, . . . by means of the (SQL or QUEL) ADD NODE command. For example:

```
ADD NODE Y
```

An entry for database S_SP_P is made in the DBDB at site Y, referring back to the entry in the DBDB at site X. Now users can operate on database S_SP_P at site Y (without explicitly having to make use of INGRES/NET) just as if S_SP_P had been defined at site Y in the first place. *Note:* There is no requirement that site Y be one of the component sites for database S_SP_P. In other words, site Y may or may not be one of the sites NS, NP, NSP.

6. Added nodes can subsequently be removed via the SQL or QUEL RE-MOVE operation:

```
REMOVE NODE node
```

The entry for the distributed database is removed from the DBDB at the specified node.

21.3   DATA MANIPULATION

The following QUEL data manipulation operations (or their SQL equivalents) are supported in the context of an INGRES/STAR distributed database:

```
RANGE
RETRIEVE (not the INTO form)
APPEND
REPLACE
DELETE
BEGIN TRANSACTION
END TRANSACTION
SAVEPOINT
ABORT [ TO savepoint ]
```

In addition, two new forms of HELP are supported:

```
HELP LINK link
HELP NODE node
```

Note: A "pass through" mode is also available, by which the user can perform QUEL or SQL operations directly on a local database without leaving the distributed database environment. In this way the user can, for example, create new tables in a database at his or her own local site and can then immediately make them accessible (via DEFINE LINK) to the distributed database.

We explain in outline what is involved in processing a query (more generally, any QUEL or SQL statement) in the INGRES/STAR environment. Suppose the query is submitted at site X. Then:

- The optimizer at site X gathers together all the dictionary information for all tables from all sites mentioned in the request and generates a *global query plan*. That plan represents the strategy that (in the optimizer's estimation) is the cheapest possible for the given query. (The cost of any given strategy is considered to be the sum of its CPU processing costs, its I/O costs, and its network communication costs.)

- The global plan is then divided into fragments, one fragment for each site that participates in the query.

- Each fragment of the plan is then converted back into SQL (or QUEL), and the converted form is shipped to the appropriate site. The advan-

tage of this "back compilation" technique is that it considerably reduces both the size and the number of messages to each participant
site.* The sequence in which such fragments are shipped is controlled
by the optimizer at site X.

- The INGRES backend at each participant site processes its own fragment of the query and sends the result back to site X.

- Site X gathers together all such results and completes processing of the
  original request as appropriate.

As explained in Chapter 2, the first version of INGRES/STAR does
suffer from one limitation—namely, that a single transaction is not allowed
to update more than one component database (of course, different transactions can update different component databases). This limitation will be
removed in the next release of the product.

We conclude this section with a brief note on the INGRES frontend
subsystems. Running a subsystem such as QBF typically involves the creation of new forms, which must be stored in the dictionary for some component database (since forms, tables, etc., "really" belong to some component database). If the user wishes to invoke such a subsystem on a
distributed database, therefore, he or she must first specify which component database's dictionary is to be used for the forms. A special SQL/
QUEL definitional operation is provided for this purpose. We omit the details here.

21.4 FUTURE DIRECTIONS

RTI has already publicly committed to a number of future enhancements
to INGRES/STAR. We summarize the most significant ones below:

- *Additional CPUs and operating systems*: Version I supports INGRES
  sites only, either VAX/VMS- or UNIX-based. Future releases will include support for MVS-, VM/CMS-, and PC/DOS-based INGRES sites
  also.

- *Additional networks*: Version I supports the DECnet and TCP/IP communication protocols only (or a combination of the two). Other protocols, including IBM's SNA (System Network Architecture), will be
  supported in future releases.

---

*Another major advantage is that (in future releases of INGRES/STAR) the par-
ticipant site need not be running INGRES, but can instead be running any DBMS
that supports the same INGRES dialect of SQL or QUEL. See Section 21.4.

- *NonINGRES sites*: Future releases will support not only INGRES sites, but "companion" DBMS sites. This support will be provided in two stages:

(a) Support for "SQL-based" companions, i.e., DBMSs that already support (some dialect of) SQL, such as IBM's DB2 and SQL/DS;

(b) Support for "nonSQL" DBMSs, such as IBM's IMS.

This support is referred to below as the INGRES/STAR *gateway* feature.

- *Multiple-database update*: A single transaction will be permitted to update data in multiple component databases.

- *Data replication*: INGRES/STAR will allow multiple physical copies ("replicates") of a given table to be kept at multiple distinct sites, thus providing greater data availability (the table remains available so long as at least one site that holds a copy of it remains available). Replicates can be created and destroyed dynamically. INGRES/STAR will keep all replicates current and consistent, by automatically propagating update operations; users and user programs thus will not have to concern themselves with such details, and indeed will not need to be aware of replication at all ("replication transparency").

- *Data fragmentation*: INGRES/STAR will allow a given table to be divided into disjoint fragments for physical storage purposes, thus allowing greater control over the physical placement of data. For example, supplier records for London suppliers can be stored in London and supplier records for suppliers in Paris can be stored in Paris (with obvious performance advantages). Refragmentation can occur at any time, and fragments can be replicated. INGRES/STAR will handle all details of the fragmentation process and will present the table to users and user programs as if it were *not* fragmented; users and user programs thus will not have to concern themselves with such details, and indeed will not need to be aware of fragmentation at all ("fragmentation transparency").

- *Gateways*: A gateway is the interface between INGRES/STAR and a nonINGRES DBMS. As such, it consists of a layer of interface code on top of the nonINGRES DBMS whose purpose is basically to make that DBMS look like INGRES for data manipulation purposes (or, at the very least, for data retrieval purposes). Its functions must include the following:

(a) Translation between INGRES/SQL (or INGRES/QUEL) and the nonINGRES DBMS's own native data manipulation language;

(b) Data type conversion between the INGRES data types and the non-INGRES DBMS's own native data types;

(c) Emulation of the INGRES dictionary (catalog tables) on top of the nonINGRES DBMS;

and miscellaneous additional functions. It is RTI's intention to provide gateways of its own for certain important nonINGRES systems, and to provide a "gateway development toolkit" to facilitate the construction of such gateways by interested parties for other systems.

APPENDIXES

Advantages of INGRES

A.1 INTRODUCTION

If the advantages of a relational system such as INGRES must be summed up in a single word, that word is *simplicity*—where by "simplicity" we mean, primarily, simplicity for the user. Simplicity, in turn, translates into *usability* and *productivity*. Usability means that even comparatively unskilled users can use the system to do useful work; that is, end-users can frequently obtain useful results from the system without having to go through the potential bottleneck of the DP department. Productivity means that both end-users and DP professionals can be more productive in their day-to-day activities; as a result, they can between them make significant inroads into the well-known application backlog problem (see Section A.7 below). In this appendix we discuss the advantages of a system like INGRES in some detail.

A.2 SOUND THEORETICAL BASE

The first point is that relational systems are based on a formal theoretical foundation, the *relational model* (discussed in detail in Appendix B). As a result, they behave in well-defined ways; and (possibly without consciously realizing the fact) users have a simple model of that behavior in their mind that enables them to predict with confidence what the system will do in any given situation. There are (or should be) no surprises. This predictability means that the user interfaces are easy to document, teach, learn, use, and remember.

Note: It cannot be denied that most systems today, even relational systems, do nevertheless display rather ad hoc and unpredictable behavior in some areas; as an example, consider the treatment of view updating in INGRES, which does display a certain amount of unpleasant arbitrariness (see Section 7.3). But such arbitrariness tends to occur precisely at those points where the implementation has departed from the underlying theory. For example, a crucial component of the relational model is the concept of *primary key* (see Appendix B). However, INGRES does not support that concept, and it is that omission that is the direct cause of the arbitrariness just referred to. INGRES is not the sole offender in this regard, of course— similar criticisms apply to most other systems at the time of writing—but it does serve to illustrate the undesirable consequences of disregarding the prescriptions of the underlying model.

Incidentally, we remark in passing that many critics of relational systems in the past have actually objected to the fact that they are based on theory! The objection seems to be that only theoreticians are capable of understanding, or need to understand, something that is based on theory. Our own position is exactly the opposite: Systems that are not based on theory are usually very difficult for *anyone* to understand. It cannot be stated too strongly that "theoretical" does *not* mean "not practical." On the contrary, considerations that are initially dismissed as being "only theoretical" (sic) have a nasty habit of becoming horribly practical a few years later on.

A.3 SMALL NUMBER OF CONCEPTS

The relational model is notable for the small number of concepts it involves. As pointed out in Section 5.5, all data in a relational database is represented in one and only one way, namely as column values within rows of tables, and hence only one operator is needed for each of the four basic manipulative functions (retrieve, change, insert, delete). For exactly the same reason, fewer operators are also needed in a relational system for all the other functions—data definition, security control, integrity control, storage mapping, etc.—that are required in a general-purpose DBMS. In the case of authorization specifically, it is the simplicity and regularity of the data structure that makes it possible to define such a sophisticated data protection mechanism (one in which, as was shown by the examples of Chapter 8, value-dependent, value-independent, context-dependent, and other constraints can be easily defined and conveniently enforced).

A separate but related point is the following: In the relational model, distinct concepts are cleanly separated, not bundled together. By contrast, the owner-member (or parent-child) link construct found in many nonrelational systems bundles together several fundamentally distinct notions: It is simultaneously a representation of a one-to-many relationship, an access path (or collection of access paths), a mechanism for enforcing certain integrity constraints, and so on. As a result, it becomes difficult to tell exactly what purpose a given link is serving (and it may be used for a purpose for which it was not intended). For example, a program may come to rely on an access path that is really a side effect of the way the database designer chose to represent a certain integrity constraint. If that integrity constraint needs to be changed, then the database will have to be restructured, with a strong likelihood that the program will then have to be rewritten—even if that program is completely uninterested in the integrity constraint per se.

A.4 SET-LEVEL OPERATORS

Relational data manipulation operations such as SELECT, UPDATE, etc., in SQL (or RETRIEVE, REPLACE, etc., in QUEL) are *set-level* operations. This fact means that users simply have to specify *what* they want, not *how* to get to what they want. For example, a user needing to know which parts are supplied by supplier S2 can simply issue the SQL query:

```
SELECT  SP.PNO
FROM    SP
WHERE   SP.SNO = 'S2'
```

INGRES decides how to "navigate" through the physical storage structure on the disk in order to respond to this query. (For this reason, as mentioned in Chapter 1, systems such as INGRES are frequently described as "automatic navigation" systems. By contrast, systems in which users have to do that navigation for themselves are described as "manual navigation" systems.) By taking this burden off the user's back, INGRES is freeing the user to concentrate on solving the real problem—i.e., on finding an answer to the query, in the case at hand, and using that information for whatever purpose it is needed in the outside world. In the case of end-users, in fact, it is automatic navigation that makes it possible for the user to use the system in the first place. It is not difficult to find a simple INGRES query for which an equivalent COBOL program would be ten or twenty pages long, and writing such a program would be out of the question for most users (and maybe not worth the effort involved even when not).

Furthermore, application programmers can take advantage of the automatic navigation feature of the system as well, just as end-users can. Application programmers too can be more productive in a system like INGRES.

A.5   THE DUAL-MODE PRINCIPLE

In INGRES the same language, SQL (or QUEL), is used for both programming and interactive access to the database. This fact has two immediate consequences:

1. Different categories of user—system and database administrators, application programmers, end-users from any number of different backgrounds—are all "speaking the same language" and are thus better able to communicate with one another. It is also easy for one person to switch between categories—e.g., to perform data definition (administrative) functions on one occasion and ad hoc query (end-user) functions on another.

2. Application programmers can easily debug the database portions of their programs (i.e., EQUEL or ESQL or OSL/QUEL or OSL/SQL statements) through the INGRES Terminal Monitor interface (INGRES/IQUEL or INGRES/ISQL). That interactive interface thus serves as a powerful and convenient program debugging aid.

A.6   DATA INDEPENDENCE

Data independence is the independence of users and user programs from details of the way the data is stored and accessed. It is critically important for at least two reasons:

1. It is important for application programmers because, without it, changes to the structure of the database would necessitate corresponding changes to application programs. In the absence of such independence, one of two things happens: Either it becomes almost impossible to make required changes to the database because of the investment in existing programs, or (more likely) a significant portion of the application programming effort is devoted purely to maintenance activity—maintenance activity, that is, that would be unnecessary if the system had provided data independence in the first place. Both of these factors are significant contributors to the application backlog problem mentioned in Section A.1.

2. It is important for end-users because, without it, direct end-user access to the database would scarcely be possible at all. Data independence and very high level languages such as QUEL and SQL go hand in hand.

Data independence is not an absolute—different systems provide it in differing degrees. To put it another way, few systems if any provide no data independence at all; it is just that some systems are more data-dependent than others. Furthermore, the term "data independence" really covers two somewhat distinct notions, namely physical data independence (i.e., independence of the physical arrangement of the data on the storage medium) and logical data independence (i.e., independence of the logical structure of the data as tables and fields). INGRES is fairly strong on both aspects, though there is undoubtedly still room for improvement in both areas (for example, it is unfortunate that the logical notion of enforcing uniqueness is bundled with the physical notion of some particular storage structure, such as an index). Basically, INGRES provides physical data independence by virtue of its automatic navigation feature, and logical data independence by virtue of its view mechanism (see Section 7.4).

A.7 EASE OF APPLICATION DEVELOPMENT

INGRES facilitates the application development process in a variety of significant ways:

1. First, as discussed in Chapter 20, the availability of the INGRES frontends—the Terminal Monitors, QBF, QBF/VIFRED, RBF, and VIGRAPH—means that it may not be necessary to develop an application program (in the traditional sense of the term) at all. The importance of this point can scarcely be over-emphasized.

2. Second, the availability of the ABF/VIFRED combination (see Chapter 20) means that if specialized, forms-based applications are needed, then they can be developed quickly and easily, still without any programming in the conventional sense.

3. Third, the high degree of data independence provided and the high level of the application programming interface (EQUEL and EQUEL/FORMS, or ESQL and ESQL/FORMS) together mean that when it *is* necessary to write a conventional program, then that program is easier to write, requires less maintenance, and is easier to change when it does require maintenance than it would be in an older, nonrelational system.

4. Last, and largely as a consequence of the previous three points, the application development cycle can involve a great deal more *prototyping* than it used to: A first version can be built and shown to the intended users, who can then suggest improvements for incorporation into the next version, and so on. As a result, the final application should do exactly what its users require it to. The overall development process is far less rigid than it used

to be, and the application users can be far more involved in that process, to the benefit of all concerned.

A.8   DYNAMIC DATA DEFINITION

We have already discussed the advantages of dynamic data definition at some length in Chapter 3 (Section 3.5), and we will not repeat the arguments here. However, we make one additional point: The ability to create new definitions at any time without having to bring the system to a halt is really only part of a larger overall objective, which is to eliminate the need for *any* planned system shutdown. Thus, for example, utilities can be invoked from an online terminal, and they can run in parallel with production work; it is possible, for example, to take a checkpoint of one database while transactions are simultaneously operating on another. Ideally, the system should have to be started exactly once, when it is first installed, and should then run "forever." (We are not claiming that this objective has yet been achieved.)

A.9   EASE OF INSTALLATION AND EASE OF OPERATION

INGRES is designed to be as easy to install and easy to operate as possible. Various features of the system, some of them touched on in previous sections of this appendix, contribute to the achievement of this objective. Details of such features (other than details already given in the body of the text) are beyond the scope of this book, but it is worth pointing out explicitly one very important consequence of them, namely the following: It requires only a comparatively small population of DP professionals (administrators, system programmers, console operators) to provide INGRES services to a very large population of users (application programmers and end-users). INGRES is an extremely cost-effective system.

A.10   SIMPLIFIED DATABASE DESIGN

Database design in a relational system is easier than it is in a nonrelational system for a number of reasons (though it may still involve some difficult decisions in complex situations).

- First, the decoupling of logical and physical levels means that logical and physical design problems can be separately addressed.
- Second, at the logical level, the data structure is just about as simple as it possibly can be.

- Third, there are some sound principles (basically the principles of *normalization*) that can be brought to bear on the logical design problem.

- Last, the dynamic data definition feature and the high degree of data independence (again) mean that it is not necessary to do the entire design all at once, and neither is it so critical to get it right first time.

A comprehensive logical design methodology that uses a combination of the principles of normalization with a top-down (entity-based) approach is described in the author's book *Relational Database: Selected Writings* (Addison-Wesley, 1986).

A.11 INTEGRATED DICTIONARY

As explained in Chapter 6, the INGRES dictionary is completely integrated with the rest of the data, in the sense that it is represented in the same way (as tables) and can be queried in the same way (via QUEL or SQL). In other words, there is no artificial and unnecessary distinction between catalog data and other data, or between data and "data about the data" (or "metadata," as it is sometimes called). This integration brings with it a number of benefits, among them the following:

1. Looking something up in the database and looking something up in the catalog are one and the same process. To see the advantage here, consider the analogy of looking something up in a book and looking something up in the table of contents for that book. It would be very annoying if the table of contents appeared somewhere other than in the book itself, in a format that required some different manner of access (for example, if the table of contents was in Spanish and was stored on a set of 3-by-5 cards, while the text of the book itself was in English). The role of the catalog with respect to the database is precisely similar to that of the table of contents with respect to a book.

2. The process of creating generalized (i.e., "metadata"-driven) application programs is considerably simplified. For example, suppose it is required to write a program that checks that every supplier number value appearing anywhere in the database also appears in the SNO column of the suppliers table S—in itself a reasonable requirement—without making any prior assumptions about the structure of the database (i.e., the program must not rely on any builtin knowledge as to what tables exist or what their columns are). More generally, suppose it is required to write a program to check that every value of type X appearing anywhere in the database also appears in some specified column Y of some specified table Z (where X, Y, and Z are parameters), again without making any prior assumptions

about the structure of the database. In both of these examples, the integrated dictionary is crucial. *Note*: Such programs may very well be needed in practice in order to enforce referential integrity. See Appendix B or the author's book *Relational Database*: *Selected Writings* (Addison-Wesley, 1986).

A.12   FORMS-BASED SUBSYSTEMS

The INGRES forms-based subsystems—INGRES/MENU, INGRES/QUERY, INGRES/GRAPHICS, etc.—are a particularly strong feature of the overall INGRES system. They are easy to learn, easy to use, effective, and well integrated with the base DBMS and with each other. Together, they illustrate very clearly the point that the relational model is *not* meant to be seen as an end in itself; rather, the ideas of the model are intended to serve as a foundation for, and a powerful unifying force in, the design and construction of higher-level interfaces—interfaces that are well engineered and truly usable by a wide variety of human users who have neither the time nor the inclination to delve into the intricacies of the DBMS per se.

A.13   DISTRIBUTED DATABASE SUPPORT

INGRES provides several levels of support for distributed processing: micro/mainframe links (INGRES/PCLINK), networking (INGRES/NET and INGRES/NET PC), and full distributed database support (INGRES/STAR). We discuss only the last of these here. INGRES/STAR represents a major technological advance in the commercial data processing world: It is the first commercially available product to provide genuine distributed *database* support (as opposed to support for distributed processing merely). The distributed database support of INGRES/STAR allows an arbitrary collection of relations from an arbitrary collection of databases on a variety of different machines, running a variety of different operating systems, and connected by a variety of different communication networks, to function as if they were all stored in a single database on a single machine. The user is completely insulated from all details of the distribution.

A.14   DUAL LANGUAGE SUPPORT

INGRES supports both QUEL and SQL. Both languages can be used:

- For interactive access to the database via the appropriate INGRES Terminal Monitor

- For programmed access to the database via one of the INGRES-supported programming languages (Ada, BASIC, C, COBOL, FORTRAN, Pascal, or PL/I)

- For defining the data to be reported on via INGRES/REPORTS

- For defining the data to be graphed via INGRES/GRAPHICS

- For OSL-based access to the database via INGRES/APPLICATIONS

As the industry standard, SQL provides the necessary base for intersystem communication: An INGRES site that supports SQL will be able to communicate via INGRES/STAR across a communication network, not only with other INGRES sites, but with any site that supports a system of any kind that supports the same SQL interface. INGRES support for SQL also raises the possibility of running third-party, SQL-based applications software on top of the INGRES DBMS. On the other hand, QUEL is a technically superior language, and many users will continue to choose it in preference to SQL for their own applications.

A.15 PERFORMANCE

It is difficult to make definitive statements regarding the performance of any given DBMS; performance is dependent on so many variables, including machine type and size, operating system, buffer parameters, number of users, and of course transaction mix. But one general point that can be made is the following: In a nonrelational system, system performance depends heavily on the quality of the application programmer; in a relational system, by contrast, it depends much more on the quality of the system *optimizer*. Indeed, it can be argued with some justification that a relational system with a good optimizer might *out*perform a nonrelational system, for at least the following three reasons:

1. The optimizer has a wealth of information available to it that an application programmer typically does not have. To be specific, it has certain statistical information, such as the size of each table, the number of values in each column, the number of times each different value occurs in each column, and so on. As a result, the optimizer is able to make a more accurate assessment of the efficiency of any given strategy for implementing a particular request, and is thus more likely to choose the most efficient implementation.

2. Furthermore, if the database statistics change significantly, then a different choice of strategy may be desirable; in other words, reoptimization may be required. In a relational system, reoptimization is trivial—it simply involves a reprocessing of the request by the system optimizer. In fact, in

a system like INGRES, such reoptimization is effectively done automatically each time the request is submitted. In a nonrelational system, by contrast, reoptimization involves a rewrite of the program, and will probably therefore not be done at all.

3. Finally, the optimizer is a *program*, and therefore by definition much more patient than a typical application programmer. The optimizer is quite capable of considering literally hundreds of different implementation strategies for a given request, whereas it is extremely unlikely that a human programmer would consider more than three or four.

For information regarding the performance of INGRES specifically, the reader is referred to RTI.

A.16   MULTIPLE ENVIRONMENTS

INGRES runs virtually unchanged in many different environments (see Appendix E). The fact that the system is thus virtually independent of its environment is the source of obvious benefits in numerous areas—for example, user education, user productivity, application portability, and distributed processing, to name but a few.

B

The Relational Model

B.1 INTRODUCTION

INGRES is a relational DBMS ("relational system" for short). The purpose of this appendix is to explain exactly what that statement means. Basically, a relational system is a system that is constructed in accordance with the relational *model* (or at least the major principles of that model); and the relational model is *a way of looking at data*—that is, a prescription for how to represent data and how to manipulate that representation. More specifically, the relational model is concerned with three aspects of data: data *structure*, data *integrity*, and data *manipulation*. We examine each of these in turn (in Sections B.2, B.3, and B.4, respectively), and then consider the question of what exactly it is that constitutes a relational *system* (in Section B.5).

Note: In this appendix we will (for the most part) be using formal relational terminology. For convenience, Fig. B.1 repeats from Chapter 1 the major relational terms and their informal equivalents.

Formal relational term	Informal equivalents
relation	table
tuple	record, row
attribute	field, column
primary key	unique identifier

Fig. B.1 Some terminology

353

B.2   RELATIONAL DATA STRUCTURE

The smallest unit of data in the relational model is the individual data value. Such values are considered to be *atomic*—that is, they are nondecomposable so far as the model is concerned. A *domain* is a set of such values, all of the same type; for example, the domain of supplier numbers is the set of all valid supplier numbers, the domain of shipment quantities is the set of all integers greater than zero and less than 10,000 (say). Thus domains are *pools of values*, from which the actual values appearing in attributes (columns) are drawn. The significance of domains is as follows: If two attributes draw their values from the same domain, then comparisons—and hence joins, unions, etc.—involving those two attributes probably make sense, because they are comparing like with like; conversely, if two attributes draw their values from different domains, then comparisons (etc.) involving those two attributes probably do not make sense. In SQL terms, for example, the query

```
SELECT P.*, SP.*
FROM   P, SP
WHERE  P.PNO = SP.PNO
```

probably does make sense, whereas the query

```
SELECT P.*, SP.*
FROM   P, SP
WHERE  P.WEIGHT = SP.QTY
```

probably does not. (INGRES, however, has no notion of domains per se. Both of the foregoing SELECT statements are legal queries in INGRES.)

Note that domains are primarily conceptual in nature. They may or may not be explicitly stored in the database as actual sets of values. But they should be specified as part of the database definition (in a system that supports the concept at all—but most systems currently do not); and then each attribute definition should include a reference to the corresponding domain. A given attribute may have the same name as the corresponding domain or a different name. Obviously it must have a different name if any ambiguity would otherwise result (in particular, if two attributes in the same relation are both based on the same domain; see the definition of relation below, and note the phrase "not necessarily all distinct").

We are now in a position to define the term "relation." A *relation* on domains D1, D2, ..., Dn (not necessarily all distinct) consists of a *heading* and a *body*. The heading consists of a fixed set of *attributes* A1, A2, ..., An, such that each attribute Ai corresponds to precisely one underlying domain Di ($i = 1,2,...,n$). The body consists of a time-varying set of *tuples,* where each tuple in turn consists of a set of attribute-value pairs (Ai:vi) ($i = 1,2,...,n$), one such pair for each attribute Ai in the heading. For any given attribute-value pair (Ai:vi), vi is a value from the unique domain Di that is associated with the attribute Ai.

As an example, let us see how the supplier relation S measures up to this definition (see Fig. 1.2 in Chapter 1). The underlying domains are the domain of supplier numbers (D1, say), the domain of supplier names (D2), the domain of supplier status values (D3), and the domain of city names (D4). The heading of S consists of the attributes SNO (underlying domain D1), SNAME (domain D2), STATUS (domain D3), and CITY (domain D4). The body of S consists of a set of tuples (five tuples in Fig. 1.2, but this set varies with time as updates are made to the relation); and each tuple consists of a set of four attribute-value pairs, one such pair for each of the four attributes in the heading. For example, the tuple for supplier S1 consists of the pairs

```
( SNO    : 'S1'     )
( SNAME  : 'Smith'  )
( STATUS : 20       )
( CITY   : 'London' )
```

(though it is normal to elide the attribute names in informal contexts). And of course each attribute value does indeed come from the appropriate underlying domain; the value "S1," for example, does come from the supplier number domain D1. So S is indeed a relation according to the definition.

Note carefully that when we draw a relation such as relation S as a table, as we did in Fig. 1.2, we are merely making use of a convenient method for representing the relation on paper. A table and a relation are not really the same thing, though for most of this book we have assumed that they are. For example, the rows of a table clearly have an ordering (from top to bottom), whereas the tuples of a relation do not (the body of a relation is a mathematical *set*, and sets do not have any ordering in mathematics). Likewise, the columns of a table also have an ordering (from left to right), whereas the attributes of a relation do not.

Notice that the underlying domains of a relation are "not necessarily all distinct." Many examples have already been given in which they are not; see, e.g., the result relation in Example 4.3.1 (Chapter 4), which includes two attributes both defined on the domain of city-names.

The value n (the number of attributes in the relation, or equivalently the number of underlying domains) is called the *degree* of the relation. A relation of degree one is called *unary*, a relation of degree two *binary*, a relation of degree three *ternary*, . . . , and a relation of degree *n n-ary*. In the suppliers-and-parts database, relations S, P, and SP have degrees 4, 5, and 3, respectively. The number of tuples in the relation is called the *cardinality* of that relation; the cardinalities of relations S, P, and SP of Fig. 1.2 are 5, 6, and 12, respectively. The cardinality of a relation changes with time, whereas the degree does not.

B.3   RELATIONAL DATA INTEGRITY

One important consequence of the definitions in the previous section is that *every relation has a primary key*. Since the body of a relation is a set, and sets by definition do not contain duplicate elements, it follows that (at any given time) no two tuples of a relation can be duplicates of each other. Let R be a relation with attributes A1, A2,..., An. The set of attributes K = (Ai,Aj, . . . ,Ak) of R is said to be a *candidate key* of R if and only if it satisfies the following two time-independent properties:

1. *Uniqueness*:
   At any given time, no two distinct tuples of R have the same value for Ai, the same value for Aj, . . . , and the same value for Ak.

2. *Minimality*:
   None of Ai, Aj, . . . , Ak can be discarded from K without destroying the uniqueness property.

Every relation has at least one candidate key, because at least the combination of all of its attributes has the uniqueness property. For a given relation, one candidate key is designated as the *primary* key; the remaining candidate keys (if any) are called *alternate* keys. *Note*: The rationale by which one candidate key is chosen as the primary key (in cases where there is a choice) is outside the framework of the relational model per se. In practice the choice is usually straightforward.

Example: Suppose that supplier names and supplier numbers are both unique (at any given time, no two suppliers have the same number or the same name). Then relation S has two candidate keys, SNO and SNAME. We choose SNO as the primary key; SNAME then becomes an alternate key. Note, however, that INGRES has no knowledge of either primary or alternate keys as such (although it is possible to enforce uniqueness via MODIFY—see Chapter 12).

Continuing with the example, consider attribute SNO of relation SP. It is clear that a given value for that attribute, say the supplier number S1, should be permitted to appear in the database only if that same value also appears as a value of the primary key SNO of relation S (for otherwise the database cannot be considered to be in a state of integrity). An attribute such as SP.SNO is said to be a *foreign key*. In general, a foreign key is an attribute (or attribute combination) of one relation R2 whose values are required to match those of the primary key of some relation R1 (R1 and R2 not necessarily distinct). Note that a foreign key and the corresponding primary key should be defined on the same underlying domain.

We can now state the two integrity rules of the relational model. *Note*: These rules are *general*, in the sense that any database that conforms to the model is required to satisfy them. However, any specific database will have a set of additional specific rules that apply to it alone. For example, the suppliers-and-parts database may have a specific rule to the effect that shipment quantities must be in the range 1 to 9999, say. But such specific rules are outside the scope of the relational model per se.

1. *Entity integrity*:
   No attribute participating in the primary key of a base relation is allowed to accept null values.

2. *Referential integrity*:
   If base relation R2 includes a foreign key FK matching the primary key PK of some base relation R1, then every value of FK in R2 must either (a) be equal to the value of PK in some tuple of R1 or (b) be wholly null (i.e., each attribute value participating in that FK value must be null). R1 and R2 are not necessarily distinct.

A *base relation* corresponds to what we have been calling a base table in the body of this book: It is an autonomous, named relation (see Chapter 3 for further discussion).

The justification for the entity integrity rule is as follows:

1. Base relations correspond to entities in the real world. For example, base relation S corresponds to a set of suppliers in the real world.

2. By definition, entities in the real world are distinguishable—that is, they have a unique identification of some kind.

3. Primary keys perform the unique identification function in the relational model.

4. Thus, a primary key value that was null would be a contradiction in terms—in effect, it would be saying that there was some entity that had no known *id*entity (i.e., did not exist). Hence the name "entity integrity."

To put it another way: *In a relational database, we never record information about something we cannot identify.*

As for the second rule ("referential integrity"), it is clear that a given foreign key value must have a matching primary key value in some tuple of the referenced relation if that foreign key value is nonnull. Sometimes, however, it is necessary to permit the foreign key to accept null values. Suppose, for example, that in a given company it is legal for some employee to be currently assigned to no department at all. For such an employee, the department number attribute (which is a foreign key) would have to be null in the tuple representing that employee in the database.

B.4   RELATIONAL DATA MANIPULATION

The manipulative part of the relational model consists of a set of operators known collectively as the *relational algebra*, together with a relational assignment operator that assigns the value of some arbitrary expression of the algebra to another relation. We discuss the algebra first.

Each operator of the relational algebra takes either one or two relations as its input and produces a new relation as its output. Codd originally defined eight such operators, two groups of four each: (1) the traditional set operations union, intersection, difference, and Cartesian product (all modified slightly to take account of the fact that their operands are relations, as opposed to arbitrary sets); and (2) the special relational operations select, project, join, and divide. The eight operations are shown symbolically in Fig. B.2. We give a brief definition of each operation below; for simplicity, we assume in those definitions that the left-to-right order of attributes within a relation *is* significant—not because it is necessary to do so, but because it simplifies the discussion.

Traditional Set Operations

Each of the traditional set operations takes two operands. For all except Cartesian product, the two operand relations must be *union-compatible*— that is, they must be of the same degree, n say, and the ith attribute of each ($i = 1,2,\ldots,n$) must be based on the same domain (they do not have to have the same name).

- Union

The union of two (union-compatible) relations A and B is the set of all tuples t belonging to either A or B (or both).

SQL example:

```
SELECT S.SNO FROM S
UNION
SELECT SP.SNO FROM SP
```

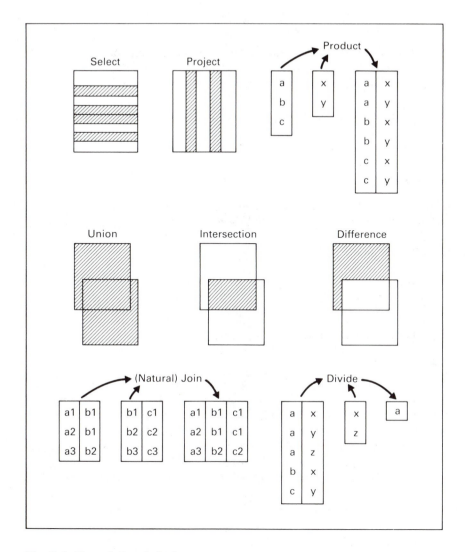

Fig. B.2 The relational algebra

- Intersection

The intersection of two (union-compatible) relations A and B is the set of all tuples *t* belonging to both A and B.
   SQL example:

```
SELECT S.SNO FROM S
WHERE   EXISTS
     ( SELECT SP.SNO FROM SP
       WHERE  SP.SNO = S.SNO )
```

- Difference

The difference between two (union-compatible) relations A and B is the set of all tuples *t* belonging to A and not to B.
SQL example:

```
SELECT S.SNO FROM S
WHERE  NOT EXISTS
       ( SELECT SP.SNO FROM SP
         WHERE  SP.SNO = S.SNO )
```

- Product

The product of two relations A and B is the set of all tuples *t* such that *t* is the concatenation of a tuple *a* belonging to A and a tuple *b* belonging to B.
SQL example:

```
SELECT S.*, SP.*
FROM   S, SP
```

Special Relational Operations

- Selection

Let *theta* represent any valid scalar comparison operator (for example, =, < >, >, > =, etc.). The theta-selection of relation A on attributes X and Y is the set of all tuples *t* of A such that the predicate "*t*.X *theta t*.Y" evaluates to *true*. (Attributes X and Y should be defined on the same domain, and the operation *theta* must make sense for that domain.) A constant value may be specified instead of attribute Y. Thus, the theta-selection operator yields a "horizontal" subset of a given relation—that is, that subset of the tuples of the given relation for which a specified predicate is satisfied. *Note*: "Theta-selection" is often abbreviated to just "selection." But note that "selection" is not the same as the SELECT operator of SQL.
SQL example:

```
SELECT S.*
FROM   S
WHERE  CITY <> 'London'
```

- Projection

The projection operator yields a "vertical" subset of a given relation—that is, that subset obtained by selecting specified attributes and then eliminating redundant duplicate tuples within the attributes selected, if necessary.

SQL example:

```
SELECT DISTINCT P.COLOR, P.CITY
FROM   P
```

- Join

Let *theta* be as defined under "Selection" above. The theta-join of relation A on attribute X with relation B on attribute Y is the set of all tuples *t* such that *t* is the concatenation of a tuple *a* belonging to A and a tuple *b* belonging to B and the predicate "*a*.X *theta b*.Y" evaluates to *true*. (Attributes A.X and B.Y should be defined on the same domain, and the operation *theta* must make sense for that domain.)
  SQL example:

```
SELECT S.*, P.*
FROM   S, P
WHERE  S.CITY > P.CITY
```

If *theta* is equality, the join is called an equijoin. It follows from the definition that the result of an equijoin must include two identical attributes. If one of those two attributes is eliminated (which it can be via projection), the result is called the *natural* join. The unqualified term "join" is usually taken to mean the natural join.

- Division

In its simplest form (which is all that we consider here), the division operator divides a relation of degree two (the dividend) by a relation of degree one (the divisor), and produces a result relation of degree one (the quotient). Let the dividend (A) have attributes X and Y, and let the divisor (B) have attribute Y. Attributes A.Y and B.Y should be defined on the same domain. The result of dividing A by B is the relation C, with sole attribute X, such that every value *x* of C.X appears as a value of A.X, and the pair of values (*x*,*y*) appears in A for *all* values *y* appearing in B.
  SQL example:

```
SELECT DISTINCT SPX.SNO FROM SP SPX
WHERE  NOT EXISTS
     ( SELECT P.PNO FROM P
       WHERE  NOT EXISTS
            ( SELECT SPY.* FROM SP SPY
              WHERE  SPY.SNO = SPX.SNO AND SPY.PNO = P.PNO ) )
```

Here we are assuming for simplicity that (a) relation SP has only two attributes, namely SNO and PNO (we are ignoring QTY), and (b) relation

P has only one attribute, namely PNO (we are ignoring PNAME, COLOR, WEIGHT, and CITY). We divide the first of these two relations by the second and obtain a result, namely a relation with one attribute (SNO) that lists supplier numbers for suppliers that supply all parts.

It is worth mentioning that, of these eight operations, only five are primitive, namely selection, projection, product, union, and difference. The other three can be defined in terms of those five. For example, the natural join is a projection of a selection of a product. In practice, however, those other three operations (especially join) are so useful that a good case can be made for supporting them directly, even though they are not primitive.

Turning now to the relational assignment operation, the purpose of that operation is simply to allow the value of some algebraic expression—say a join—to be saved in some more or less permanent place. It can be simulated in SQL by means of the INSERT... SELECT operation. For example, suppose relation XYZ has two attributes, SNO and PNO, and suppose also that it is currently empty (contains no tuples). The SQL statement

```
INSERT INTO XYZ ( SNO, PNO )
       SELECT S.SNO, P.PNO
       FROM   S, P
       WHERE  S.CITY = P.CITY
```

assigns the result of the SELECT (namely, a projection of a join) to the relation XYZ.

By way of conclusion, Fig. B.3 summarizes the major components of the relational model.

Data structure

    domains (values)
    n-ary relations (attributes, tuples)
    keys (candidate, primary, alternate, foreign)

Data integrity

    1. primary key values must not be null
    2. foreign key values must match primary key values
      (or be null)

Data manipulation

    relational algebra
      union, intersection, difference, product
      select, project, join, divide
    relational assignment

Fig. B.3 The relational model

B.5 RELATIONAL SYSTEMS

We are now (at last) in a position to define exactly what we mean by a *relational database management system* (relational DBMS, or relational system for short). The point is, *no* system today supports the relational model in its entirety (several come close, but most systems fall down on the integrity rules if nowhere else). On the other hand, it would be unreasonable to insist that a system is not relational unless it supports every last detail of the model. The fact is, not all aspects of the model are equally important; some of course are crucial, but others may be regarded merely as features that are "nice to have" (comparatively speaking). We therefore define a system as *relational* (minimally so) if and only if it supports at least the following:

- Relational databases (i.e., databases that can be perceived by the user as tables, and nothing but tables);

- At least the operations select, project, and join of the relational algebra (without requiring any predefinition of physical access paths to support those operations).

Note carefully that a system does not have to support the select, project, and join operators *explicitly* in order to qualify as relational. It is only the functionality of those operators that we are talking about here. For example, INGRES provides the functionality of all three of those operators (and more besides) within the SELECT operator of SQL. More important, note that a system that supports relational databases but not these three operators does not qualify as a relational system under our definition. Likewise, a system that allows (say) the user to select tuples according to values of some attribute X only if that attribute X is indexed also does not qualify, because it is requiring predefinition of physical access paths.

We justify our definition as follows:

1. Although select, project, and join are less than the full algebra, they are an extremely useful subset. There are comparatively few practical problems that can be solved with the algebra that cannot be solved with select, project, and join alone.

2. A system that supports the relational data structure but not the relational operators does not provide the productivity of a genuinely relational system.

3. To do a good job of implementing the relational operators *requires* the system to do some optimization. A system that merely executed the exact operations requested by the user in a comparatively unintelligent fashion would almost certainly not have acceptable performance. Thus, to imple-

ment a system that realizes the potential of the relational model in an efficient manner is a highly nontrivial task.

INGRES is a relational system according to our definition (even though there are several aspects of the relational model that it does not support). But there are a number of systems on the market today that advertise themselves as "relational" that do not meet the criteria defined above. As we have tried to suggest, those criteria are useful as a means of drawing a sharp line between systems that are indeed genuinely relational and systems that are merely "relational-like." "Relational-like" systems do not truly provide the benefits of the relational model. The distinction is thus worth making, as it ensures that the label "relational" is not used in misleading ways.

Note: For further discussion of what it means for a system to be relational, the reader is referred to a recent paper by E. F. Codd, "Is Your DBMS Really Relational?" (see Appendix F).

C

Syntax of QUEL
Data Manipulation
Operations

C.1 INTRODUCTION

We give a BNF grammar for the four data manipulation operations of
QUEL (RETRIEVE, REPLACE, DELETE, and APPEND) described in
this book. The grammar makes use of the following convenient shorthand:

- If "xyz" is a syntactic category, then "xyz-list" is a syntactic category
  consisting of a list of one or more "xyz"s in which each pair of adjacent "xyz"s is separated by a sequence of characters consisting of
  zero or more spaces, followed by a comma, followed by zero or more
  spaces.

The categories "constant", "table-name", "column-name", and
"range-variable-name" are terminal with respect to this grammar. In particular, certain so-called "system constants" (such as USERNAME) are not
explicitly defined.

C.2   SCALAR EXPRESSIONS

```
scalar-expression
    ::=  scalar-term [ arithmetic-operator scalar-expression ]

scalar-term
    ::=  [ + ¦ - ] scalar-value

scalar-value
    ::=     constant
         ¦  NULL
         ¦  column-reference
         ¦  scalar-function ( scalar-expression )
         ¦  aggregate-operator ( aggregate-argument )
         ¦  aggregate-operator ( aggregate-function-argument )
         ¦  ( scalar-expression )

column-reference
    ::=  range-variable-name . column-name
```

```
scalar-function
    ::=     ABS       ¦ ASCII     ¦ ATAN     ¦ CONCAT    ¦ COS
         ¦  DATE      ¦ DOW       ¦ EXP      ¦ FLOAT4    ¦ FLOAT8
         ¦  INT1      ¦ INT2      ¦ INT4     ¦ INTERVAL  ¦ LEFT
         ¦  LENGTH    ¦ LOCATE    ¦ LOG      ¦ LOWERCASE ¦ MOD
         ¦  MONEY     ¦ PAD       ¦ RIGHT    ¦ SHIFT     ¦ SIN
         ¦  SIZE      ¦ SQUEEZE   ¦ SQRT     ¦ TEXT      ¦ TRIM
         ¦  UPPERCASE ¦ _BINTIM() ¦ _DATE()  ¦ _TIME()
```

Note: CONCAT, INTERVAL, LEFT, LOCATE, MOD, RIGHT, and SHIFT each take *two* scalar-expression arguments, separated by a comma.

```
aggregate-operator
    ::=     COUNT ¦ COUNTU
         ¦  SUM   ¦ SUMU
         ¦  AVG   ¦ AVGU
         ¦  MAX   ¦ MIN
         ¦  ANY

aggregate-argument
    ::=  scalar-expression [ WHERE predicate ]

aggregate-function-argument
    ::=  scalar-expression BY column-reference-list
                         [ [ ONLY ] WHERE predicate ]

arithmetic-operator
    ::=  + ¦ - ¦ * ¦ / ¦ **
```

C.3   PREDICATES

```
predicate
    ::=     comparison
         ¦  comparison AND predicate
         ¦  comparison OR predicate
         ¦  NOT predicate
         ¦  ( predicate )
```

```
comparison
    ::=    scalar-expression comparison-operator scalar-expression
         ¦ scalar-expression IS [ NOT ] NULL
```

Note: Certain character string constants have a special interpretation in the context of a "comparison"—details beyond the scope of this grammar.

```
comparison-operator
    ::=  =  ¦  <>  ¦  <  ¦  <=  ¦  >  ¦  >=
```

C.4 STATEMENTS

```
statement
    ::=    retrieve-statement
         ¦ replace-statement
         ¦ delete-statement
         ¦ append-statement

retrieve-statement
    ::=  RETRIEVE [ [ INTO ] table-name ]
                 [ UNIQUE ] ( target-list )
                 [ WHERE predicate ]
                 [ SORT [ BY ] sort-item-list ]

target
    ::=    range-variable-name . ALL
         ¦ column-reference
         ¦ column-name = scalar-expression

sort-item
    ::=  [ range-variable-name . ] column-name [ : A ¦ : D ]

append-statement
    ::=  APPEND [ TO ] table-name [ UNIQUE ] ( target-list )
                 [ WHERE predicate ]

replace-statement
    ::=  REPLACE range-variable-name ( target-list )
                 [ WHERE predicate ]

delete-statement
    ::=  DELETE range-variable-name [ WHERE predicate ]
```

D

Syntax of SQL
Data Manipulation
Operations

D.1 INTRODUCTION

We give a BNF grammar for the four data manipulation operations of SQL (SELECT, UPDATE, DELETE, and INSERT) described in this book. The grammar makes use of the following convenient shorthand:

- If "xyz" is a syntactic category, then "xyz-list" is a syntactic category consisting of a list of one or more "xyz"s in which each pair of adjacent "xyz"s is separated by a sequence of characters consisting of zero or more spaces, followed by a comma, followed by zero or more spaces.

The categories "integer", "constant", "table-name", "column-name", and "range-variable-name" are terminal with respect to this grammar. In particular, certain so-called "system constants" (such as USER-NAME) are not explicitly defined.

Note: Aspects of the four statements not described in the body of the book (e.g., the comparison operators >ANY, =ALL, etc.) are ignored. In

the interests of clarity and brevity, moreover, the grammar does not accurately reflect the SQL language but is instead slightly permissive, in the
sense that it allows the generation of certain constructs that are not legal
in SQL. For example, it allows the argument to a function such as AVG to
consist of a reference to another function such as SUM, which SQL does
not permit.

D.2 SCALAR EXPRESSIONS

```
scalar-expression
   ::=  scalar-term [ arithmetic-operator scalar-expression ]

scalar-term
   ::=  [ + ¦ - ] scalar-value

scalar-value
   ::=    constant
        ¦ NULL
        ¦ column-reference
        ¦ scalar-function ( scalar-expression )
        ¦ set-function-reference
        ¦ ( scalar-expression )

column-reference
   ::=  [ range-variable-name .] column-name

scalar-function
   ::=    ABS      ¦ ASCII    ¦ ATAN     ¦ CONCAT    ¦ COS
        ¦ DATE     ¦ DOW      ¦ EXP      ¦ FLOAT4    ¦ FLOAT8
        ¦ INT1     ¦ INT2     ¦ INT4     ¦ INTERVAL  ¦ LEFT
        ¦ LENGTH   ¦ LOCATE   ¦ LOG      ¦ LOWERCASE ¦ MOD
        ¦ MONEY    ¦ PAD      ¦ RIGHT    ¦ SHIFT     ¦ SIN
        ¦ SIZE     ¦ SQUEEZE  ¦ SQRT     ¦ TEXT      ¦ TRIM
        ¦ UPPERCASE ¦ _BINTIM() ¦ _DATE() ¦ _TIME()
```

Note: CONCAT, INTERVAL, LEFT, LOCATE, MOD, RIGHT, and
SHIFT each take *two* scalar-expression arguments, separated by a comma.

```
set-function-reference
   ::=    COUNT ( * )
        ¦ set-function-name ( scalar-expression )
        ¦ set-function-name ( DISTINCT column-reference )

set-function-name
   ::=  COUNT ¦ SUM ¦ AVG ¦ MAX ¦ MIN

arithmetic-operator
   ::=  + ¦ - ¦ * ¦ / ¦ **
```

D.3 SELECT-EXPRESSIONS

```
select-expression
   ::=  select-clause
        from-clause
        [ where-clause ]
        [ grouping-clause [ having-clause ] ]

select-clause
   ::=  SELECT [ DISTINCT ] select-spec

select-spec
   ::=  * | select-item-list

select-item
   ::=    range-variable-name . *
        | scalar-expression

from-clause
   ::=  FROM from-item-list

from-item
   ::=  table-name [ range-variable-name ]

where-clause
   ::=  WHERE predicate

grouping-clause
   ::=  GROUP BY column-reference-list

having-clause
   ::=  HAVING predicate
```

D.4 PREDICATES

```
predicate
   ::=    condition
        | condition AND predicate
        | condition OR predicate
        | NOT predicate

condition
   ::=    compare-condition
        | between-condition
        | like-condition
        | in-condition
        | exists-condition
        | ( predicate )

compare-condition
   ::=    scalar-expression compare-operator scalar-expression
        | scalar-expression compare-operator
                         ( column-select-expression )
        | scalar-expression IS [ NOT ] NULL

compare-operator
   ::=  = | <> | < | <= | > | >=
```

```
column-select-expression
    ::=  column-select-clause
         from-clause
         [ where-clause ]
         [ grouping-clause [ having-clause ] ]

column-select-clause
    ::=  SELECT [ DISTINCT ] scalar-expression

between-condition
    ::=  column-reference [ NOT ] BETWEEN scalar-expression
                                     AND scalar-expression

like-condition
    ::=  column-reference [ NOT ] LIKE scalar-expression

in-condition
    ::=  scalar-expression [ NOT ] IN ( set-of-scalars )

set-of-scalars
    ::=    constant-list
        ¦ column-select-expression

exists-condition
    ::=  EXISTS ( select-expression )
```

D.5 STATEMENTS

```
statement
    ::=    select-statement
        ¦ update-statement
        ¦ delete-statement
        ¦ insert-statement

select-statement
    ::=  union-expression [ ordering-clause ]

union-expression
    ::=  select-expression [ UNION union-expression ]

ordering-clause
    ::=  ORDER BY order-item-list

order-item
    ::=  ordering-column [ ASC ¦ DESC ]

ordering-column
    ::=  column-reference ¦ integer

update-statement
    ::=  UPDATE table-name [ range-variable-name ]
         SET column-assignment-list
         [ where-clause ]

column-assignment
    ::=    column-reference = scalar-expression
        ¦ column-reference = NULL

delete-statement
    ::=  DELETE FROM table-name [ range-variable-name ]
         [ where-clause ]
```

```
insert-statement
    ::=   INSERT INTO table-name [ ( column-reference-list ) ]
                     source-values

source-values
    ::=      VALUES ( insert-item-list )
          ¦ select-expression

insert-item
    ::=   constant ¦ NULL
```

E

INGRES Environments

At the time of writing, INGRES runs in the environments shown in Fig. E.1. Note, however, that RTI is constantly working with other vendors to make INGRES available on additional machines and under additional operating systems, and hence that the list of environments supported is constantly being extended. *Note*: The term "UNIX" includes both AT&T System V UNIX and UC Berkeley 4.2 BSD UNIX, as well as proprietary UNIX systems from other vendors.

Vendor	Processor	Operating System
Alliant	FX8, FX1	CONCENTRIX
Amdahl	58xx, V-x	VM/CMS,MVS,UTS
Apollo	DN series	UNIX
AT&T	3B series	UNIX
Burroughs	XE550	CENTIX
Computer Consoles	Power 6/32	UNIX
Computervision	CDS 3000	UNIX
Convergent	Megaframe	CENTIX
DEC	VAX series	VMS,UNIX,ULTRIX
DG	MV series	DG/UX
Elxsi	6400	ENIX
Gould	PN 6000, PN 9000	UTX
HP	9000 series	HP/UX
IBM	370,43xx,30xx	VM/CMS,MVS,UTS
IBM	PC/XT,PC/AT	PC/DOS,MS/DOS
IBM	RT PC	AIX
ICL	Series 39	VME
ICL	CLAN series	UNIX
NAS	6000, 8000, 9000	VM/CMS,MVS,UTS
NCR	Tower series	UNIX
Pyramid	all	OSx
Sequent	Balance 21000, 8000	UNIX
Sperry	7000/40	UNIX
Sun	SUN-2, SUN-3	SUN OS

Fig. E.1 INGRES environments

F

Bibliography

We present a short list of selected further reading.

Relational Technology Inc.: *The INGRES Documentation Set.* Available from Relational Technology Inc. (RTI), 1080 Marina Village Parkway, Alameda, Calif. 94501.

An extensive set of manuals on all aspects of the Commercial INGRES product.

E. F. Codd: "A Relational Model of Data for Large Shared Data Banks." *Communications of the ACM,* Vol. 13, No. 6 (June 1970); reprinted in *Communications of the ACM,* Vol. 26, No. 1 (January 1983).

This was the paper that (apart from some early internal IBM papers, also by Codd) first proposed the ideas of the relational model.

E. F. Codd: "Relational Database: A Practical Foundation for Productivity." *Communications of the ACM,* Vol. 25, No. 2 (February 1982).

The paper that Codd presented on the occasion of his receiving the 1981 ACM Turing Award for his work on relational database. The definition of "relational system" in Appendix B of the present book is taken from this paper. See also the next reference below.

E. F. Codd: "Is Your DBMS Really Relational?" (*Computerworld,* October 14, 1985); "Does Your DBMS Run by the Rules?" (*Computerworld,* October 21, 1985).

These two papers include proposals for a more stringent definition of what it means for a system to be relational in the mid to late 1980s.

Michael Stonebraker (ed.): *The INGRES Papers*: *Anatomy of a Relational Database System* (Addison-Wesley, 1985).

A comprehensive collection of papers on the University INGRES prototype and related research and development activities. The book also includes one paper discussing the evolution of the prototype into the Commercial INGRES product.

C. J. Date: *An Introduction to Database Systems*: *Volume I* (4th edition, Addison-Wesley, 1985); *Volume II* (1st edition, Addison-Wesley, 1983).

These two volumes between them provide a basis for a comprehensive education in most aspects of database technology. In particular, they include a very detailed treatment of the relational approach.

C. J. Date: *Relational Database*: *Selected Writings* (Addison-Wesley, 1986).

A collection of papers on various aspects of relational technology, including several on the SQL language and one (rather long) on a relational database design methodology.

G

List of Acronyms

We list below some of the more important acronyms introduced in the text, together with their meanings.

ABF	Applications-By-Forms
ANSI	American National Standards Institute
BNF	Backus-Naur Form
DBA	Database Administrator
DBMS	Database Management System
DBDB	Database Database
DCLGEN	Declarations Generator
EQUEL	Embedded QUEL
ESQL	Embedded SQL
GBF	Graph-By-Forms
I/O	Input/Output
INGRES	Interactive Graphics and Retrieval System
IQUEL	Interactive QUEL
ISQL	Interactive SQL

JoinDef	Join Definition
MST	Multi-Statement Transaction
OSL	Operation Specification Language
PFKey	Program Function Key
QBF	Query-By-Forms
QBFName	QBF Name
QUEL	Query Language
RBF	Report-By-Forms
RTI	Relational Technology Inc.
SQL	Structured Query Language
SQLCA	SQL Communication Area
SST	Single Statement Transaction
TID	Tuple ID
VIFRED	Visual-Forms-Editor
VIGRAPH	Visual-Graphics-Editor
WYSIWIG	What You See Is What You Get

Index

381